"Yudkin applies her usual intuitive marketing acumen and savvy business knowledge as she acts as coach and brainstorming partner to improve existing Web sites or create dynamite new ones. There are money-making ideas galore here for veteran and neophyte alike. And the Makeover Checklist alone is worth the price of the book."

—Marilyn Ross, author, *Jump Start Your Book Sales*
and *Shameless Marketing for Brazen Hussies*

"I didn't even know I needed a makeover until I read the book. My site has been up a couple of months. During that time not even one order has been placed. Of course I wasn't pleased with the results. I now have a chance to do a makeover before I have an actual grand opening of my store. I felt like we had a one-on-one private lesson as I read the book. The book is written in simple terms for everyone to understand and follow."

—Crystal Eleby, CE Books and Gifts, http://www.cebooksandgifts.com/

"This book is a must-have for anyone who wonders why their Web site isn't generating the kind of money, traffic and rave reviews they expected. Regardless of size or standing, your Web site is one of millions. This book shows you how to make it one in a million! Filled with common sense and uncommon insights, *Poor Richard's Web Site Marketing Makeover* explains how to transform your site into one that is easier to navigate, more inviting, and more profitable."

—Drew VanKrevelen, Graphic Designer/Web Designer/Manager,
Minnesota State Lottery, http://www.mnlottery.com/

"The information in *Poor Richard's Web Site Marketing Makeover* seemed to be written just for me. I now understand what was unappealing about my site."
  —Brian Dunphy, HomePro Inspections, http://www.homepro-kamloops.com/

"This book is filled with excellent information about marketing any web site. It's well-written, and very easy to understand. There is something for everyone in this book, regardless of what kind of web site they have. I personally have a site where I sell a number of related products, and this is the first book I've read that really addresses that kind of web site."
  —Linda Ditz, Twin Creek Farm Seasonings, http://www.TwinCreekFarm.com/

"A clear concise guide loaded with practical tips and traps to avoid when optimizing your site for e-commerce."
            —Florrie Kichler, Patria Press, Inc., http://www.patriapress.com/

"I feel as if I hired an Internet Marketing Consultant instead of reading a book. The advice and examples are clear and understandable."
                  —Bill Sefton, Seftek, http://www.Seftek.com/

"As a former college professor (and a very demanding one at that), I approached Ms. Yudkin's book with a somewhat cynical and aggressive mindset. Here was another book which was the 'be-all-to-end-all' in the subject of *not* website design but rather in the area of remedial work to correct a below average website. Amazingly such was not the case. The book set forth it's purpose and then in a straightforward manner introduced the reader to common website failures and pitfalls and thereafter, in an equally forthright manner, proposed remedies and sources for those remedies."

—Reg Tarleton, CEO, Tarleton Custom Homes,
http://www.TarletonCustomHomes.com/

"After recently doing a complete makeover of my web site with input from a well-known guru, I started reading Marcia Yudkin's *Poor Richard's Web Site Marketing Makeover* with the idea that I wouldn't learn anything new. I couldn't have been more wrong! Marcia covered everything from making the web site easier to navigate, to content. And threw in ideas for keeping in contact with your visitors that I had not even considered. This is a must read for anyone in business on the Internet—even if someone else designs your site!"

—Terri Robinson, President, http://www.recruit2hire.com/

"A must-have book for anyone in charge of their company's Web site or considering creating a company Web site. A great tool for conducting an audit of any existing Web site!"

—Tom Anderson, SpaceAge Control, Inc.

"I really liked this book! I've been online since 1995, but only recently put up my own website. I've read a few books on website design, but they were mostly a collection of links with commentary from individual webmasters, and no real direction on what to do with the information once you got it. Sometimes the information conflicted, which left me no further ahead. This book provides good suggestions with clear reasoning behind those suggestions. It also articulated some things that I was vaguely unhappy about with my own website, but couldn't quite put my finger on."

—Trudy W. Schuett, Publisher, The DesertLight Journal,
http://www.desertlightjournal.homestead.com/

"Marcia Yudkin's book, *Poor Richard's Website Marketing Makeover* clears up the confusion. Pick up a copy of this book and learn how to find the weak spots in your design and layout. Learn the value of easy navigation, how to use keywords and phrases, how to translate features into benefits."

—Yvonne DiVita, Marketing/Sales Manager, http://www.Annexa.net/

Praise for other books in the Poor Richard's Series . . .

Poor Richard's Web Site

"Makes it possible for ordinary people to set up effective business websites without going broke or spending forever online. It's a great read for anyone who wants to build a business site, and it becomes a part of our recommended library."
—CMPnet's Techweb

"A good source with easy step-by-step directions."   —*Publishers Weekly*

"Offers clear advice to help you defend against jargon-happy sales people and computer magazines."   —Fortune.com

"If you really want to build a functional Web site [this] might just be the book for you."   —CNN Interactive

Poor Richard's E-mail Publishing

"The single most authoritative and helpful guide an entrepreneur can turn to when it's time to move beyond a Web site."   —*The Newsletter on Newsletters*

"Unites commonsense advice with clear explanations of e-mail technology . . .The book is packed with marketing know-how and tells you how to make money with your newsletter . . .Don't click Send without [this book]."   —*PC World*

"Transforms what could be boring technical jargon into an easy-to-understand tutorial on the ins and outs of Email publishing."
—*Website Success Monthly* newsletter

Poor Richard's Building Online Communities

"An extensive course on creating a vital Web community."   —Entrepreneur.com

"Create a web community for a business or family using the power of the Internet and this *Poor Richard's* guide, which focuses on inexpensive methods of achieving such a goal. From locating and participating in mailing lists to joining web-based communities for business and pleasure, this imparts the basics of understanding how such groups function."   —Review's Bookwatch

"Another great book from the *Poor Richard's* Series. This book will help the novice or expert build a online community that will make the most out of the different components that turn a Web site into a community."
—Nathan Allan, Community Development Manager, Sausage Software

POOR RICHARD'S WEB SITE MARKETING MAKEOVER

by
Marcia Yudkin

2001

TOP FLOOR
PUBLISHING

Poor Richard's Web Site Marketing Makeover:
Improve Your Message and Turn Visitors into Buyers

Copyright © 2001 Marcia Yudkin

SAN#: 299-4550
Top Floor Publishing
8790 W. Colfax #107
Lakewood, CO 80215

Feedback to the author: feedback@topfloor.com
Sales information: sales@topfloor.com
The Top Floor Publishing Web Site: http://TopFloor.com/
The Poor Richard Web Site: http://PoorRichard.com/
Cover design/illustration by Marty Petersen, http://www.artymarty.com

Library of Congress Catalog Card Number: 2001096342

ISBN: 1-930082-16-9

03   02   01   6 5 4 3 2 1

ACKNOWLEDGMENTS

I'd like to send thanks to those who allowed their Web sites to be used for instructional purposes in Part II, "Putting It All Together: Sample Makeovers": Nancy Hendrickson of **The Family Tree Guide to Internet Genealogy** (http://genealogytutor.com/order/guide.cfm); Megan Cunningham of **Magnet Media** (http://www.digitalmediatraining.com/); Jean Sifleet, Esq. of **Smart Fast** (http://www.smartfast.com/); Jim Verzino of **Jerboa, Inc.** (http://www.jerboa.com/); Trina Dunbar of **ComputerAthlete.org** (http://www.computerathlete.org/); Kathy Brady-Romanelli of the **Boston Learning Society** (http://www.bostonlearning society/); Carol Duke of **Carol Duke Flowers** (http://www.caroldukeflowers.com/); and Ronni Rhodes of **WBC Imaging** (http://www.wbcimaging.com/). Naturally, the comments and observations accompanying the makeovers or discussion of their sites are solely my responsibility.

Those who worked on this book include J.W. (Jerry) Olsen, project manager and developmental editor; Sydney Jones, copyeditor; Missy Ramey, publisher and layout artist; and Joann Woy, proofreader and indexer. Special thanks to Syd for sensitive copyediting and to Missy for creative layout solutions.

Thanks as well to my sister JJ for continued advice on contracts and other legal matters related to my writing career; to my sister Gila for detailed and useful feedback on my work; to my mother, Florence, for being my best fan and supporter; and to my husband, Chen, for helping to resolve my computer headaches when I ask him nicely enough.

ABOUT THE AUTHOR

A freelance writer since 1981 and marketing consultant since 1991, Marcia Yudkin is an expert in turning words into money. She is the author of 11 books, including *Six Steps to Free Publicity* (Plume/Penguin), *Internet Marketing for Less than $500/Year* (Maximum Press), and *Freelance Writing for Magazines & Newspapers* (HarperCollins and a Book-of-the-Month-Club Selection). Her articles have appeared in hundreds of magazines and at scores of Web sites, from the *New York Times Magazine* and *Psychology Today* to *Business 2.0, Publish,* and ClickZ.com. She has also delivered commentaries on National Public Radio.

Marcia Yudkin's clients around the world range from therapists and attorneys to sales executives and Internet entrepreneurs. She maintains an active seminar and speaking schedule, and publishes a free weekly newsletter, *The Marketing Minute*. For more information, see http://www.yudkin.com or contact her at marcia@yudkin.com.

CONTENTS AT A GLANCE

TABLE OF CONTENTS

PREFACE

"My Web site isn't working!" It's an endemic complaint, and usually it involves a site where the visitor can get around fine by clicking here and there. The Web paraphernalia functions fine. But visitors are not turning into subscribers, hot leads, or buyers.

Sometimes the problem has to do with folks not knowing the site exists. Site logs show that visitors aren't coming. In that case, the cure lies in site promotion, a process described by many of the books listed in Appendix B, *Recommended Books and Web Resources*. Sometimes the design is so awful that visitors flee without exploring or vanish before making a commitment. That's surprisingly rare, considering how much site owners agonize over design.

Most often, the explanation pertains to confusion, boredom, or apathy in the user. The site hasn't reached out and moved the visitor to care, to trust, and to act. That's where a Web site marketing makeover comes in.

A marketing makeover looks at an existing Web site from the point of view of a visitor who's never seen it before and suggests changes that will better orient, interest, and persuade him or her. You'll encounter a lot of wording changes in this book, rooted in issues concerning audience, purpose, and the psychology of business. Recommendations here sometimes involve format and layout to make sure that the Web site elements come across with the proper emphasis. In a marketing makeover, however, aesthetics take a back seat to making sure that the site communicates quickly, clearly, and powerfully.

This Book Is for You If...

If your Web site has been up for a while and you're not happy with the results, this book will lead you by the hand toward a more effective strategy and implementation. If your site brings in business but you suspect it could do better, this book will help you identify improvements that will make a difference. If you have not yet constructed and launched a site, this book will put you on the right track from the get-go. Do you design sites, advise companies on Web projects, or devise marketing plans or marketing communications? Then this book is for you, too.

Few of the remedies in this book require monetary expenditures—just energy and intelligence. So, you can take these makeover principles and run with them whether you comprise a company of one or work alongside a staff of thousands. They also apply whether you seek customers or clients only on the Internet, or you're adding a Web presence to a bricks-and-mortar operation. And whether you are selling pet treats, blast furnaces, or accounting services, or are trying to change society and are not selling anything, you'll find suggestions here you can use.

You won't need a penetrating understanding of programming or HTML coding to follow the guidelines here to revamp your site. Whatever your Web proficiency, you'll at least be able to reconstruct and rewrite your pages and hand your makeover to someone with a mastery of technicalities to execute the changes.

Your Guide

And from what fount of knowledge am I leading the way? I have 20 years of experience as a professional wordsmith. Originally I worked as a freelance magazine writer, convincing editors who didn't know me to assign me articles. I published everywhere from the *New York Times Magazine* to *New Age* to *Cosmopolitan* and still go that route when I have topics I'm eager to tackle for wide audiences. In the last 10 years, however, you'd more often find me identifying the implicit benefits of a product or service, conceiving creative outreach strategies for a company, and crafting materials that make orders or appointment requests pour in.

I've worked with physicians and attorneys, software firms and industrial suppliers, plumbing contractors and sculptors, and trade associations and publishers, ranging from a solo shop to an outfit with 15 to 25 employees. I got my feet wet with Internet marketing in 1994, and before e-commerce and the World Wide Web existed, I figured out ways to use online discussion boards and e-mail lists to attract business. While I'm familiar with expensive, cutting-edge marketing tools, I favor inventive strategies that have a modest cost and a disciplined implementation and that work because they connect solidly with the way the target market thinks and acts.

Although the Web is a distinctive medium with characteristic protocols and opportunities, my recommendations for Web-site improvement resemble the kinds of suggestions I make for old-fashioned brochures, news releases, and sales flyers. Just as with traditional marketing vehicles, a commercial Web site should not be a monument to someone's personal or corporate ego. Except for someone in the business of making and selling cool things, a Web site shouldn't evoke a "Wow!" or call attention to its aesthetic or technical ingenuity. Its job is to communicate and persuade and to enable visitors to learn, understand, and take actions that benefit both themselves and the Web site's owner.

How to Use This Book

Details matter immensely on the Web, and you'll discover throughout this book scores of nuances and particulars to pay attention to. The order in which the visitor encounters information or requests can make an enormous difference, as can whether and how a site uses jargon. I value findings about what actually works and doesn't on the Web, and I've included the insights of usability researchers like Jakob Nielsen and Jared Spool where they're relevant.

Because you could easily become discouraged by the amount of change your site needs as you delve into this book, please keep in mind that a Web site is always a work in progress. At one stage, you're rightly delighted to have gotten it up at all. Then you can go back at it armed with feedback and analysis and make it better. Then you can repeat the process and overhaul or fine-tune the site further.

I recommend you read this book with highlighter, pen, or sticky notes in hand, jotting down ideas and options you might want to or need to implement. You don't need to digest the chapters and sections consecutively. Feel free to home in first on a factor that has been troubling you, or to study one or two of the makeovers in Part II, *Putting It All Together*, before turning back for a more systematic, step-by-step discussion.

In the Introduction, I discuss the basic set of questions you need to address before embarking on your Web site makeover. Part I takes you step by step through the elements of most Web sites, showing how to use each to best advantage. Part II provides a more integrated look at several distinctive types of sites, and you should expect useful discoveries from studying the makeovers for sites different from yours. In the appendixes, I've collected suggestions, including reminders not appearing elsewhere in the book, that you can use as a checklist for your own makeover, along with recommended resources and a glossary of Web-related terminology. Since everyone wants his or her Web site to get exceptional results, I've tried my best to maintain a constructive tone while discussing the pervasive marketing mistakes that can be found all over the Web. It's difficult for any individual or company to think objectively about the best way to communicate with its target market and to channel initial interest into a definite lead or a sale. But armed with the principles and examples in this book, you'll find this easier, and you'll profit when you change your Web site accordingly.

I'd like to extend heartfelt thanks to all the individuals and organizations that agreed to serve as guinea pigs for the makeovers in my book. When you visit their sites, you may discover differences from figures in the book for a variety of reasons. Naturally, I alone am responsible for my makeover suggestions and how they appear in the Web pages as presented in the pages that follow.

What You'll Learn in This Book

And now, to encourage you to dig in with your reading and study right away, here's an overview of some of the lessons lying in wait for you in this book:

- Why and how you must help first-time visitors understand at a glance where they are when they've landed at your site
- How to ensure that when people search among the offerings at your site, they receive an adequate response to their search
- How to use a six-step process for arriving at optimal navigation links for your site
- Why and how to translate features of what you're marketing into benefits
- Why contact information is indispensable
- How to avoid using site elements that elevate or damage visitors' trust
- What kinds of content can attract repeat traffic
- Which do's and don'ts to observe for subscription and order forms
- How to employ techniques that make site content more readable and inviting

In addition, you'll find scores of helpful illustrations along with the nitty-gritty details for remaking specific sites.

Send me the URLs of sites that you've made over by following my suggestions. Who knows, you might end up in a future edition of this book! Good luck!

Marcia Yudkin
Boston, MA
marcia@yudkin.com
http://www.yudkin.com

INTRODUCTION

Amarketing makeover of your Web site begins with two fundamental questions that are rarely as simple as they seem:

- What results would you like your site to achieve?
- Who are your audiences; what are their needs, expectations, and assumptions?

Plopping a site on the Net just to have a site is a recipe for disappointment. Before you can achieve Web-site success, you must decide as precisely as possible what you would like to see happen because of your site.

If you're not sure what you'd like your site to achieve, you're hardly alone. Barb Leff, whose company, Legal Web Works, creates sites for solo attorneys and small law firms, says that most of those approaching her for a site have no clue when she asks what they want to accomplish. "When I ask if their target markets are prospective clients, existing clients, or referral sources, they're usually either vague or they say 'OK'—which isn't exactly an answer," she says.

Even when you have an answer like "We want to increase sales," you'll see more progress when you refine your purpose in more particular goals. "No matter how deeply clients may have probed in coming up with goals for their Web site, we help them probe even deeper," says David Weltman, Chief Operating Officer of Future Now, an online sales consulting firm. "For example, we helped a discount magazine-subscription site identify its most profitable market segments and its most profitable product. We also helped them with more targeted product and pricing strategies, new sales copy, and a more efficient marketing plan. As a result, their conversion rate—the percentage of visitors who buy—quadrupled, from 1.21% to 4.97%."

In this introduction:
- *Why it's essential to articulate the purpose of your Web site*
- *How to plan for multiple audiences*
- *Why you should usually avoid jargon at your site*
- *What you must understand about the Web as a communication vehicle*

Articulating Your Purpose

Whether you prefer hard-nosed quantitative targets or softer, nonnumerical goals, here are some appropriate answers to the first fundamental question, about desired results:

From a speaker's bureau: "I'd like the site to bring me requests for speakers from organizations that have sizable budgets, and I'll then follow up by e-mail and phone to close the deals."

From a local hardware store: "We see the site as a way to position ourselves as the convenient, community-minded alternative to the home-improvement superstores. We'd like to be able to get orders from our regular customers and deliver that same day. It would be nice, too, to showcase our community involvements and provide a forum where experts and enthusiasts answer questions about construction, plumbing, and repair."

From a spice dealer: "We want the site to sell, sell, sell our stuff to retail or wholesale customers who are interested in gourmet spices anywhere in the world. Doubling our sales in the next six months would make us ecstatic."

From a computer training firm: "We'd like our site to answer routine questions from our regular clients, inform them about upcoming seminars, and enable them to sign up for programs online, saving us time, energy, and postage. If the site brings us new clients, that's a bonus."

From a book publisher: "Our site should increase our overall book sales and serve as a media resource to help our authors get booked on talk shows and interviewed in newspapers and magazines. It should also reduce the number of inappropriate submissions we receive by telling prospective authors what we want and don't want to look at."

From a psychotherapist: "I want the site to funnel leads to me for coaching clients around the country whom I can coach by phone, so that I can give up my bricks-and-mortar office within six months."

From a graphic design firm: "We see our site as an inexpensive but extensive 24-hour-a-day, full-color portfolio that demonstrates what we do for our clients. We would like it to upgrade our image so that organizations that think we're too small to handle their account will take us seriously."

From a bed and breakfast: "By the end of the year, we'd like the Web site to be bringing us at least 50% of our guests. We would like an online booking system so that people planning a trip can know instantly whether the dates they have in mind are available and then reserve rooms using their credit card."

From a museum: "Our Web site should serve the public with accurate information about our hours, how to find us, and our current and future exhibits. It should also boost our membership renewal rate, recognize our corporate donors with links, and bring in enough product sales to at least pay for the site."

Did you notice how diverse purposes can be? The more specific your goal, the better your chances of fashioning targeted solutions that bring you those results. For instance, when Barb Leff learned that a family-law firm she worked with, **Gevurtz, Menashe, Larson & Howe, P.C.** (http://www.gevurtzmenashe.com) wished that prospective clients could be better screened, she was able to create an online intake form and a booklet request form that helped qualify prospects. (See Figures I.1 and I.2.)

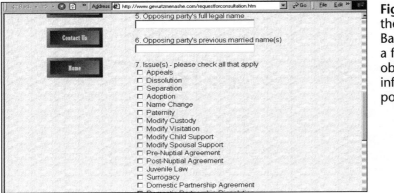

Figure I.1: Part of the intake form Barb Leff created for a family-law firm to obtain fuller information on potential clients.

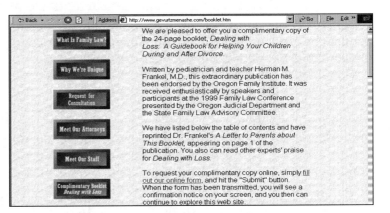

Figure I.2: Note how much information this page provides about a free booklet, increasing its chances of attracting the attention of the firm's target market, parents with divorce and custody issues.

On the other hand, don't beat yourself up if you can't right now put into words the results you'd like. A Web site is something that can naturally evolve as you become more comfortable with the medium and compare the results you do get to your vague hopes and fantasies.

Several years ago, I had a site hosted at the site for a TV show on which I regularly appeared. When I finally created my own site, I saw it as a draw for people seeking marketing information, functioning much like my articles in magazines, my books, and my appearances at the podium. In other words, the site would increase sales of my books, bring inquiries from potential consulting clients, and attract new business opportunities.

Those things did occur, but more than a year went by before I realized that I should focus more on funneling as many site visitors as possible into subscribing to my weekly *Marketing Minute* e-mail newsletter, whose special offers had proved popular and lucrative. Someone who visited once and thought the site a marvelous resource didn't do me nearly as much good as someone who visited once, thought the site a marvelous resource, and subscribed to receive a marketing tip from me every week. So I added an invitation to subscribe at the bottom of all the informative articles at the site. (See Figure I.3.)

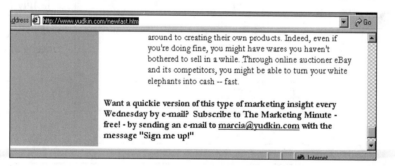

Figure I.3: Adding this paragraph at the bottom of all the articles at my Web site boosted the number of subscriptions to my newsletter from the Web site, which in turn increased sales of my products and services.

I also realized I lacked any way to feature anything new, current, or upcoming. Reorganizing the home page from two columns to three increased sales of the products, services, and seminars I placed in the center column. (See Figures I.4 and I.5.)

If you can't articulate specific purposes for your site now, pay special attention to your reactions as you encounter the examples I've collected for you. Noticing which features prompt you to think, "Hey, I could do that!" can serve as the trigger for changes that refine your results.

Figure I.4: My old home page lacked a way to highlight anything new, upcoming programs, or special offers.

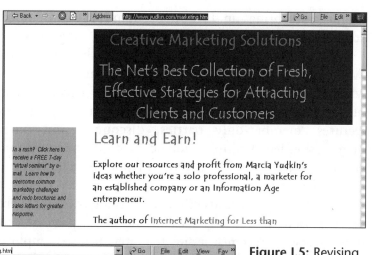

Figure I.5: Revising my home page (see Figure I.4) from two columns to three enabled me to shine a spotlight on certain products and services.

Identifying Your Audiences

Some of the answers collected in the preceding section begin to address the second essential question mentioned in the opening of this Introduction about your target audience or audiences. Being equally specific about whom you'd like to serve enables you to construct the site to attract the right people and turn their interest to your benefit.

For example, suppose a local museum analyzed its attendance and realized that a growing number of in-person visitors came from foreign countries. What features at the Web site would meet their needs? Many visitors would appreciate basic information about the museum in their own language, with directions and maps geared to their unfamiliarity with the surroundings. Links to other attractions in the museum's city would appeal to this population, too. The Louvre museum site, **Site officiel du musée du Louvre,** (http://www.louvre.fr/) reaches out to foreign visitors on its home page, which is in French, by offering links to versions in English, Spanish, and Japanese. Clicking the Japanese-language link brings up the Louvre's home page content fully translated into that language, along with links to the other three languages.

Yet tourists from abroad don't comprise the only audience for the museum's Web site, and their needs differ greatly from those of another audience—locals who either are or could be persuaded to become members. Members and prospective members would want to know more about special events, exhibits, lectures, member-only parties, discounts, and other benefits of their membership fee. Multiple audiences are extremely common for Web sites, and you must plan carefully to avoid inappropriately tilting your Web site to one group, ignoring the needs of an important constituency, or even turning off a category of people, because they see nothing there for them. The solution might be as obvious as dividing part of the home page in half, as did **eWork.com** (http://www.ework.com/), a site that matches self-employed professionals with companies needing freelance help. (See Figure I.6.) Or you might devote most of the home page to the needs of one group and catch the attention of your other audience with a subhead in a boxed-off area. (See Figure I.7.)

Figure I.6:
eWork.com serves two audiences and gives them equal billing so that visitors can choose the appropriate pages for their situation.

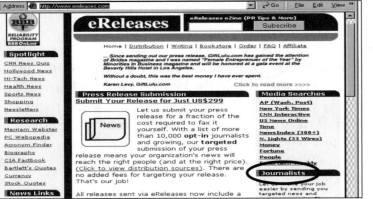

Figure I.7: eReleases, which distributes press releases for those seeking publicity, catches the attention of its secondary audience—journalists—via the heading "Journalists" and a box of copy directed at them.

Sometimes you have an audience whose needs you want to satisfy, but you don't want to be so obvious about it. For example, a man running a site for a learn-to-read system hoped the site would not only produce sales but also attract and address the concerns of investors. Although this didn't warrant an explicit section for potential investors, it did call for a thorough profile of those running the company and a convincing section on what made this learn-to-read system superior to competitor's systems—more information on each of these elements than doting parents would ordinarily need.

Once in a while you'll have a particular group whose needs you most definitely do not want to satisfy at your site. Perhaps, like a wine merchant or a political fundraiser, you can legally carry on business only with those over a certain age and living in certain countries, states, or counties. Or perhaps your firm is licensed to perform services only in specific geographical areas. Possibly ethical scruples lead you to reject some kinds of businesses, such as pornographers or spammers, as clients. Or you just don't want to be bothered with inquiries from people in some category or other, such as headhunters or students working on school papers. Sometimes the solution to such limitations lies in a clear, prominently placed, positively worded statement about who your audience is. For example, **SeniorNet** (http://www.seniornet.com/) heads off questions about how "senior" visitors have to be to use the site with a reference to adults 50+ smack in the center of its home page. **ParentCenter.com** (http://www.parentcenter.com/) uses a different solution. (See Figure I.8.)

Figure I.8: ParentCenter.com makes its audience clear through the buttons 2 through 8 near the bottom of this screen shot and through its referral to babycenter.com in the upper left.

Other times you can specify your disqualifying conditions close to the text that invites prospects to get in touch or submit their order. (See Figure I.9). In still other cases, you simply try to identify which features of your site are attracting the wrong crowd and change them appropriately.

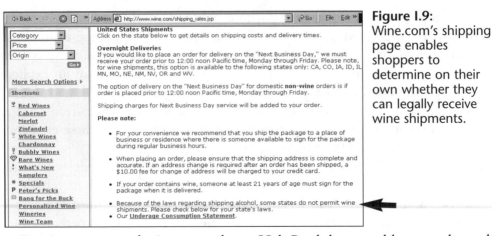

Figure I.9:
Wine.com's shipping page enables shoppers to determine on their own whether they can legally receive wine shipments.

For instance, marketing consultant Hal Pawluk was able to reduce the number of inquiries he received from cheapskates and increase those from firms with sizable budgets by stating his fees at his Web site. "Since posting my rates I have had nothing but real leads, great projects, and contacts from companies with seven-figure ad accounts. I even raised my day rate," says Pawluk.

Knowing your audience is essential for properly describing your products and services to the group you want to attract. As we'll see throughout this book, one prevalent pitfall is using insider language—jargon—that puts off some or most of the individuals the Web site is trying to serve.

In the last few years, for example, readers of *Fast Company* and other "with it" business magazines have encountered the term "free agent" to denote self-employed professionals or those who move from one project-focused contract to another. Yet there are plenty of freelancers and consultants who associate the term free agent with sports figures rather than themselves. Thus a site like **Freeagent.com** (http://www.freeagent.com/) that depends on this language without any helpful paraphrases (as shown in Figure I.10) unnecessarily excludes people in its target market who just don't know the insider lingo.

Figure I.10:
Freeagent.com assumes that visitors know what a free agent is. This page is especially confusing because freelancers and consultants do not have employers.

The solution lies either in choosing terms understood by everyone in your audience, providing an unobtrusive explanation to clue in the uncool (see Figure I.11), or inserting a link with a definition for outsiders (see Figure I.12).

Figure I.11: Freeagentnation.com provides an unobtrusive, clear paraphrase on its masthead for those unfamiliar with the lingo.

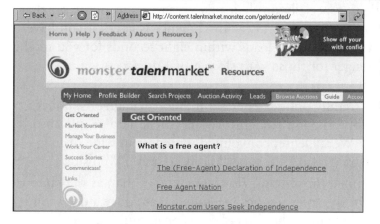

Figure I.12: Monster Talent Market provides this primer on free agents from a home page link called "Learn more about free agency in the Free Agent Guide."

Understanding the Medium

Brochureware is a derogatory term invented by Internet old-timers to denote company Web sites that use pre-existing copy from print brochures almost word for word. Such a strategy not only fails to acknowledge the distinctive nature of the World Wide Web, it tends to foil the expectations of site visitors. Before turning to specific ways in which you can do a better job of marketing online, let's consider ways in which the medium of the Web shapes encounters between sites and users:

- Because of the way search engines and links function, people may first land on other pages besides the one you've planned as the home page. When this happens, they need a quick orientation to whose site they're on and signposts showing them how to locate what they're looking for. By contrast, people looking at a brochure almost always see the front or cover before the inside contents.

- Similarly, people can and will view pages in the order in which they feel like looking at them, not the order you've planned for them. So when something crucial is explained somewhere other than on the page where the visitor has the question, dissatisfaction and confusion can occur. On the Web, explanations must be accessible—even better, obvious—from the page where the visitor experiences the uncertainty.

- Unlike printed sales letters or brochures, you won't have control of who views your information—or when. It's not possible to ensure that only the right people visit your site or that they do so after hearing your explanation of what they need to know to appreciate and use the site. Also, you're not there to show them around and provide commentary. All visitors have to go on is what they find on the Web page.

- People are impatient, especially on their first visit to a site. Some say that if a site doesn't load in eight seconds, your audience is gone. If you have high-speed Internet access, what loads within eight seconds for you might take many times longer for those with slower, dial-up access via a traditional modem.

- People don't read carefully online. They skim. Short paragraphs, bullet points, frequent subheads, and straightforward syntax help people absorb information on the Web. Dense, convoluted sentences in wide or long blocks of text that are passable on paper kill interest at a Web site.

- Web visitors are primed for mistrust. Everyone knows that, as the famous cartoon puts it, "On the Internet, no one knows that you're a dog" (said by a dog). Visitors don't have the three-dimensional, multisensory impressions of you and your company that they would have in real life. So unless you provide every reassurance you can, they're quick to draw the conclusion—fairly or not—that you don't deserve their trust.

- People may not have the ideal computer setup. Perhaps 90% of those who arrive at your site are using the latest browser version and have the right plug-ins to view or hear multimedia already installed. Among the remaining 10% there may be a CEO on vacation surfing on his sister-in-law's old computer or an entrepreneur, seeking investment opportunities, whose browser reads text to her out loud because she can't see. The only excuses for such access barriers involve either lack of familiarity with the ins and outs of the Web or some designer's ego.

Throughout the book we'll return to the implications of these points when discussing how you should structure and word your Web copy. You ought to be working with, not against, the psychological and technical facts of life of the Internet medium.

PART I

Crucial Web Site Elements

CHAPTER ONE

The Name Plate

It's next to impossible to perceive ourselves as others do. Mirrors don't reflect precisely what others see, because they reverse left and right. Photographs either flatter or distort our looks by using a particular angle, depth of field, and composition. Tape recorders supposedly capture what we sound like, but the medium can introduce pops and wheezes that listeners wouldn't hear. Besides, most of us don't believe we truly sound the way we do on tape, so differently does a recording come across from the way we normally hear ourselves speak.

Likewise, we can't easily put ourselves in the place of first-time visitors to our site. Since we know who we are and what we do, we can forget to set up our site properly for people who wander in without that knowledge. Task number one for your Web site is to properly orient everyone who happens by so that they feel comfortable and know where they are and within whose auspices they find themselves.

A name plate and headline can create near-instant orientation on your site, but that sets just a minimum standard for getting off on the right foot with a first-time visitor. To make the site truly achieve your marketing purpose, you also need to ensure that orientation information, repeating from page to page, makes clear who the site is for and why people should spend their valuable time there.

In this chapter:
- *Why and how to orient first-time visitors to your site*
- *What a site's name plate should consist of*
- *Which uses of jargon you should avoid*
- *Why you should use a benefit, not your company name, as a headline*

Helping Lost Souls

Once you realize that someone can land at your site through an imperfect search engine, an ambiguous link, or even by accident, you can better appreciate why you need to head off their bafflement about where they are. One day, clicking links at an adventure travel site brought me to **global-village.net** (http://www.global-village.net/). A picture of a ship at sea, the line, "Follow your path, know where you're going," the phrase "global village," and where I'd come from gave me the strong impression that this company offered some kind of travel advisory services.

Wrong! Clicking the Services link brought to light that I'd been radically misled, because the company dealt with software development, not leisure-time trekking. Afterward, I realized that the term "global village" derived from media critic Marshall McLuhan's label for the way the media has created worldwide connections. No wonder, though, that when I went back to take a screen shot for this book of what had so misdirected me, I found a site that had eliminated the confusing ship and travel terminology. (See Figure 1.1.)

Figure 1.1: Global Village Consulting's new site, minus misleading travel images and terminology.

Serious confusion hit me as much as 20% of the time when I served as a site reviewer for the 2001 Webby Awards. They were not a random assortment of sites but those nominated as excellent. Yet sites, such as **Craig's List** (http://www.craigslist.com/), didn't immediately clue in first-time visitors, who were apt to wonder, "What is this? Who's running this? What is someone supposed to do here?" Even though I had a vague memory of people I knew recommending this site for something or other, I still couldn't find my footing until I clicked around a bit. Similarly, people happening upon **accenture.com** (http://www.accenture.com/, shown in Figure 1.2) would not find one single line or phrase of copy on the home page explaining what kind of company this was. Sure, they could click around to figure it out, but it's arrogant and foolish to assume they would.

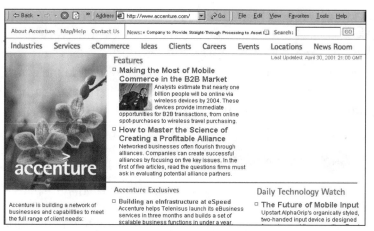

Figure 1.2: Accenture is a powerhouse consulting firm formerly known as Andersen Consulting. You wouldn't be able to figure that out from its home page.

The judging also sent me to several locally focused sites that included only the town or county name and not the city, state or province, and country. The **City of Trail** at http://www.trail2001.com/ was celebrating a centennial, but was it in New Mexico, Australia, or Costa Rica? Only the Contact Us page answered this question. (It's in British Columbia.)

On the other hand, numerous sites made me completely comfortable the second I arrived through a clear, concise statement of purpose that captured immediate attention. **Allrecipes.com** (http://www.allrecipes.com/), for example, has a head start with a nicely descriptive domain name and makes its purpose totally clear with its tag line, "Your home for great recipes, meal ideas, and cooking advice." (See Figure 1.3.)

Figure 1.3: Allrecipes.com's tag line makes the site's purpose unmistakable.

DiamondReview.com (http://www.diamondreview.com/) does this differently, forgoing a tag line but achieving the same clarity with a brief statement of purpose smack in the center of the home page. (See Figure 1.4.)

Figure 1.4: Note the crystal-clear explanation of purpose at the center of DiamondReview.com's home page.

Successful at-a-glance orientation for first-time visitors most commonly occurs through a site's name and tag line, which together repeat on every page. (See Figure 1.5.) Following nomenclature for print newsletters, let's call this element the name plate. Note how **Clicktime.com** (http://www.clicktime.com/) provides basic orientation in a thin banner at the top of each page, leaving ample space for communicating the details of what it provides customers.

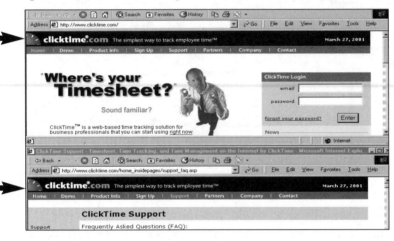

Figure 1.5: Note how the logo and tag line use little space to provide a stable identity for Clicktime.com from the home page (top) to subsequent pages (bottom).

Web designers who routinely repeat the name plate on every page may do so thinking that it gives the site needed visual unity—which it does. Just as important, though, it ensures that Web surfers don't encounter mystery meat like that shown in Figure 1.6.

Figure 1.6: Linda Formichelli produced and publicized a terrific resource for writers to learn how and where to submit review copy requests, but nowhere on this page can a reader find her authorship or her credentials.

The Jargon Trap

Either a tag line that sums up the purpose of the site, a brief, eye-catching explanation on the home page, or both sets visitors at ease by identifying the informational space in which they find themselves. Make sure that your words truly get the message across to your target audience, which means beware of jargon. Terminology that a select in-group habitually uses often gets in the way of communication with people who don't know much about your products and services, but who need them. Jargon is epidemic on Web sites for computer-related products and services. When you're certain that purchasers would be technologically well informed and up on the latest buzz words, jargon may communicate with your audience. But most companies underestimate the need for explanations of terminology that they toss around among themselves without a second thought.

For instance, **WebTrends** (http://www.webtrends.com/) announces itself as "The world's leading provider of Enterprise Solutions for eBusiness Intelligence and Visitor Relationship Management." What does "enterprise solutions" mean? "eBusiness intelligence" doesn't convey anything specific, either. "Visitor relationship management," just barely saves this tag line from being a total washout.

Likewise a company called **Carpio Helpdesk** (http://www.carpiohelpdesk.com/) uses a tag line that you may be able to translate, but many other business owners who need their product can't: "CRM for SmallBiz." Not until five paragraphs later does the marketing copy explain what "CRM" stands for—customer relationship management.

Trendy language and acronyms make some feel part of an in crowd, but without paraphrases or clarifications close by, they exclude potential buyers who know they have a problem yet don't read trendy magazines. Remember, if you're trying to make your Web marketing pay off, you want to capture the attention of your entire market, not just the most savvy segment of it. An example of a home page that uses jargon, but remains accessible to the uninitiated, is **Commission Junction** (http://www.commissionjunction.com/), which realizes that a good number of potential customers need a definition of *affiliate marketing*, and it provides a prominent link to a clear, expansive explanation. Those puzzled can click *What is Affiliate Marketing?* while those already in the know can ignore that link.

Jargon sometimes involves ordinary words used in specialized ways. Bob Marstall illustrates nature books for young adults. When I visited him after not having seen him for years, he showed me books on butterflies and deep sea creatures he'd recently worked on and mentioned that he'd developed an enjoyable extra stream of income by serving stints as artist-in-residence for school systems around the country. Then he showed me his Web site, **Bob Marstall, Visiting Artist** (http://www.marstallstudio.com/), with the site's name in big letters at the top. (See Figure 1.7.) Although I understood the words *visiting* and *artist* separately, I couldn't wrap my mind around the phrase. "Visiting? Where are you visiting? I don't get it."

Figure 1.7: The phrase *Visiting Artist* is less appealing and less widely understood than *Award-Winning Nature Book Illustrator*.

It took a couple more minutes of conversation before understanding dawned. When he served as artist-in-residence for a school system far from his home base, he became a visiting artist. The title referred to his role after being hired. But librarians, teachers, and school personnel wouldn't hire him for a residency because they were looking for a visiting artist but rather because his work fascinates school children. *Bob Marstall, Award-Winning Nature Book Illustrator* would thus be much more appealing for his audience. Marstall could then explain his role as an artist-in-residence in more detail elsewhere on his site. The general principle here is to lead with the concepts that make the most sense to your target market, not your own lingo.

More Name Plate Don'ts

Another kind of problem turns up when you click a recommended link from an e-mail newsletter and arrive at **jargonfreeweb.com** (http://www.jargonfreeweb.com/, shown in Figure 1.8). Here, you'll realize that you've arrived at a site devoted to exposing and eliminating fashionable but meaningless or overused buzzwords in public-relations writing. However, although right under the site title it reads, "The Gable Group, Public Relations Marketing Communications," you won't find a link or any other information anywhere on the page that lets you know who the Gable Group is, and where, and how this public service fits in with its own PR outreach. Not knowing this dominates an exploration of the site.

Double-checking the Gable Group site for this book, I later discovered that the links that would have answered my overpowering questions, which did not show up in Netscape in Figure 1.8, did show up in Internet Explorer. (See Figure 1.9.) Check your site in many browsers!

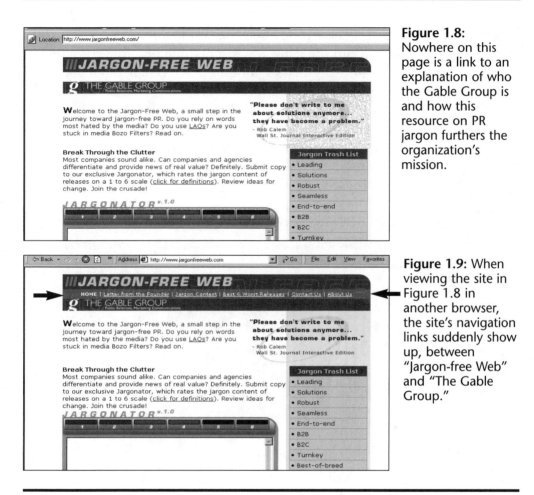

Figure 1.8: Nowhere on this page is a link to an explanation of who the Gable Group is and how this resource on PR jargon furthers the organization's mission.

Figure 1.9: When viewing the site in Figure 1.8 in another browser, the site's navigation links suddenly show up, between "Jargon-free Web" and "The Gable Group."

Avoid Browser Surprises—*An inexpensive product called Browser Photo shows you exactly what your site looks like in 14 browsers or browser versions, including WebTV Viewer, Version 2.0, Netscape Navigator, Version 4.7 for iMac, AOL, Version 6.0 for the PC, Internet Explorer, Version 4.0 for the PC, and others. It's sold by NetMechanic (http://www.netmechanic.com/browser-index.htm).*

Also distracting is seeing the name of the site spelled differently on the page and in the URL. Where are you, at Jargonfreeweb or Jargon-free Web? Interestingly, the first site mentioned in this chapter also had inconsistent hyphens: "Global Village Consulting" as the company name and "global-village" in the domain name. This might seem overly nitpicky, but misspelling of URLs is fatal to your traffic-building efforts. If you saw a screen shot of the Jargon-free Web page without the browser's address line, you would probably try the URL with a hyphen and encounter a Site Not Found message. Maintain uniformity in the identity your visitor sees at your home page.

Advertisers may like their banner ad appearing at the top of your home page, but by allowing that, you run the danger of visitors thinking that the ad refers to your company since normally that's a location reserved for the name plate. Similarly, Figure 1.10 shows a site that gives out conflicting cues as to whose site it is. Yet another site, for a gift company, was so focused on Valentine's Day when I happened to look at it that at first I thought the site offered only Valentine's Day gifts and cards, and not items suitable for a birthday or housewarming that happened to take place at the same time of year. Never allow timely content to overpower the lasting purpose of your site.

Figure 1.10: Typing *http://www.printable expressions.com/* opens a page that sort of belongs to hp photo (Hewlett-Packard) and sort of to something else called "cartogra." **Confusing!**

Beyond Who and What to Why

For your site to function optimally from a marketing point of view, you want your name plate to communicate in an eyeblink not only the basic identity of the site, but also why someone would want to do business with you. To do this well, you need to go beyond what you're promoting at the site and who you are to who would benefit from this site and how. Why should visitors bother spending time here? What help do you provide to users that competing sites don't?

Please be sure you're sitting down, because I'm going to make a suggestion that some people find shocking. If you want your site to create rapport with potential customers from the get-go, do not feature your company name in the name plate. Instead, accentuate the benefit your target market gets out of doing business with you. For some businesses, this distinction evaporates because their company name expresses the firm's benefit for clients. But if that isn't the case, lead with the benefit statement or an equally compelling marketing pitch, rather than your company's name.

To understand why, consider which line of the following pairs has marketing appeal:

Pipkind & Garvey, P.C.
Get and Keep Custody of Your Children

Steamboat Springs Spa Supply
Everything for the Commercial Spa or Home Hot Tub

Dibble Design
Inventing Your Image in Print and On the Web

In each pair, the second line reaches out and touches the reader, while the first line evokes either indifference or just mild curiosity. When you state a promise instead of just saying who you are, you stimulate interest and thereby make it plain why the folks whom your Web site is designed to attract should bother reading on. That promise provides the rationale for the Web site. In contrast, the name of an organization usually prompts a neutral feeling or impatience to find out from other elements at the Web site whether or not it will prove beneficial in some way. If you devote the biggest amount of space in your name plate to your company name, you are delaying and diluting your site's marketing impact. Figure 1.11 shows how I executed the strategy I'm recommending at **Published! How to Reach Writing Success**, my site for freelance writers (http://www.yudkin.com/publish.htm).

Figure 1.11: I named and headlined this site to place more initial emphasis on how the audience would benefit from my advice than on me.

If this feels too radical to you, or if you feel committed to branding your company name along with your benefit for customers, then see the solution in Figure 1.12. There **Harbinger Press** (http://www.harbpress.com/) puts its company name discreetly in the background while its marketing message, "Welcome to the home of the finest books on issues around the child–parent bond," fills the foreground. When using this combination strategy, make the most of prime Web space by making your benefit statement larger or more prominent than your business name.

Figure 1.12: This publishing company's name, Harbinger Press, sits discreetly in the background while its purpose takes center stage.

Creating a Clever Tag Line

Let's suppose that you're now convinced that you need an alternative or supplement to your company name to lead off your Web site. How do you come up with something catchy, compelling, and comprehensible? While inspiration needs to pay you a visit, there's a lot you can do to encourage the Muse in charge of tag lines to come calling. Try these steps, condensed from my **Business Name and Tag Line Generator** at http://www.yudkin.com/generate.htm.

1. Brainstorm a list of keywords related to your business. The more words, the better—verbs, nouns, and adjectives. For instance, keywords for a fence company would include fence, boundary, perimeter, surround, keep in, keep out, bounds, picket, enclose, yard.

2. Look up all the keywords in a thesaurus, or synonym finder, and add other words you see that relate to your business. For an online thesaurus, consult **Thesaurus.com** (http://www.thesaurus.com/). When you look up the keywords in Step 1 for the fence company, you can add lots more to the collection: limits, border, verge, hem, frontier, edge, pen, coop, wall, corral, pound, hutch, rampart, moat, ring, and more.

3. Try combining words on your list. Sometimes this alone sparks a winner; for example combining the previous words you could come up with Frontier Fence or Boundary Keepers. When any idea feels promising but not quite right, be sure to write it down.

4. Consider whether any of the words on your list have a homonym—another word that sounds the same but is spelled differently. If so, add the homonym to your list. For example, one keyword for a human resource company is "hire," which sounds the same as "higher." You can find 706 sets of homonyms at **Alan Cooper's Homonym List** (http:// www.cooper.com/ alan/homonym_list.html).

5. Look through your list of keywords, and see if any suggest common sayings, mottoes, or clichés. For instance, for a custom tailoring shop, you would spot the word *stitch* and jot down A Stitch in Time, In Stitches, and Stitched Together. The **Cliché Finder** at http://www.westegg.com/cliche/ lists clichés.

6. Now write down words that represent the benefits and results your clients and customers receive from your product or service. A financial software manufacturer might cite these: speed, convenience, and accuracy. Repeat Steps 3, 4, and 5 for these words.

7. Next, ask yourself what qualities characterize your clientele. For a yacht chartering concern, you might reply exclusive, busy, demanding, tasteful, famous, private, wealthy, multilingual, and cosmopolitan. Here the fence company might add either home or industrial to its list. Look for combinations of these new terms with the old ones.

8. Add your own name, if you're the business owner, to the brew. Does it suggest a homonym or pun? Publishing guru Dan Poynter calls his newsletter Publishing Poynters.

9. Since we assume you wish to be the best of your kind, consider words that imply mastery, excellence, superiority, biggest, and best. Also, think of what the best or top ones of different sorts are called, such as king, big fish, pinnacle, mogul, goddess, roof, and so on. Do these words, in combination with previous ones, have sparkle, as in Queen of Clean?

10. Now brainstorm what your customers and clients are trying to avoid or get rid of when they buy from you. For an embezzlement detection and prevention firm, it's theft, cheating, cons, and loss: Loss Busters. For a house cleaning service that straightens up as well as cleans, it's chaos: We tame the chaos.

11. What wishes, no matter how far-fetched, do clients often voice? Write these down and play around with them. For example, a word-processing service might call itself Done Yesterday. A used auto-parts shop claiming to be the biggest in the area could use this tag line: Everything but the kitchen sink.

12. Go back through your collection of keywords and find or create alliteration—combinations of words beginning with the same letter or same initial sound. Frontier Fence works better as a business name than Borderline Fence. Similarly, the tag line for Amazon Drygoods, an Iowa company that sells Victorian-era clothing and patterns, gives it an authoritative ring: Purveyors of the Past.

13. Similarly, try rhymes and near-rhymes for your keywords. **RhymeZone**, an online rhyming dictionary, should help (http://www.rhymezone.com/). After looking for rhymes, a tourism TV channel might select as its tag line The Vacation Station.

14. Construct a paradox by linking two concepts that could be considered opposites. For instance, an Italian pastry shop could boast of the most heavenly cannolis on earth. Look back through words and phrases you've previously jotted down and ponder their contraries.

15. Sometimes an evocative business name or tag line uses figures from ancient mythology. A Web site known for breaking stories that conventional news media won't touch might style itself: Newspapers' Nemesis, or, for a moving company, The Hercules Crew with the Touch You Can Trust. **Brewer's Phrase & Fable** dictionary at http://www.bibliomania.com/2/3/255/frameset.html will help with this step.

16. Combine and recombine. And finally, make sure your top candidate is distinctive, communicates what you want to convey to your target audience, and isn't already in use elsewhere online. Then congratulations— you've got a new tag line!

Action Steps:

• Show your home page to a couple of people who don't even know what business you're in. After a quick look, can they state the purpose of your site? If not, get busy making changes.

• Identify every instance of jargon on your home page. Unless close to 100% of your target visitors understand your terminology, reword or add explanations.

• Consider your site's headline and tag line. Do they merely identify you or do they start marketing for you in a powerful way? In the former case, begin brainstorming new possibilities.

CHAPTER TWO

Navigation Labels and On-Site Searches

Imagine driving out of the airport in a part of the world you've never before visited. You come upon a fork in the road with two stark choices: North and South. Your destination is downtown, and in the few seconds before you must go one way or the other, you seem to recall that downtown is East. Frustrated, you choose North and fail to find any turnoff for downtown or see any facility where you can ask directions. Even if you finally make it downtown with sanity intact, you'll consider the area cursed and won't be eager to return and explore without a guide.

This story dramatizes, with only slight exaggeration, the predicament many users encounter in their first or subsequent visits to many Web sites. Navigation labels, the words or phrases on a site's major internal links, function like signposts that should tell us where to turn at a fork in the road. All too often, however, they provide a bad match with visitors' mental maps. Sometimes they make no sense at all to newcomers. The disorientation repeats with another popular tool for finding one's way around sites, the Search box.

In this chapter:
- *What researchers have learned about how people find their way around a site*
- *How to arrive at appropriate navigation categories, step by step*
- *How to lay out navigation options on your Web page*
- *Why you should include tips for searching along with a Search box*
- *When to structure searches with specific options*

The Importance of Navigation Labels

Research by usability guru Jakob Nielsen reveals that when visitors arrive at a Web site, about half head straight for the Search box to find what they are looking for, one-fifth depend on the navigation links, and the rest switch between searching and following links. These numbers may understate the importance of navigation labels. Because the categories represented by these labels are often just as visible on the home page as the site's name plate, they help orient visitors whether they prefer starting off at the Search box or choosing navigation links.

Usability Resources—By watching people try to accomplish certain tasks at Web sites, usability researchers discover which factors make sites easier to use and which frustrate users. Learn more about such findings at these information-packed sites: Usable Web (http://www.usableweb.com/); Useit.com (http://www.useit.com/); and User Interface Engineering (http://www.uie.com/).

Consider visitors interested in mutual funds who land at a site called Fifi Financial. If navigation tabs like New Investors, Your Account, and About Us catch their attention, they'll either begin typing in the Search box or select a link. But if the tabs read About Pet Plots, Web Memorials, Pet Insurance, and Financing Your Purchase, they'll realize at a glance that they're at the wrong place and will back out without using either the Search box or the links.

Coming up with the ideal set of top-level navigation choices is not easy, whether you're starting from scratch or revising a site that's been up for a while. One common pitfall to stay away from is replicating your internal company structure in the main choices on your site. See Figure 2.1 for an example of a top-level navigation system constructed from company divisions rather than the needs of potential clients.

Figure 2.1: I arrived at Visx International (http://www.visx.com/) after selecting #16 on *Fortune* magazine's list of fastest growing companies. Why should I have to select either U.S. users or International Users before learning what the company does?

Figure 2.2 shows another site with a startlingly fractured set of main choices that don't make sense from the site visitor's point of view. Nielsen reports that one e-commerce project showed a ninefold increase in usability when a site switched from categories derived from the way the manufacturer thought about its products to a scheme reflecting users' mental model of the product lines.

Figure 2.2: If you didn't already know what Berkshire Hathaway (http://www.berkshirehathaway.com/), one of America's 10 most admired companies, does, its home page would only deepen the mystery. Why does it give as much weight to ads for Geico car insurance and Borsheim's jewelry as to the company's annual report?

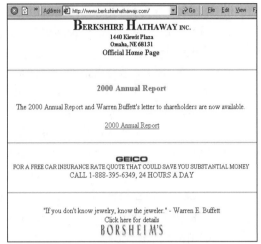

Effective navigation choices indicate to your target audience where they should click to find the items or information they're looking for. Annual tests of e-commerce sites by a firm called Creative Good show findability of items by online shoppers getting worse rather than improving. Paying close attention to this factor alone can help your site soar above the competition.

Six Steps to Top-Level Navigation Categories

Arriving at good top-level link labels involves a combination of approaches. Using only one method, you run too great a risk of leaving out or obscuring options that matter to your visitors. Some steps in the following list may seem to duplicate other steps, but I urge you to stick with the instructions to make certain that you end up with categories that funnel visitors to the parts of your site that pay off both for you and for them:

Step 1—Make a list of kinds of visitors to your site, breaking the list into as many categories as you can think of. For example, for a smallish bank with several local branches, the list might include current depositors and borrowers, local people shopping for a new bank, newcomers to the area, consumer and commercial customers, kids, students, wage earners, seniors, and the media.

Step 2—For each group you identified in step 1, brainstorm a list of activities people might want to perform at your site—actions they'll want to accomplish. Include actions visitors might want to take but you don't plan to accommodate for now. This list will contain verbs, such as the following, for a car dealer's site:

- Find out about available cars
- Learn the features of current models
- Find out about available financing

- Book a repair appointment
- Determine warranty periods and policies
- Find directions, service hours, and phone number

Step 3—Now create a list of items and features you already have at the site or plan to provide there. For a graphics software company, this list might include these things, among others:

- Information about the programs
- Information about program updates
- Technical support FAQs (frequently asked questions)
- Technical support hours, phone numbers, and e-mail addresses
- Additional company information
- Online order forms

Step 4—Where possible, consult your e-mail, phone, and in-person customer-service records to note what people have been looking for at your site that wasn't there or what needs they've had that they couldn't satisfy at the site. Sometimes this step makes obvious something that didn't come up on the other lists.

Step 5—Now pool all the information from Steps 1 through 4 and devise five to seven top-level categories that enable visitors to accomplish their goals and find the materials you want them to locate on your site. Often site teams come up with these central categories through scribbles, circles, and arrows on white boards. Others arrange and rearrange self-stick notes to do this, either on poster board or on the wall. A corkboard and pushpins gets the job done, too. My favorite organizational tools are index cards. I write each item on a separate card and sort related cards into piles. Each pile then represents a category, for which I create a name.

Step 6—Test and revise. It's essential to learn whether the labels you've come up with make as much sense to your audience as they do to you. You don't need to design and code those labels into a Web site to test them, however. You can get valuable answers from giving five or six people in each target market a paper-and-pencil quiz. Give them a small number of tasks to imagine performing, or a number of items to find, and ask them to check off which link they would choose to accomplish each task. The last option in each set of responses should read something like, "I'm stumped." If testers select the correct options, the associated categories will probably work well at the site. But if testers make lots of mistakes or report confusion, you should create a new set of labels and test again.

Keep in mind that the top-level navigation represents just the beginning of a workable Web structure, since users often have to drill down several levels to find what they are looking for. Getting lost halfway to one's destination is as serious as being baffled at the outset. If you have a large or medium-sized site with a great variety of elements, you'll want to repeat this exercise to end up with a complete, well-organized configuration of categories. Many site builders convert their arrangement of self-stick notes or their white-board sketch into a multilevel diagram resembling an organizational chart. (See Figure 2.3.)

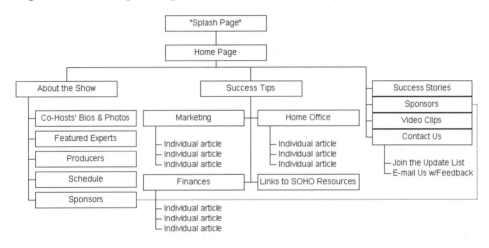

Figure 2.3: This is a schematic diagram of the Web site for a proposed TV show called "Soho Success."

Category Problems and Solutions

Let's look at some common shortcomings for navigation labels and how to remedy the flaws. Unless you are 100% certain that anyone who might realistically do business with you understands your specialized or trendy terminology, beware of jargon. Buzzwords, or fashionable phrases that convey little except "We're cool," hold special irritation for journalists. A group of writers for *Forbes, Fortune,* and *eCompany Now* singled out these offenders, among others, at **Buzzkiller** (http://www.buzzkiller.net/buzzsaw.html):

- Mission-critical
- Scalable
- Next-generation
- Web-enabled
- B2B, B2C

- Leading
- Leverage (used as a transitive verb)
- End-to-end
- "The ___ space"
- Incent

However, even terms that have been around for a generation can get in the way of communication if they represent language understood by those selling the product or service but not by those buying. For example, marketers sometimes call brochures "collateral," which to many business owners evokes associations of collateral damage, not vehicles for getting a company's message across. Likewise, financial planners are comfortable talking about irrevocable trusts and limited partnerships, but clients don't usually know what such terms mean.

Jargon often creeps into Web sites in the form of navigation labels comprised of names or concepts invented by the company. For instance, **Drugstore.com** (http://www.drugstore.com/) has an option under Service Center that reads *eMedAlert*. (See Figure 2.4.) That, it turns out, is a free e-mail alert service for product warnings, updates, and recalls. But how would you know that unless you'd already visited the page that explains it? More people would click the link if it said, *Free Product Safety Alerts*.

Figure 2.4: The ineffective link for eMedAlert in the left column would more effectively read Free Products Safety Alerts.

Avoid the temptation to come up with cute titles for navigation options or with phrases so pithy that they're confusing. Numerous sites have seen sales pick up when they changed some creative moniker, such as *shopping sled* or *wheelbarrow*, to the standard label, *shopping cart*.

Similarly, when I visited the site for the **Weather Channel** (http://www.weather.com/), I had to scratch my head at a link labeled, Wireless

Weather. I know what Boston Weather or World Weather would lead me to, but would Wireless Weather tell me about atmospheric static affecting wireless reception? Nope. It tells how to receive weather reports on a wireless device. Accordingly, Weather by Wireless would be much clearer and more effective.

According to usability expert Jared Spool, longer links orient users significantly better than those consisting of just one or two words. Granted, longer labels can pose design challenges, but what's the point of an aesthetically perfect home page with options that perplex visitors? The six-step process outlined earlier in this chapter can help you arrive at more effective options.

Categories that appeal to one audience and not another can also cause problems. Most sites for leading camera stores provide options similar to those shown in Figure 2.5. For sophisticated buyers who know what they want, navigating according to manufacturer and model number is perfect. However, people who have no idea whether they want a 35mm or digital camera, much less the make and model number, will go elsewhere when encountering only such choices. To welcome less knowledgeable shoppers, these sites merely have to add a top-level link, "Which camera?" leading to a page recommending certain cameras for family, vacation, or business use. Don't be afraid of adding information geared to a less advanced audience so long as experienced visitors can zoom in right away on their quarry.

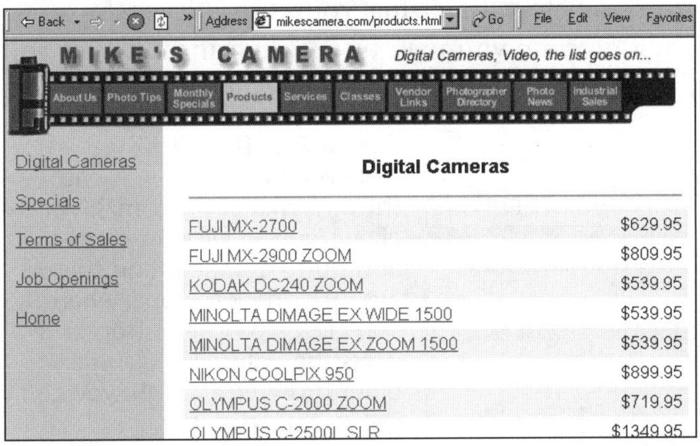

Figure 2.5: Like most camera-store Web sites, Mike's Camera (http://www.mikescamera.com/) presents cameras only by manufacturer and model number, which is unhelpful for someone who has no idea what to buy.

Another prevalent blunder involves missing information. I once decided to find out whether I could eliminate monthly service charges on my checking account by shifting money I had on deposit elsewhere to a money-market savings account connected to my checking account. Naturally, I'd want to do this only if subtracting the service charge and comparing interest rates kept me roughly in the same financial situation I was already in. A visit to the bank's Web site raised and then dashed my hopes of getting my question answered there.

Although the home page for the bank did not include a clear option for rates, clicking any of the link options on the home page brought up a new set of links, including one for Rates. When I clicked this very promising link, however, there was no mention of savings rates, only mortgage rates. In fact, savings rates were not mentioned anywhere at the site. A bank representative said savings rates weren't posted at the site because they varied from state to state and week to week. Still, how much interest someone gets on deposits is a common enough concern that copy on the Rates page should have said something, such as "Call for current savings rates." Leaving this out was a flaw in the site's navigation, which would have been prevented by brainstorming a full list of bank services.

Navigation Formats

Conventionally, sites display the main navigation options either just below the name plate, vertically along the left margin, or both. Graphically, tabs, buttons, words encased in a horizontal colored bar, or simple underlined hyperlinks usually display the choices. Since these formats work not because they're intrinsically intuitive but because they've become widespread, you normally can't go wrong by imitating the format used by the Web's most popular sites.

Drop-down menus are another way to provide navigation choices, but be sure to test these with older browsers before finalizing your site. Newer browsers enable a visitor to select from a drop-down menu by highlighting a choice and then pressing the Enter key or clicking a mouse button. (See Figure 2.6.)

Figure 2.6: The ClickZ Network's drop-down menu (http://www.clickz.com/), which allows you to click an author and go to a page listing that author's articles, works when you click a mouse button or press the Enter key. Using an older browser, though, you can't get to the articles.

An older browser may require a Go button for a drop-down menu to do its thing. (See Figure 2.7.)

Figure 2.7: Adding a Go button to open a drop-down menu, as Intuit.com (http://www.intuit.com/) does, makes it work for users of older browsers.

Many sites furnish the main navigation options in a cluster of links at the bottom of every page in addition to under the name plate or along the left side. Don't worry about the apparent duplication of having more than one set of links! I've never heard of a user complaining because of too many routes leading to their destination, although the opposite problem rears its head frequently. Having two or even three—top, left side, and bottom—overlapping batches of navigation choices simply increases the odds of visitors finding their way without having to scroll or click around too much.

In line with usability expert Jared Spool's discovery that links with more words tend to work better than compressed two-word phrases, some sites do well with hyperlinks containing more than five words or even an entire sentence. (See Figure 2.8.)

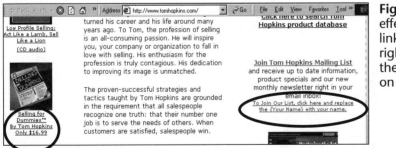

Figure 2.8: Note the effective use of long links both in the right column and in the book captions on the left.

Likewise, at an information design seminar, Yale professor Edward Tufte showed the opening screen of **Excite.com** (http://www.excite.com/) that served as a gateway for no less than 162 links. (See Figure 2.9.) Such densely packed but logically organized information there does not overwhelm the viewer.

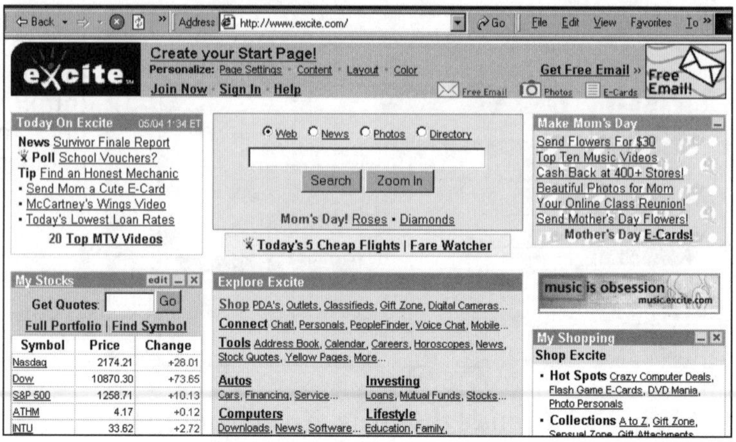

Figure 2.9:
Excite.com displays dense, but well-organized links.

The more link choices you offer, however, the more vital it is that they be chunked in scannable groups of links under subheads. (See Figures 2.10.) More than seven items together in one list makes most people's eyes glaze over. When you do offer many options, try to cluster them either thematically or chronologically. Alphabetical lists rarely work well.

Figure 2.10: I count the successful use of at least four types of subheads at Yahoo!

When you can't easily summarize an offering or a section of information with a couple of words, consider getting your point across with a headline, a block of text, and a link people can click to learn more. (See Figure 2.11.) This technique is often used for news items and ads, but there's no reason you can't use it for major options on a home page. Remember, no one gives prizes for managing to reduce your directional signals to just one word or two. The reward of increased leads and sales from your site will often require clearer, longer labels than that.

Figure 2.11: The InternetContent.net site sets up links to its main articles with a clickable headline and a blurb consisting of a sentence or two.

What about graphic icons instead of text link labels? Ordinarily, words communicate much more clearly to first-time visitors than images do. Icons also present a barrier to visually impaired computer users, unless the images bear HTML Alt tags—text associated with the images that is accessible to a nongraphical browser.

Navigation Aids

Helping visitors find their way around your offerings and treasures is so vital that you should consider a few additional techniques that help orient and direct people at your site. For a site containing more than 10 or 15 pages, particularly with a lot of different types of content, a site map shows at a glance the categories and subcategories. Usually a site map displays just the structure of the site with a phrase summarizing each page, but Figure 2.12 shows a more creative format for a site map, helping newcomers understand what they can find where at the site.

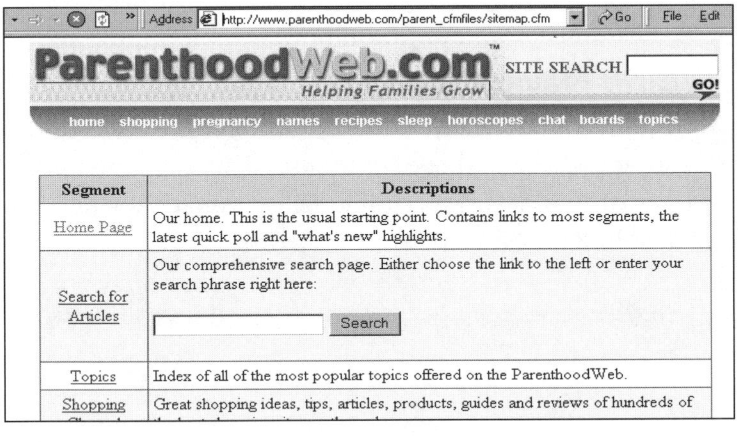

Figure 2.12: ParenthoodWeb.com's site map (http://www.parent hoodweb.com/) not only displays the categories of content available at the site, but also explains how each benefits visitors.

If you have a deeply structured site, with visitors able to delve further and further into one category at a time, you might want to provide "bread crumbs," which show the path just taken through ever narrower categories (see the top line of text in Figure 2.13). Named after the trail markers used by Hansel and Gretel in the well-known fairy tale, a breadcrumb system reminds visitors exactly how they've drilled down and where they'll go if they hit their browser's Back button.

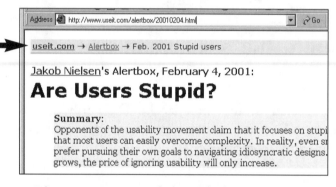

Figure 2.13: The bread crumbs

"Useit.com→Alertbox→ Feb. 2001 Stupid users"

indicate that the user started at the home page of Useit.com, clicked Alertbox, and then clicked the Feb. 2001 issue, Stupid users.

It's customary to code hyperlinks to change color after they are clicked, so that visitors can see which links they have already visited and which they have not. I received complaints from users when the first version of my Web site didn't include a color change for visited links.

Even if you've indicated an area of your site in your main navigation system, both in top and side or bottom sets of links, you may be wise to insert yet another textual link exactly where the reader would naturally begin thinking along those lines. For example, **eReleases** (http://www.ereleases.com/), a company that writes and delivers news releases to the media, has an excellent FAQ (Frequently Asked Questions) page that needs to be mentioned more prominently on the page where visitors are ready to place an order and may have questions. (See Figures 2.14 and 2.15.)

More Tips for Wording Navigation Links

Whether displayed horizontally or vertically, a set of navigation links should conform to some niceties we expect of a table of contents, which it functionally resembles. For instance, the words and phrases should be grammatically parallel. Consider the following set of links for a graphic design firm:

- What We Do
- Who We Are
- Our Portfolio
- Contact Us

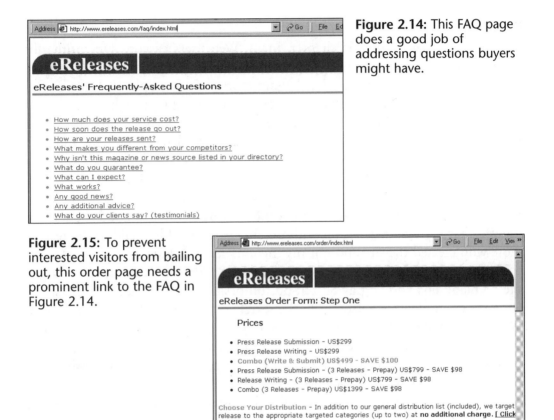

Figure 2.14: This FAQ page does a good job of addressing questions buyers might have.

Figure 2.15: To prevent interested visitors from bailing out, this order page needs a prominent link to the FAQ in Figure 2.14.

This list would be more effective if converted to the following:

- What We Do
- How We Do It
- Who We Are
- How to Reach Us

Before finalizing your list of links, think about the order in which you put them. When the order on the Web page matches some sequence in the visitor's mind or the process someone is likely to follow at your site, the links are easier to use. At most shopping sites, for example, having Place Your Order as the first link doesn't make sense, since visitors first need to look around to see what, if anything, they want to buy. On the other hand, at a business-to-business site where most visitors arrive knowing what they want to buy, a Place Your Order link might indeed be the first logical option.

Helping Searchers

As mentioned earlier in this chapter, many Web users explore sites primarily through entering terms representing what they're looking for in a Search box. Naturally, this applies only to sites having more than a couple of dozen pages. Many site builders devote next to no energy to ensuring that such a Search box actually helps visitors find the pages that meet their needs. As a result, the search box usually frustrates rather than helps. When I asked six prominent Internet industry commentators how well they thought the average Search box worked, five of the six said it worked extremely poorly most of the time. The sixth said that Webmasters usually didn't try to make it work well; but when they did, results could be quite accurate. This consensus made me feel good, because it showed that my own frustration with on-site search could be laid at the feet of those who created the site and not my incompetence as a user.

First, consider the bare-bones setup you'll find at many mid-sized or larger sites: a blank box with a gray Search button beside it. This takes up little space but gives no guidance whatsoever to the searcher. If you're looking for articles by but not about about Tom Peters, what exactly are you supposed to type into the little box? According to the experts, there is no standard answer to this question. I, as a long-time Web user, have no idea how to phrase this search; newer users are undoubtedly equally in the dark.

Theoretically, it's simple to eliminate this obstacle: Directly under the blank box insert a link that reads, Search Tips or How to Search. (See Figure 2.16.) This shouldn't muck up anyone's design. Such a link should lead to a set of instructions in ordinary language, with examples: If you're looking for _____, type in _____. The next part may not be so easy. To write user-friendly instructions for your visitors, you need to understand how the search engine you are using works. If you're using the Search box that comes with your Web authoring software, you may have to figure that out on your own. For instance, FrontPage 2000 makes it easy to create a Search box and says, "If you add a search form to an existing page using the following procedure, be sure to type instructions for site visitors on how to use the search form, and then create the search form immediately following the explanatory text." Nowhere does the program provide such instructions.

You're equally on your own for user-friendly search instructions if you install a third-party Search box at your site. I visited eight Web sites using different kinds of third-party on-site Search boxes, all of which create an index of words and phrases for your site that your visitors search through a box the third party gives you to install. None of the eight sites said anything about user instructions for using these Search boxes, either in their marketing copy, in their demos, or in their FAQs. Two

Figure 2.16: By adding a simple link such as Search Tips below a plain-vanilla search box, WorkZ.com would be able to clue in flummoxed searchers.

strategies might help you overcome this obstacle. You might simply install a Search box on your site, create the index, try a lot of searches for material you know is or isn't on your site, and then write clear instructions yourself. Or you can find a site comparable to yours in size that has good search instructions, get the particular Search box they use and adapt their instructions for your visitors. (See Figure 2.17.)

***Free Site Search Engines**—These eight sites offer free on-site Search boxes for which they create and host the index. They provide you with a Search box to install on your site and usually enable you to customize various aspects of searching, such as how results are displayed. Some charge to host your Search box if you have more than 500 pages at your site or if you would like their ads removed from the search display.*

> *Atomz, http://www.atomz.com/*
>
> *Bravenet.com, http://www.bravenet.com/*
>
> *FreeFind, http://www.freefind.com/*
>
> *FusionBot, http://www.fusionbot.com/*
>
> *Master.com, http://www.master.com/*
>
> *PinPoint, http://www.pinpoint.netcreations.com/*
>
> *POPaccount.com, http://www.popaccount.com/*
>
> *SiteLevel.com, http://www.sitelevel.com/*

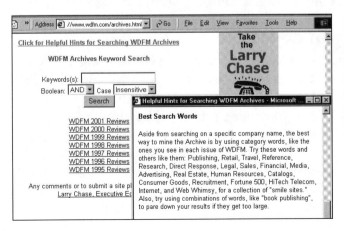

Figure 2.17: Larry Chase's Web Digest for Marketers (http://www.wdfm.com/) offers search tips that Chase obviously wrote himself. He says he got the Search box script from Matt's Script Archive (http://www.world widemart.com/scripts/).

Along with installing a Search box and providing general guidance for those who need help using it, offer suggestions on the page displaying the results. Figure 2.18 shows what typically happens when the user's first request doesn't succeed. Not very helpful! Users may also need help when a search request returns too many results. Third-party site search engines allow you to customize the copy on the search display page, so again the challenge is figuring out what to say. Something like the following might work there:

Too many results? Try using a phrase (such as "wedding flowers") rather than just a word ("flowers"), or linking two words with "and" ("wedding and flowers").

Too few? Try synonyms and related words ("bouquet" instead of "flowers").

Irrelevant results? Try excluding what you don't want with "not" ("justice of the peace and not bail and not traffic violations")

Figure 2.18: After an unsuccessful search, Entrepreneur.com left me wondering whether my search technique was at fault or there really is nothing along the lines I was searching for.

A final common and easily remediable fault with Search boxes is hiding them rather than making them available from every page of the site. Don't hide yours on some obscure back page! Either insert the Search box in the same spot on every page or offer Search as one of your main navigation options.

Drop-Down Menus and Keywords

Some searches should be more highly structured for the visitor using a different interface than a Search box. For example, let's suppose that you provide a directory of properties available for rent on Cape Cod. Much better than a Search box would be a set of drop-down menus from which users could choose the month they wanted to rent, how many bedrooms they needed, any particular town or towns they had a preference for, and an acceptable price range. See Figure 2.19 for an example of this approach used by **eCapeCod.com** (http://www.ecapecod.com/).

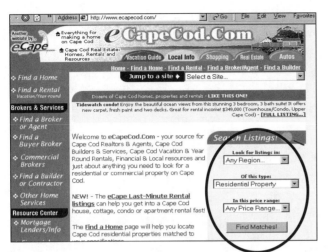

Figure 2.19: The drop-down menus on the right enable users to specify the area of Cape Cod to search, whether they're seeking a house, land or something else, and their price range.

The structured search approach may work especially well for e-commerce sites where it's unlikely that visitors will be able to accurately type in the name or kind of item they're searching for. You can also offer a set of options when a regular search doesn't succeed. Offering options in a drop-down menu steers them to the right department, so to speak, where they can peruse a limited selection of items, such as in Figure 2.20. It also works well for situations where pages don't necessarily contain the exact words matching the category under which they conceptually fall. For instance, I have written marketing articles that never use the word "marketing" as well as articles on online marketing that use the words "Internet" or "Web" rather than "online." The drop-down menu approach ensures that documents come up by category rather than according to words contained in them.

Judicious use of a drop-down menu requires two steps: first, anticipating the categories your visitors will use to search, and second, programming the drop-down menu so that it directs users to the proper pages. The latter involves techniques involving scripts and databases that are beyond the scope of this book but that most Web developers and designers can implement.

For structured searches to work properly, each document or item for sale must be coded with keyword metatags corresponding to the categories in the drop-down menu. Metatags are special insertions in HTML coding that visitors never see on the page but that determine which pages come up in a search. Figure 2.21 shows a database entry interface that ensures the proper placement of keywords behind the scenes. For sites with a constantly changing inventory of items or an ever-growing collection of documents, it's best to develop a discipline of adding the keywords as a part of adding any new item or page to the site. Web authoring programs generally provide a way to add keywords to a page invisibly.

Figure 2.20: Through drop-down menus, this portion of the home page of Outpost.com (http://www.outpost.com/) offers structured choices to shoppers who need help deciding what to select as a gift.

Consider adding common misspellings to the keywords. You can't reasonably expect everyone to know that a well-known book on Web usability is not by Jacob Nielson but by Jakob Nielsen. On the other hand, you don't want to misspell this name on your Web site. Interestingly, the first (wrong) spelling of Nielson's name calls up his books at **barnesnadnoble.com** (http://www.barnesandnoble.com/) but not at **amazon.com** (http://www.amazon.com/).

Having both a Search box and drop-down menus enables you to fine-tune your on-site search to increase the success rate of visitors' searches. Most of the third-party site search engines enable you to keep tabs on what people are typing into the Search box, so that you can incorporate new phrases and common misspellings into the keywords. If the search reports say that

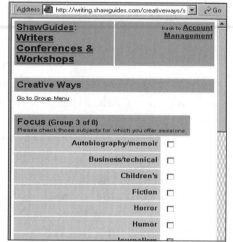

Figure 2.21: To make seminars properly come up during relevant searches, Shaw Guides (http://writing.shawguides.com/) asks seminar providers to select one or more seminar categories.

people were looking for sales force software at your site, and you'd been calling it sales automation software, you'd know how to steer those using the former term toward the proper offerings. You can also add content to your site to satisfy visitors searching for material you don't yet have.

Remember, you want your site to manifest the principle, "Seek and ye shall find!"

Action Steps:

• List five common tasks someone might want to perform at your site. Then show your home page to several people who have never seen it. Can they quickly find their way around to accomplish those tasks? If not, rethink your main navigation categories.

• Put yourself in the place of each audience you're trying to serve at your site and imagine whether they would easily find what they need. Restructure your navigation accordingly.

• Do you assume visitors arrive already knowing everything that you know? If so, consider providing other navigation routes to your resources and offerings.

• If you have a multitude of navigation choices, group them under headings.

• Add user-friendly instructions for your Search box, if you have one.

• For a shopping site or a content site, consider directing visitors' choices through drop-down menus.

CHAPTER THREE

Marketing Copy

The actual wording at many Web sites comes into being without much thought or consciousness. Someone lifts phrases and paragraphs from print marketing pieces or slaps something together under the pressure of a frantic deadline. Just because it looks acceptable to the Web team and company executives approve, doesn't mean the text will accomplish its purpose.

Although the World Wide Web has barely a decade of history so far, most of the principles for writing copy that communicates clearly and persuasively online carry over from other media. Applying these principles to your Web copy will make a just-OK site hum with impact and results.

In this chapter:
- *How to brainstorm a clear, crisp, concise headline*
- *Why* you *works better than* we *in marketing copy*
- *How and why to articulate the benefits of products and services*
- *Which details to include in descriptions of your offerings*
- *What you must include to persuade Web visitors to get in touch or buy*

Clear, Crisp, Concise Headlines

It's challenging to come up with one line that sums up the appeal of your product, service, or company for prospective customers. Indeed, this task usually takes a disproportionate amount of time and energy when I'm working on a makeover. Sometimes I find compelling words or phrases buried somewhere in the copy. Other times I need to translate a vaguely conveyed idea into clearer terms. I make notes, circle words that seem especially promising, try various combinations, and then let it all simmer in the back of my mind as I work on something else. The answer may pop up within hours, or I may need to repeat these steps and let the mix simmer again. So don't be chagrined if you find this part of your makeover difficult. Give it time.

For instance, take a look at the home page copy for **MangoSoft** (http://www.mangosoft.com/) in Figure 3.1. You need to read past the tag line, past the vague initial statement of purpose, and at least halfway into each boxed description to grasp what this company does. "Software solutions that improve the utility and effectiveness of Internet-based business applications" badly needs a tuneup. I suspect the writer had trouble coming up with an umbrella concept under which to fit both of the company's products, and this is not a problem we can easily solve, either. However, it's easy to see that the central attraction of the product on the left is increased speed. For the product on the right, we can generate a list of phrases describing its distinctive appeal:

- No extra hardware
- Convenient file sharing
- Flexible file access
- Virtual private network
- Internet-based

Figure 3.1: See how long it takes you to grasp what this company does.

The last phrase seems closest to the answer, especially once we add in a few more of the previous words. For this audience, Internet-based private network would communicate that colleagues could share files privately without having to install network hardware. Thus, to replace the introductory sentence we can use this headline, which is punchier, more specific, and more tantalizing than the original.

Providing Speeded-up Internet Access and Internet-based Private Networks

Let's do this again with a site called **VirtualAdagio** (http://www.virtualadagio.com/), whose mysterious name serves as the headline at its home page. (See Figure 3.2.) To come up with an appealing headline, we need to figure out the purpose of this site and what it has to offer that's different from similar sites. Site owner Diane Duncan explained to me that she was creating a more personal, more intimate Internet directory than, say, **Yahoo!** (http://www.yahoo.com/) or **Librarians' Index to the Internet** (http://www.lii.org/). People can use **VirtualAdagio** in several ways: They can search its categories (Arts and Entertainment, Commerce, Educational, etc.) for Internet resources, they can request a free custom search if **VirtualAdagio** does not yet include the kind of resources they're hunting for, and they can pay to request inclusion of their commercial site in the directory. Diane Duncan's vision is of a directory that lists quality sites only and that encourages serendipity.

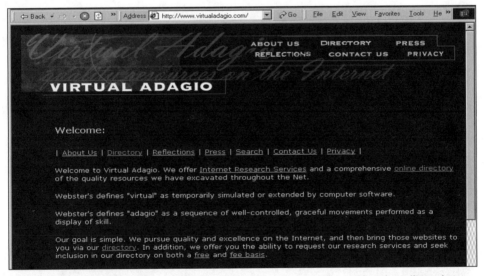

Figure 3.2: VirtualAdagio (http://www.virtualadagio.com/) needs a headline that succinctly describes what one can do there.

We need a headline that accurately and invitingly describes the purpose of this site, so let's next brainstorm words and phrases denoting a search site:

- Search site
- Mini-Yahoo!
- Directory
- Index
- Register
- Search engine
- Catalog
- Guide
- Listings
- Gateway
- Portal

For legal reasons, of course we couldn't really use *Mini-Yahoo!*, and because of the personal screening, **VirtualAdagio** is technically a directory rather than a search engine, but during brainstorming, write down everything that comes to mind. Feel free to wander around in a thesaurus for related words and phrases, so long as you also include top-of-your-head associations. You could also look at similar sites to see what words and phrases they use to describe themselves.

To make clear how this site differs from other indexes or directories, we also need words or phrases denoting screening for quality, such as the following:

- Exclusive
- Excellent/excellence
- Screened for quality
- Selective

Next comes an intuitive process of mixing and matching the brainstormed words and phrases until one combination jumps out as both appealing and accurate. For instance:

The Selective Search Portal

Figure 3.3 shows my revision of the **VirtualAdagio** home page, after repeating the brainstorming process to arrive at another phrase that emphasized the idea of quality and the ways that visitors would use the site.

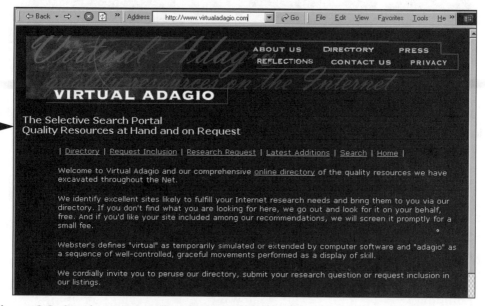

Figure 3.3: See the new headline for VirtualAdagio (http://www.virtualadagio.com/) as well as other changes in the home page copy.

From *We, We, We* to *You, You, You*

The next factor to work on in revising your marketing copy is to address the readers directly and to express what your organization, product, or service does for them. Instead of talking endlessly about *we* and *us*, your site should use an implicit or explicit *you*. Copy loaded with the word *we* requires readers to guess what it means for them. They must invest time and effort to translate what *we* means for them. On the other hand, the word *you* transmits your message directly and powerfully. As some marketers put it, people listen most to radio station WIIFM (What's In It For Me), and this is even more true for impatient Web surfers than for other audiences.

One home page uses *our* or *we* 15 times in just 423 words and mentions the name of their product or the company 5 times. The word *you* doesn't appear even once. Such self-absorption implies that *we*, meaning the company, matter more than *you*, the customer, do. Another site with a comparable percentage of the word *we* also placed its About Us navigation button first, before Our Services and filled the rest of the home page with the titles of five media releases, each beginning with the name of the company. That's egomania, and sites like this go "we, we, we" all the way to oblivion.

In comparison, on the home page of **Netflix** (http://www.netflix.com/), which rents DVDs by mail, you'll find 18 explicit or implicit *you's* and just 3 *we's*. Similarly, **Popula** (http://www.popula.com/), a vintage auction site, uses *you* 17 times and *we* only 4 times in the marketing copy at the bottom of its home page. In doing so, both companies communicate an inviting, client-centered attitude. You may believe that using *you* makes you sound unsophisticated and hucksterish. **Fencepost** (http://www.fencepost.com/), a site for New Zealand farmers that is as businesslike as they come while using a second-person orientation, should disabuse you of that notion. (See Figure 3.4.)

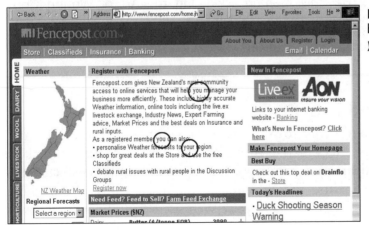

Figure 3.4: This businesslike site uses a *you* orientation.

Let's illustrate the process of translating *we* or *they* copy into *you* now with an example. The "Before" version that follows, from **PC Support Center's** home page (http://pcsupport.com/) is the sort of text found all over the Web. It's cold and bureaucratic and fails to convey that the firm truly cares about solving the computer-related confusions of its customers or about making organizations more productive. Notice how the tone warms up with minimal revision into *you* mode.

> **Before—PCsupport.com's** suite of help desk services, the MyHelpDesk system, combines assisted support services and computer self-help resources delivered, 24x7, via a Web-based application with complete reporting and administrative capabilities.
>
> Whether providing a complete help desk solution or supplementing an internal help desk, the MyHelpDesk system enables corporations to dramatically reduce the costs of providing technical support services to employees while increasing productivity across the organization and improving the overall support experience.
>
> **After—PCsupport.com's** suite of help-desk services, the MyHelpDesk system, provides you with assisted support services and computer self-help resources delivered via a Web-based application. You receive support 24 hours a day, 7 days a week along with complete reporting so that you can identify and track trends in your support needs.
>
> Whether you need a complete help-desk solution or supplementation for your internal help desk, the MyHelpDesk system enables your organization to dramatically reduce the costs of providing technical support services to employees while enjoying increased productivity and improved morale.

Copywriting Tips—Want to learn more about writing dynamic headlines and persuasive marketing copy? These three classic books got me started putting words together to get action: Herschell Gordon Lewis, On the Art of Writing Copy (Amacom, 2000); Richard S. Hodgson, The Greatest Direct Mail Sales Letters of All Time (Dartnell, 1986—available through the DMA Bookstore (http://www.the-dma.org/bookstore/); John Caples, Tested Advertising Methods (Prentice Hall Trade, 1998).

Both Features and Benefits

Web visitors also respond better to your site when you highlight the "so what" of your products and services instead of merely the "what." Marketers make a useful and important distinction between features, the descriptive characteristics of something, and benefits, the advantages the user enjoys from those characteristics. Emphasizing benefits at your Web site adds tremendous power and immediacy, motivating visitors to find out more. Take time to create a simple chart with two columns, listing the features of your product or service in the left column and the benefits of each feature in the right. To arrive at the benefit, ask yourself, "What's the good of that feature? What does it give me? What's the real reason I'd want that feature?"

For example, before its launch, **24/7Sitewatch** (http://www.247sitewatch.com/) included a list of benefits of its site monitoring service on its home page. (See Figure 3.5.)

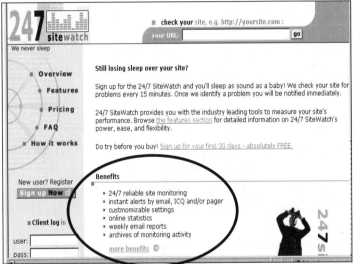

Figure 3.5: The benefits listed here needed some further analysis and rewording.

However, practically everything on the list was a feature and not a benefit. To make clearer to site owners why the service offered great value, I created a feature-benefit chart:

FEATURE	BENEFIT
24/7 reliable site monitoring	You get reliable detection of site problems so you can fix them as quickly as possible.
Instant alerts by email, ICQ, and/or pager	You can choose the most convenient way to be notified immediately of problems.
Customizable settings	You get information about problems in the format you prefer.
Online statistics	You have the convenience of being able to view site reliability statistics online.
Weekly email reports	You stay up to date on patterns of problems.
Archives of monitoring activity	You can look up past problems whenever you want.

Figure 3.6 shows how I integrated the benefit of each feature into the list to eliminate the need for the visitor to figure out why each feature matters. I did the same with a bullet farther down the home page under Pricing, changing Monthly membership subscription to Monthly membership—start and stop when you like.

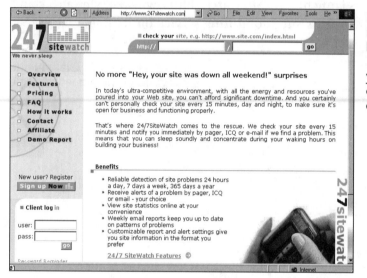

Figure 3.6: My rewording of the benefits from Figure 3.5. (Look closely and you'll note other changes I made in the copy, too.)

Let's run through the process again in slow motion for some features offered by a personal coach who does most of her coaching sessions by phone. Note that sometimes the first stab at a benefit doesn't adequately answer the client's paramount question "What's in it for me?" and you have to dig deeper for the real benefit. For each feature, the goal is to come up with a benefit whose appeal is so obvious that you don't get anywhere by asking again, "What's good about that? Why do people really want that?" These benefits then become raw material for your marketing copy.

Feature—50-minute telephone sessions.
Benefit—Convenient, compact help.
What's the benefit of that?—Advice sessions that you can easily fit into your current schedule without having to worry about traffic or weather.

Feature—$300 for three sessions a month.
Benefit—Affordable; continuity that facilitates focus and personal growth.

Feature—Free half-hour introductory session.

Benefit—No-risk way to find out whether there's a good match; opportunity to get your questions answered.

What's the benefit of that?—When we formally get started, we can get right down to business.

Feature—Masters degree in psychology and 20 years of experience as therapist.

Benefit—Although coaching isn't therapy, these credentials bespeak good listening skills, an ability to read between the lines, and knowledge of ways to facilitate personal change.

What's the benefit of that?—You get sensitive feedback and constructive direction that helps you reach your goals.

This exercise would then enable you to go from the "Before" to the "After" marketing statements below:

Before—I offer coaching in 50-minute telephone sessions, for $300 for three sessions a month.

After—Coaching in 50-minute telephone sessions provides advice and support that you can easily fit into your current schedule without having to worry about traffic or weather. At just $300 for three sessions a month, coaching offers an affordable way for you to stay focused and promote your personal growth.

Before—I offer a free half-hour introductory session.

After—A free half-hour introductory session gives you a no-risk way of getting answers to your questions about coaching and deciding whether we're a good match for one another. If you decide to proceed, we can then get straight down to business.

Before—I have a masters degree in psychology and 20 years of experience as therapist.

After—Coaching is more practical and goal-oriented than therapy. Nevertheless, as my coaching client, you get the benefit of my previous training in supportive listening, sensitive feedback, and facilitation of personal change. My two decades as a therapist ensure that you get constructive direction that helps you reach your goals.

When I do this exercise with a group during a seminar, I allow plenty of time for questions and discussion, because lots of participants need help putting into words what's beneficial about a certain feature on their list. Often outsiders to their industry can do it better than the company owner or employee. Ask friends and relatives for help filling out your chart if you get stumped. Also, use this list of common benefits to prompt your thinking:

- Save time
- Save money
- Gain convenience
- Avoid problems
- Gain security
- Avoid surprises
- Remain competitive
- Increase personal satisfaction

If thinking about benefits is new to you, you'll be shocked how much more enthusiastic a response you can get when you emphasize benefits in your Web-site copy. As one marketing writer put it, people looking for an electric drill don't really want the drill. They want the ability to make holes. Therefore when you underscore how easy and fast making holes becomes with the DRX45 drill, you do better than when you put the stress on the exact size and weight of the drill and the metallic composition of its 12 drill inserts. Benefits go straight to that part of the brain that motivates buying.

Thorough Descriptions

Whether you're selling products or services or persuading people to support a worthy cause, people want to know what they'll be getting when you ask them to take action. According to usability researcher Jared Spool, incomplete information is a major cause of people leaving a site without buying. Often the picture is too small or too fuzzy to see what the product really looks like, or the copywriter said it's available in "winesap, plum blossom, and winter wheat." (What colors are those?) Or the product description neglected to say whether the software works with a Mac and how much hard disk space it needs. At a site selling electronic booklets, none of the blurbs made it clear how short these items were for $4.77, so I just went away.

In addition to knowing what they're buying, people want to know the price before they commit themselves to the purchase. Too often, that information is available way too late in the ordering process. A good model for constructing an online catalog is a print mail-order catalog from a well-established company. A product description paragraph in a catalog typically includes measurements or sizes available, materials, price, and some tantalizing words that tickle the imagination. In addition, every print catalog page includes the company's toll-free number (corresponding to a Submit or Order button for a Web site), and the shipping charges are easy to find on the order form. See Figure 3.7 for an online catalog page that includes practically anything a potential buyer would need to know: the item's features, the company's 800 number, a way to order a color swatch for the bathing suit, a way to get immediate live help through online chat, the price, size charts, that this suit is imported, requires hand washing, is made of 83% nylon and 17% Lycra spandex, and is slimming.

Figure 3.7:
This catalog page on the Lands' End web site (http://www.landsend.com/) includes practically anything a buyer needs to know.

At times, the most basic product information is omitted from Web sites because the marketer mistakenly thinks something is too obvious to say. For instance, **Aquent.com** (http://www.aquent.com/) once sent an e-mail inviting me to subscribe to their new magazine for independent professionals, *1099*. Nowhere in that e-mail or on the Web site elaborating the free subscription offer did it state clearly whether the magazine in question was print or Web-based. I sent an e-mail asking which it was and they then added an explicit line at the site, "Free subscriptions to our new print magazine."

Another time, a guy sent me an enthusiastic e-mail telling me he liked my most recent book so much that he added it as a must-read to the recommended books at his site. I took a look, and became absorbed in his descriptions of other business books. But none had prices listed. "I have high-speed access and it's really tedious to click to the **Amazon.com** page to find out how much each book is," I wrote him. "This must be sheer torture on dial-up." The guy said this hadn't occurred to him, and he quickly added the prices and upped his odds of making sales.

If you sell just a few related services or products, another model besides catalogs can work for you: describing your offerings in narrative form, along with a readily available Frequently Asked Questions (FAQ) file that includes the same and perhaps additional information in question and answer format. (See Figures 3.8 and 3.9.) Some people skip immediately to the FAQ because one particular question is burning uppermost in their mind or because they just prefer to read questions and answers.

Figure 3.8: This marketing copy in narrative form provides the broad outlines of what someone gets when buying the online version of *Writer's Market* at Writersmarket.com (http://www.writersmarket.com).

In the process of constantly refining your marketing copy, pay attention to questions that you receive from customers. Don't take yourself off the hook because you can point to the answer appearing somewhere or other at your Web site. The fact that an interested customer didn't see it indicates that the information should probably be reworded, moved, or changed in its visual presentation. In one test performed by **Deloitte & Touche** (http://www.dttus.com/) usability specialist Tom Weathington, people couldn't find certain details about Ford trucks that were right on the screen in front of them because beautiful graphics diverted their attention from the text.

Figure 3.9: The FAQ here repeats some of the information in Figure 3.8 and adds more in easy-reference format.

When working on the copy for a brand-new Web site, you can increase persuasiveness by imagining the questions, worries, or doubts site visitors might have. And before questions and responses start rolling in, you can improve the clarity of your marketing copy by asking yourself, "What does this really mean?" Tune up its relevance to the visitor by posing skeptical objections like "Who cares?"

The Crucial Call to Action

Political candidates learn early on that no matter how on target their platform is and how well they connect with audiences, one rhetorical move is indispensable if they want to win: They must ask for the voter's vote. The same goes for you if you're a business trying to woo clients into your camp: You must ask the site visitor to take action, to sign up, to inquire about their needs, to buy.

This is a difficult point to grasp, especially for new marketers. Isn't it just obvious that you're going to all the trouble of describing your offerings because you want readers to do business with you? Well, apparently it's not obvious enough. Direct response marketers have proven again and again that you get much better results when you explicitly ask readers to take some action. And you get even better results when you ask that more than once.

So don't let those interested visitors slip away. Tell them unequivocally what you want them to do, whether that's "Call now," "Fill out our needs survey," "Please give as much as you can afford," or "Become a member today." (See Figure 3.10.)

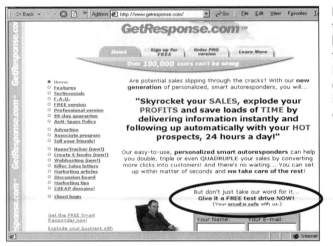

Figure 3.10: Besides the call to action visible at the bottom of this Web page, the long home page for Get Response (http://www.getresponse.com/) includes at least seven more calls to action.

One final option for organizing marketing copy to get action, which you should consider when selling a single product, is a sales-letter format, usually with a hard-sell tone. Imagine the kind of multipage sales letter you get in the mail imported onto a Web page or a sequence of them, with all the same elements: a headline, date, salutation, typewriter-style font, direct address to the reader, a closing, handwritten signature, and a "P.S." See Figure 3.11 for an example that grabs readers by the throat right from the start and leads them in unrelenting linear fashion right up to the order form.

A quick reminder: The special price of $49.97 is only guaranteed if you order by midnight Saturday, April 28, 2001 . Otherwise you'll have to pay the regular price of $99.95. **If you are serious about succeeding in your business, you need this CD-ROM. Don't delay a moment longer. Order now!** **Two Easy Ways to Order** You may order the CD-ROM directly using our online Secure order form, or through a toll free phone number. Sincerely, *Meir Liraz* President, BizMove.com **P.S.** The Managing a Small Business CD-ROM will make a huge difference. You risk nothing. The CD-ROM is not the original price of $99.95, but only $49.97 (if you order by midnight Saturday, April 28, 2001) and comes with a one year money back guarantee. And you get 7 free bonuses which you may keep regardless. Don't delay a moment longer, order now! **P.P.S.** By the way, the Managing a Small Business is a tax-deductible purchase on Schedule A of your tax return.	**Figure 3.11:** The end of an online sales pitch using classic sales letter techniques at BizMove.com (http://www.bizmove.com/).

Why does this approach get spectacular results for some entrepreneurs on the Web? A well-written sales letter represents the most intimate kind of marketing pitch, from a seemingly authentic persona with a name, a personality, and often one or two disarming weaknesses in a direct, explicit appeal one-on-one to the reader. In short sentences and a long succession of brief paragraphs, the online sales letter builds a detailed case for the product or service at hand, anticipates objections, offers bonuses for immediate action, and closes the sale. Since it requires just one service or product as a focus and most sites have a panoply of offerings, however, this format has limited applicability online.

Action Steps:

• Assess how often you use "we" or "I" rather than "you." Make changes so that readers feel the site is addressing them and their concerns.

• If you don't have a headline for your home page, brainstorm a list of the most important aspects of your site and combine the elements until you arrive at an inviting summary.

• Identify each spot at your site where you cite a feature and either substitute or add the corresponding benefit.

• Pretend to order something at your site and make sure that the most likely questions have obvious answers available before you have to enter your credit card information.

• If you have a Frequently Asked Questions page, make it readily available from every other page where visitors might have questions.

• Check whether you have adequately headed off questions or doubts people might have about your products or services.

CHAPTER FOUR

Who Are We?

In Chapter 3, *Marketing Copy*, I advised you to not to communicate your Web site's marketing message in terms of *we, we, we*, but of *you, you, you*. Now I'm going to speak out of the other side of my mouth. A Web site that only pitches its wares to *you* and says nothing at all about *we* or *I* won't reach its goals. Both direct address and self-presentation—in proper proportion—are necessary for a successful site.

People get drawn into your marketing proposition more easily when you make clear what's in it for them. But before they take action, whether that's calling you to become a client or typing in their credit card information, they usually want to know who you are. Leaving out adequate biographical or company information makes your site run roughly, as if one cylinder out of four isn't contributing its share of oomph. First, I describe the minimum factors necessary for this aspect of your Web site to operate smoothly. Then, I explain additional ingredients that make it even more well oiled for sales and opportunities.

In this chapter:
- *Why contact information is essential for every site*
- *How to write compelling individual and company bios*
- *What information to include specifically for the media*

The Minimum: Contact Information

When someone calls you and refuses to provide a name or return number, you know that something is awry. You want to know whom you're dealing with. It's just as natural for people asked to perform any sort of transaction with a Web site to look around to make sure that the individual or entity behind the site is identified. Finding a name, location, and contact information provides reassurance and psychological grounding so that the interested visitor is more likely to proceed. A Web site without identity and contact information listed anywhere might as well post a sign saying, "Trust me at your own risk."

I can't begin to count how many times I've run up against a brick wall in attempting to e-mail or phone someone running a site. On many sophisticated sites of multinational companies as well as homemade setups, contact mechanisms are nowhere to be found. One study gave 20 journalists a list of 10 prominent companies and their URLs and asked them to find a public-relations contact for each company. They could complete that task only 60% of the time.

Web forms that force all inquiries into the same little boxes and shoot off to somewhere in cyberspace when visitors click a Submit button do not satisfy this need. They don't indicate in what legal jurisdiction the site is based. They don't enable immediate contact with someone, and they don't offer any reason to believe that an urgent question submitted via an all-purpose Web form would get to the right person or get to anyone that day. (See Figure 4.1.) They also don't address the desire most of us have to know the identity of those with whom we do business.

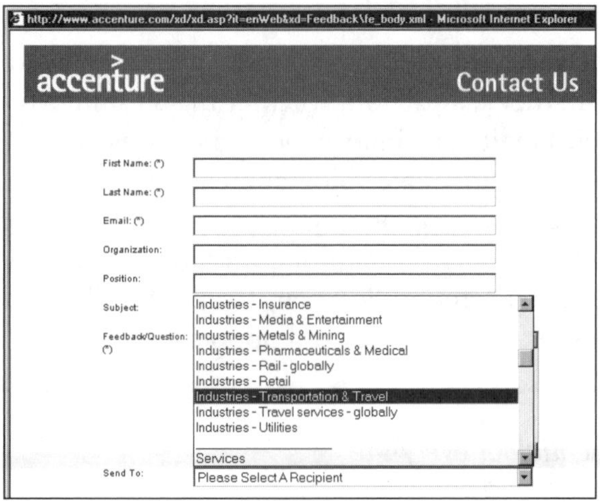

Figure 4.1: You can select a topic for an inquiry to Accenture (http://www.accenture.com/), but it's not clear to which of the firm's 137 offices it would be directed or when, if ever, you could expect to receive a response.

Some site owners probably just overlook this element without any rationalization for doing so. On the other hand, some defend providing only Web forms for visitors to get in touch as essential for them to keep up with a flood of inquiries. Richard Hoy, CEO of **Booklocker.com** (http://www.booklocker.com/) doesn't go quite that far, but close. "I think you should take your phone number off your Web site and force people to communicate with you via e-mail," he wrote in an article for small-business owners. "Set up e-mail addresses for specific types of correspondence (example: sales@yourdomain.com, support@yourdomain.com). It is a million times easier to filter all the incoming e-mail that way. When possible, use Web forms, which forces people to include all the necessary information you need to respond to their query."

Imagining that you can channel all needs into rigid and limited conduits presupposes that you can anticipate all the possible reasons someone would want to reach you. Sure, it's easy enough to foresee that people will want to submit orders, questions about their orders, pre-purchase questions about products and services, feedback about the site, and inquiries along the way to becoming a client. Here are some additional purposes you may not have considered, though:

- Someone wants to let you know right away that your site appears to have been hacked.
- Someone wants to buy your company.
- Someone wants to invite you to fill in for a cancelled speaker—tonight.
- Someone wants to license your content.
- A law enforcement official has concerns that your site might be breaking the law and wants to discuss it with you immediately, off the record.
- A reporter on deadline wants to speak with you.

Contact information also reassures prospective buyers that you're on the up and up and helps to ensure prompt, satisfactory customer service. Although Web forms can help you route and keep track of routine inquiries, you must also make clear how to phone, fax, and e-mail your company.

"Contact Us" Made Easy

One satisfactory way to provide contact information is in an unobtrusive footer appearing along the bottom of every page on the site. (See Figure 4.2.) Equally good is a Contact Us button visible on every page—so long as that button brings up a page containing actual contact information and not a form to fill out and submit.

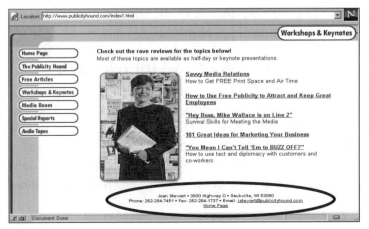

Figure 4.2: The three lines at the bottom contain contact information for The Publicity Hound (http://www.publicityhound.com/) and appear on every page of the site.

If you have more than a handful of employees, you might give thought to a categorized set of contact names, e-mail addresses, and phone numbers. See Figure 4.3 for an example of how you can suggest proper routing of an inquiry.

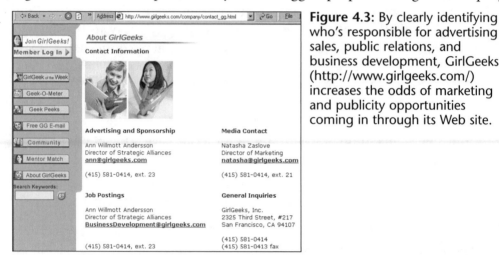

Figure 4.3: By clearly identifying who's responsible for advertising sales, public relations, and business development, GirlGeeks (http://www.girlgeeks.com/) increases the odds of marketing and publicity opportunities coming in through its Web site.

If you're outsourcing some company responsibilities, such as is frequently done with public relations, make that clear on the contact page, as you'll see in Figure 4.4.

Figure 4.4: 2Roam (http://www.2roam.com/) not only makes it clear that media interviews should be arranged through its public relations firm, but also provides the contact person's name, address, phone number, and e-mail address.

Most people who need to get in touch use the phone or e-mail, but your physical address not only anchors all the contact information with credibility, it also indicates implicitly your general hours of availability. Customers several time zones apart from you who left an urgent message with no reply may not panic or get angry if they realize that it's still the wee hours of the morning where you are.

Company and Individual Bios

Most often, you'll find biographical information about a company and its owners or executives from a main navigation button called About Us. Whether your navigation options run vertically or horizontally, don't put this button first. Normally it belongs toward the end of the list.

If you're a solo operation, About Us would normally lead to your business bio. This should be a narrative paragraph or several of them telling the story of what qualifies you to deliver the products or services that you provide. Instead of organizing such a bio chronologically, lead off with a summary statement that explains in a nutshell your unique combination of skills and experience. Then furnish the most pertinent facts that round out the picture. The following two abbreviated examples should give you a clearer idea. Notice how they offer just enough detail to make claims believable and concrete:

> *MaryAnn Gerhardt's 22 years of design experience encompass media ranging from print to outdoor signage to television. As the owner of Gerhardt Design, she works with clients to create, extend, and change corporate identities. Trained in illustration at the New York Museum School, she has received 17 awards for client work, 3 gallery exhibitions, and scores of mentions in national publications. Gerhardt lives and works in a Victorian mansion that she redesigned and that also serves as a showcase for her work.*

> *Harold Wen has been called "a lifesaver," "a miracle worker," and "a revival artist" for his ability to revive companies near death. His 37 years in finance, marketing, and operations give him an unusually broad base of experience with which to diagnose and remedy a company's problems. Clients run the gamut from food processing firms and family farms to Fortune 100 conglomerates.*

As with the other sorts of marketing copy, for a client's business bio, I begin by making notes on the most important points and look for ways to group related items into a broader statement. The overview sentence is the hardest part to compose; but once that arrives from the muse, the rest usually comes together quickly. Remember to emphasize the aspects of your story that appeal most to your target market. Photos can add warmth and personality to the words. (See Figure 4.5.)

For a professional firm comprising less than a dozen practitioners, you'd usually present a grouping of these sorts of individual bios on an About Us page. A bigger firm might split the bios according to practice area—all the chiropractors on one page, the naturopaths on another, and the energy healers on a third, for instance.

When you have a large organization or a company that you want to be perceived as a team, not a collection of individuals, you should present a biography of the company, analogous to the samples shown previously. For example:

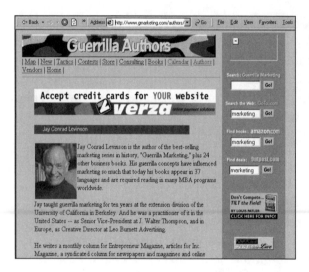

Figure 4.5: Guerrilla marketing guru Jay Conrad Levinson becomes more approachable through the photo accompanying his online bio at Guerrilla Marketing (http://www.gmarketing.com/).

In its two years since launch, eLusivv.com has built a worldwide reputation for organizing and running Internet scavenger hunts. Its experiential braintwisters usually require topical knowledge, ingenuity, and Web navigation skills, generating tremendous enthusiasm and participation in target populations. eLusivv.com's client list ranges from the Disney corporation to the National Association of Orienteers, and its events have been featured on CNN, CNBC, and Fox News as well as in the Dallas Morning News, Family Fun, *and* People *magazines.*

Even when you want to place the company identity at center stage, consider also offering bios and perhaps accompanying photos of founders and key executives. This humanizes the organization for users and adds credibility, which can be particularly important if you'd like to attract interest from investors without being too obvious about it.

A company bio becomes particularly important when you've taken over or renamed Web sites that previously had a significant reputation. The old URLs may circulate in books and on other Web sites for years, and people who type *www.softlock.com* and get *www.digitalgoods.com* will feel initially bewildered. The conspicuous About Us link on the **Digital Goods** site that appeared did lead to one page that mentioned SoftLock, but at the **Digital Goods** site SoftLock's e-book services referred to in the manual were nowhere to be found. This could confuse visitors about whether this company has just changed its name and hidden its old services somewhere at the site or been swallowed up by a larger company that discontinued what had been popular with the former one. A brief company history in the About Us copy might have solved that problem.

Client Lists and Portfolios

For high-level professional firms, the question of "Who Are We?" is partly addressed by a list of clients they have served. A roster of blue-chip companies, national agencies, international governments, or high-profile celebrities speaks volumes about your capabilities and influence. Just don't go overboard by creating an ever-expanding, bloated list. Select a spectrum of exemplars—less than a dozen—to avoid overwhelming your site visitor. (See Figure 4.6.)

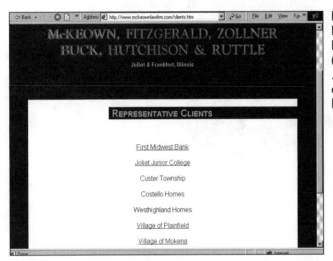

Figure 4.6: This law firm, McKeown, Fitzgerald, Zollner, Buck, Hutchison & Ruttle (http://www.mckeownlawfirm .com/), got it right—just enough names on the client list to impress, not too many.

Those who provide visual services have another convenient tool for explaining who they are at their Web site: a portfolio of work samples. Think carefully about the categories of work that the clients whom you want to attract will find persuasive. Although some shoppers browse your samples trying to get a sense of your style and approach to design, others examine your portfolio for evidence that you've handled projects similar in type and scope to theirs. Thus you need to include a representative range of project types as well as work that you know looks impressive. For instance, include one house photo, a group portrait, and an individual portrait rather than three individual portraits that happen to be your favorites. And rather than assume pictures are self-explanatory, include a verbal synopsis of the challenge posed by each project, your solution, and, where available, your client's results. (See Figure 4.7.)

To show off photos of your work samples at best advantage, make certain that the photographs or screen shots as viewed on a typical monitor flatter the work rather than raise doubts about its quality. Some kinds of creative work, such as jewelry, sculpture, and interior design, are difficult to capture and show off in small photographs. A common answer is small photos, or thumbnails, on which the viewer can click to see a larger version.

Tips for Design Firms and Visual Artists—For more ideas on how to promote your visual work through collective portfolio sites as well as your own Web site, along with plenty of examples in sumptuous color, see Ilise Benun, Self-Promotion Online: Marketing Your Creative Services Using Web Sites, E-mail and Digital Portfolios (North Light Books, 2001).

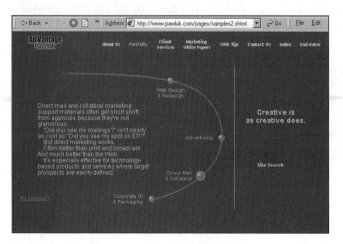

Figure 4.7: AdVantage Pawluk (http://www.pawluk.com/) presents samples of its work in four categories, with a philosophical introduction explaining its approach to each type of work.

Press Rooms

Another tool that helps flesh out a company's identity is a section of the Web site set aside for media-related or media-oriented information. Some examples consist of information for the press, while others compile media mentions and provide links to press coverage. Still others combine those ingredients. (See Figure 4.8.) If you have achieved press coverage, collecting references to it in one place impresses potential customers, investors, and subsequent visitors who represent other media outlets. As some like to put it, "Them that gots, gets."

Because most people perceive the press as an independent voice, its implicit endorsement of businesses it covers makes the media coverage count as more compelling than the company's own words in its marketing or public relations copy. Even so, the contents of your self-generated press releases often tell a story about what you're up to, so they have value when featured and archived at your site.

Remember that most media reports, whether written or spoken, are covered by copyright, so you need permission from the copyright holder—which could be the newspaper, Web site, or the author—to post the whole article or news clip at your site. In most cases, links to the articles are perfectly acceptable, as is providing the headline, source, date, the first few sentences, and a link back to the original version. Check with your attorney, of course, about how to handle a specific situation.

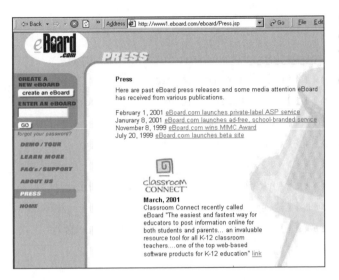

Figure 4.8: eBoard (http://www.eboard.com/) combines press releases and links to media coverage on one press page.

Copyrights and Wrongs—Unsure about whether or not something is protected by copyright? Need guidance on how to ask permission to quote from or reuse material? These sites help keep you on the right side of the law: The Copyright Website (http://www.benedict.com/); *MIT's Copyright FAQs* (http://web.mit.edu/cwis/copyright/faq.html); *and the U.S. Copyright Office FAQ* (http://www.loc.gov/copyright/faq.html).

According to Joan Stewart, mastermind of **The Publicity Hound** (http://www.publicityhound.com/), a Web site, and print newsletter, some creative and productive ways to use a press room include the following:

- List company experts at your site and invite the media to call on them for commentary, background, and story ideas.
- Post story ideas about your company.
- Provide a company history, fact sheet, frequently asked questions, and anything that's available in your printed media kit.
- Offer digital photos of yourself, other key executives, and your products.
- Post white papers and articles, and let the media know which ones are available for reprint in their own publications.
- Invite media visitors to let you e-mail them when you have new content at your site that might interest them.
- Archive CEO speeches and industry statistics at your site.
- Make it possible for media visitors to request that you send a press kit via snail-mail. Some reporters still prefer to get material the old-fashioned way.

Action Steps:

- Add complete contact information, if you don't already have it, so that visitors can find it from any other part of the site.
- Make sure people wanting to know about your company or personal background can find it, in an engaging, reader-friendly style.
- Consider adding a client list if you don't have one, or trimming yours if it's very long.
- Would an online portfolio of work samples bolster your credibility? If so, provide samples in several categories.
- Think about adding a special area of your site geared to the needs of visiting reporters.

CHAPTER FIVE

Trust-Building Elements

Most of us do not walk, filled with fear and suspicion, into a three-dimensional, tangible store. On the Net, however, such emotions are commonplace. Without the presumptive stability of a physical location and the myriad sensory cues that convey legitimacy, visitors to a Web site worry. How do you know this wasn't put up yesterday by two teenagers who think this is a cool way to steal credit card numbers? Or by a database developer whose listed qualifications hardly contain an ounce of truth? Or by a dot-com so disorganized that you'll never get what you ordered or your money back? To paraphrase Gertrude Stein, we fret that there may not be any real *there* there.

Because sensory evidence of trustworthiness is sparse online, sites must undertake mighty efforts to prove they deserve the confidence of strangers. It's impossible to go overboard on the measures in this chapter if you want your site to inspire a torrent of leads or orders. Implement as many of the trust-building elements described here as you can.

In this chapter:
- *How to undermine or increase site visitors' confidence in you*
- *Which common mistakes drive wary Web users away*
- *Why you need an explicit privacy policy at your site*

Basics That Affect Confidence

First impressions count. Plenty of times you'll land at an unfamiliar site and fairly or not, within less than a minute, form a judgment and bolt. Here are some of the ingredients that might provoke such a negative snap assessment:

Garish color combinations with big, thick letters and an awkward-looking page layout—Some sites like this appear to have been put up in the early days of the Web, back in 1995, and barely touched since then. Tastes change fast online!

Clear-cut evidence that the site has not been kept up to date—Such a site might show a line such as "Last updated, September 17, 1997."

Glaring typos and flagrant page formatting errors—Would you trust a site with visible computer code and columns overlapping each other—the on-screen equivalents of a job applicant showing up with clothing askew?

Site features that don't work, especially features central to the site's mission—(See Figure 5.1.) Would you stick around to watch a juggler who proclaimed, "Now watch me juggle four balls" and then dropped two of them?

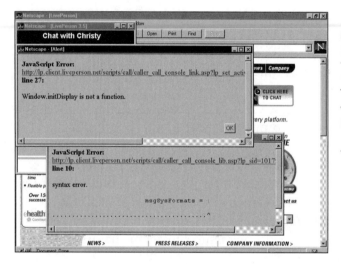

Figure 5.1: Here's what might happen when you follow LivePerson's invitation to test its live chat at http://www.liveperson.com/. The marketing copy says it works with "standard Web browsers (Navigator 3.0+ and Explorer 3.0+)." It doesn't work with Navigator 3.

A demand for personal information or the installation of plug-ins before the site has even presented what it's all about—This resembles someone asking you to buy a ticket or sign on the dotted line before describing the performance or explaining the contract.

Design at odds with the industry or expertise of the site owner—One management consultant used a pleasing color scheme and attractive fonts that gave the wrong impression at first glance, because they seemed more appropriate to a breath-of-fresh-air beginner than a well-credentialed $200/hour professional.

Experts and ordinary Web users alike draw quick, sweeping conclusions from limited evidence. When Ray Bernard, a product development consultant in Laguna Hills, California, tested a financial services site for a client, navigation blunders, broken links, and spelling mistakes caused users to stop dead in their tracks. Independently, all the testers declined to continue out of fear that the site would lose or steal their money.

Not only must basics, such as proper spelling and formatting, full functionality, and acceptable aesthetics, be in place to earn visitors' trust, the overall gestalt must be consistent with the kind of organization the site purports to represent. A cartoony collage of primary colors and a backward "S" in a logo might strengthen credibility for a daycare center but undermine it for an investment firm. Remember that if you participate in the creation of the site, you'll find it impossible to objectively assess the sort of initial impression it makes. Get independent feedback on this, such as from a group of noncompeting business owners or marketing managers who get together monthly to provide one another with advice and support.

Hidden Threats to Credibility

In addition to the at-a-glance factors outlined in the preceding section, several less obvious site flaws tarnish your image in the minds of visitors and may drive them away. If you're guilty of any of the techniques covered in the following sections, you're letting business slip through your fingers.

Overuse of Cookies

Perhaps you've never given any thought to cookies, little data files that a site inserts onto the visitor's hard disk, to help keep track of the identity of that visitor or record which pages he or she viewed. Perhaps you don't even know whether your site uses cookies. Find out! Savvy Web surfers who are concerned about invasions of their privacy have configured their browsers so that they're warned when a site is attempting to send a cookie to their hard drive. (See Figure 5.2.)

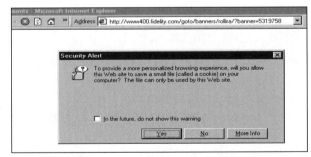

Figure 5.2: Here's what it looks like to enter the Fidelity Investments site (http://fidelity.com/) when someone has asked to be alerted when a site tries to set a cookie. Some sites require a noncookie user to click a No button more than two dozen times.

Both Netscape Navigator and Internet Explorer allow users to prompt a cookie alert—the former by clicking Options, Network Preferences, and Protocols to find the cookie options and the latter by clicking Internet Options and Custom Level, then scrolling down to the cookie settings. You may be surprised at the use of cookies on your own site (if someone else constructed it) and on others you frequent. I've set my browser to alert me to cookies for the last year, and sometimes I have to click the No button on the Alert box more than a dozen times before the site allows me to proceed.

Advertising networks set cookies to record which pages and ads were viewed, and many content sites use them for storing registration or password information. Sites with affiliate or commission arrangements use them to track where buyers came from to share revenues. E-commerce sites use cookie files to address return visitors by name, present them with specials likely to be of interest, and call up previous purchases and credit card numbers. Training sites and others with fancy interactive features use cookies to deliver advanced services.

Sometimes a site posts the equivalent of a Keep Out sign to those who have disabled cookies. (See Figure 5.3.) This is especially troubling and off-putting when it's hard to think of a legitimate reason for the site tracking a visitor, especially one walking in the virtual door for the first time. To get on the good side of those who have a horror of Big Brother, avoid gratuitous use of cookies, and be candid about what you're up to and why in your privacy statement, discussed in the final section of this chapter.

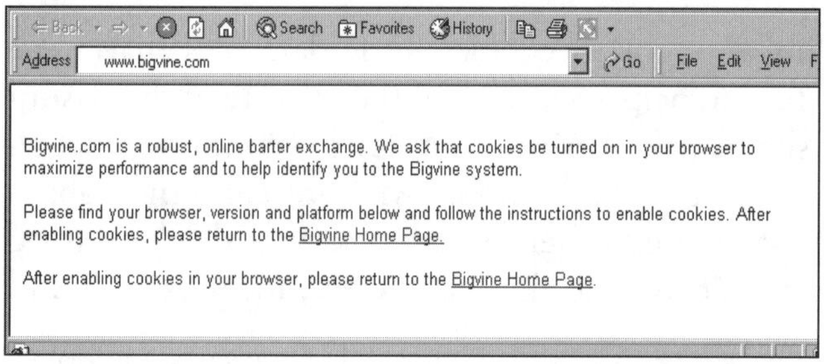

Figure 5.3: If you have not yet visited Bigvine.com (http://www.bigvine.com/), this message does not provide any reason to change your cookie settings or to trust what the site does with the cookie.

Premature Requests for Credit-Card Information

Proper timing of this step is crucial. Usability researcher Jared Spool performed a test for a computer accessory site in which a user put a color printer into his shopping cart and then backed out of the purchase when the site asked for his credit card. "The site hadn't revealed the shipping charges, and in the user's mind, entering credit-card information was the point of no return. Actually, the next screen contained shipping information and would have told the user that two-day shipping was free for orders over $1,000. Not explaining the shipping fees before asking for the order accounted for $24,000 in lost revenue in one month," says Spool. We'll discuss this again in Chapter 8, *Order Forms and Customer Service*.

Omission of Security Signals

Although in fact, a merchant runs a much higher risk of being shafted by credit-card fraud than does a buyer, online shoppers have an inordinate fear of credit card theft. You can help reassure them by making sure your site displays the secure-server icons whenever visitors are asked to submit credit-card information. (See Figure 5.4.) Security-conscious shoppers expect to see one of these when asked for their credit card. Normally the icon shows up automatically when all of the page elements for the order page, including graphics, are housed on the secure server. It's also helpful to state explicitly on your secure-server pages that they are secure.

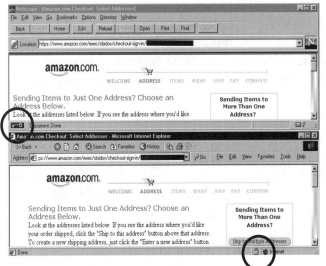

Figure 5.4: In the Netscape browser on top, the secure-server icon is a skeleton key in the lower left. In the Internet Explorer browser on the bottom, the secure-server icon is a padlock in the lower right.

Inaccurate Information

Someone who's reading along and encounters the Hudson River referred to as part of New England or *E. coli* called a virus although it's actually a bacterium feels glimmers of doubt about everything else at the site. In one of usability guru Jakob Nielsen's studies, a map that failed to show a recently constructed bridge caused users to lose faith in the rest of the site.

Lack of Contact Information

According to search engine specialists, the top search engine **Yahoo!** (http://www.yahoo.com/) won't list any sites that omit ways to contact those behind the site by phone and e-mail. Fill-in-the-blank Web forms sent to who knows where aren't a substitute for company name, address, phone, fax, and e-mail. Remember, shoppers and information seekers are wary online and feel reassured when they have the means to follow up apart from the site itself.

Failure to specify the identity and location of the site builders raises suspicion: Is there some shady reason you're attempting to remain unreachable? Contact information should either appear on every page or be accessible from a Contact Us link on every page.

Unresponsiveness

Visitors may also lose trust in a site when they pursue an inquiry by phone or e-mail to no avail. Your non-Web behavior, like not answering the phone or not answering e-mail, influences the perception of your Web site, and not only with a visitor who got no reply. Word gets around!

Measures That Bolster Trust

Earning trust involves much more than staying away from all the "don'ts" discussed in the earlier sections of this chapter. The following sections cover some features that reach out in a positive way and boost your trust quotient.

Media Coverage

When you've been featured in *USA Today*, your local paper, *TradeShow News*, or CNBC, let your site visitors know. The average person assumes that someone singled out by media reporting has a more reputable and outstanding business than competitors. In fact, the one in the spotlight might not be a better dry cleaner or illustrator—only better at getting ink and air time. If you've got gobs of media mentions, you might create a separate section of your site to house them, as mentioned in Chapter 4. Consider highlighting the latest or the best media appearance on your home page. (See Figure 5.5.)

Figure 5.5: The quoted magazine endorsement at the top of Blue Cat Design's home page (http://www.blue-cat.com/) brings instant credibility.

Because of copyright restrictions, you need express permission to repost an entire article or an audio or video clip at your site. Inserting a link to the original location is the safe alternative. See Appendix C, *Recommended Resources*, for books that explain how to earn your turn in the media spotlight. The gains in credibility make media coverage more than worth the effort.

Testimonials

A surprising number of companies ignore the tremendous clout of from-the-client's-mouth testimonial quotes. Visitors know to discount any self-praise woven into your marketing copy. After all, the horn is being tooted by you. But when outsiders say wonderful things about you and stand behind the words with their name and identifying information, the content becomes many times more believable.

Good testimonials consist of just one to two sentences, concluding with the person's full name, city, and state or province, and where appropriate, their title and company. You might feature such blurbs on a page of their own, on the home page (see Figure 5.6), or contextually positioned, with a quote adjacent to the product or service praised. (See Figure 5.7.)

Four Ways to Get Great Testimonials for Your Site

Unsolicited comments—When people send e-mail praising you to the skies, ask whether you can quote the comments and use their names. The same goes for comments heard over the phone. Just ask, "May I quote you on that?" Ninety-nine times out of a hundred, people agree.

Feedback requests—When you deliver your product or service, ask for feedback. Provide a special e-mail address, a postage-paid form, or a fax-back survey for customers to fill out. Identify the best quotes and ask for permission to use them at your Web site.

Solicited comments—Ask longstanding customers why they enjoy doing business with you, and ask permission to quote them at your site. Some people prefer to say this verbally for you to write down, while others want to compose a blurb and send it back to you.

Write something rough yourself—For clients you know really well, you can write something up yourself and ask if they'd put their name on something like it. Some will say okay; others will recast what you wrote in their own words.

Guarantees

"Satisfaction guaranteed or your money back." A rocket full of credibility is packed into that promise. When shopping online for a computer, you'll find the no-strings, no-restocking-fee return policy of **Outpost.com** (http://www.outpost.com/) for hardware elevating it miles above its competitors. The more generous your

Figure 5.6: The CEO quote in the lower left shaded panel sets a credible tone for Joan Holman's home page (http://www.holman.com/).

Figure 5.7: When I have them, I include testimonial quotes along with program descriptions on my seminar page.

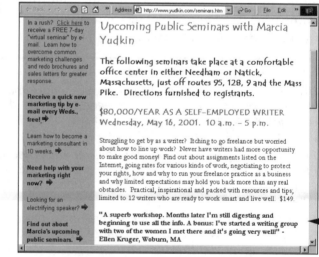

guarantee, the more trust you earn from honest Web users wary of choosing vendors online. Explicitly spell out exactly how you stand behind your products or your work. (See Figure 5.8.) Even if the guarantee is a matter of law that you would assume everyone knows, such as U.S. bank deposits being guaranteed by the FDIC up to $100,000, state it on the site.

Conformity to Industry Guidelines

EHealthstores (http://www.ehealthstores.com/) ensures that every health products e-commerce site it constructs includes a statement saying that it follows the

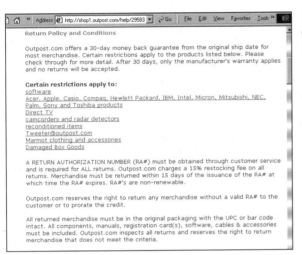

Figure 5.8: Outpost.com's detailed guarantee policies, spelled out at http://www.outpost.com/.

guidelines for trustworthy medical information of the Health on the **Net Foundation** (http://www.hon.ch/). For literary agencies, the counterpart would be adherence to the ethical principles of the **Association of Authors' Representatives** (http://www.publishersweekly.com/AAR/). If your industry or trade association has guidelines that you follow, let users know, and either restate the most important tenets or include a link to the entire ethical code.

Disclaimers

It might seem odd to consider "We're not responsible for..." legal notices as a credibility booster, but in certain professions, such as legal services or investments where savvy users know they're standard, their obvious presence helps reassure visitors that you're on the up and up. (See Figure 5.9.)

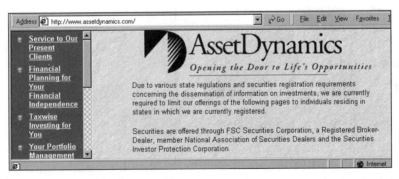

Figure 5.9: If someone searching for an investment firm did not find a disclaimer like this one at the site of AssetDynamics (http://www.assetdynamics.com/), the site might come under suspicion.

Good Product Photos

Online shoppers want to know what they'd be getting if they order, and often the pictures provide little or no help. Fuzzy, undecipherable photos undermine your credibility. High-quality photography is indispensable, and to prevent the illustrations from inordinately slowing down the page loading, offer a small photo on which users can click to open up a larger image. (See Figure 5.10.)

Finding Out More About Photos—*Consult these sites to learn more about advisable photo formats, resolution, file compression, editing, and converting print photos for use on the Web:*

> *About.com's Web Design Site*
> (http://webdesign.about.com/compute/webdesign/)
>
> *ZDNet Developer—Graphics*
> (http://www.zdnet.com/devhead/filters/0,9429,2133231,00.html)
>
> *Webmonkey—Cheap and Cool Photos*
> (http://hotwired.lycos.com/webmonkey/99/23/index3a.html?tw=design/)

Figure 5.10: ArtNet (http://www.artnet.com/) strikes the proper balance between showing several images at once and enabling a look at detail by using smaller images that the viewer can click to see in a larger version.

Consumer Advocate Memberships

One of the most famous names in consumer protection, the Better Business Bureau, offers the BBBOnLine Reliability seal, which online merchants who have met its stringent examinations can display at their sites. (See Figure 5.11.) Its rigorous criteria for acceptance into the Reliability Seal program include membership in one's local Better Business Bureau chapter, having been in business for at least one year, adherence to strict guidelines about advertising claims, and having a satisfactory record of handling complaints. The other seal widely respected online is from **TRUSTe** (http://www.truste.com/), which certifies that you have an explicit, adhered-to privacy policy, discussed in the final section of this chapter. If you've earned such seals, flaunt them on your home page.

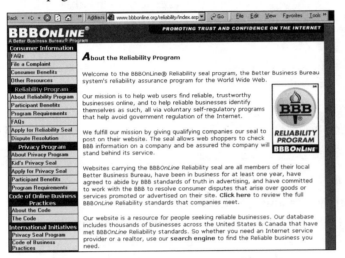

Figure 5.11: The eye-catching Reliability Program seal of BBBOnline (http://www.bbbonline.org/), a division of the Better Business Bureau, carries tremendous weight with consumers.

Partnerships with Well-Known Brands

Have you, as a small fry, teamed up with some big-shot firm like Coca-Cola or Fidelity Investments? If so, saying so can give you a boost in the eyes of Web users learning about you for the first time.

FAQ

A Frequently Asked Questions page that clears up confusions about your services, procedures, and policies implies that you care about dealing fairly and in an above-board fashion with your clientele. A similar FAQ about the features of your product or service shows that you want to make sure people know what they'll be getting. (See Figure 5.12.) Some users click to the FAQ first rather than read your conventional marketing copy, so include a link to your FAQ on your home page.

Content Demonstrating Your Expertise

Chapter 6, *Content as Bait*, describes many kinds of content that attract Web visitors and keep them coming back. The kinds that bolster your credibility with readers include samples of your work, such as a portfolio for a graphic design firm or ad agency, case studies that reveal how you solved difficult problems for clients, and articles or white papers that show you really know your stuff. A client list that includes lots of famous names can make the same sort of impact.

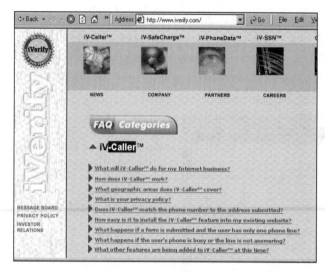

Figure 5.12: The FAQ for iVerify's iV-Caller (http://www.iverify.com/) is set up in traditional FAQ fashion: initially, a list of the questions, with each question a clickable link that brings the reader to the answer.

Company Information

If you assume that everyone who's anyone already knows and trusts you, you'll be in good company—and you'll be wrong. In fact, no matter how well-known you are in your niche, people who have never heard of you will find your site. They may need information about the company's ownership, its longevity, and your qualifications—discussed in detail in Chapter 4, *Who Are We?*—to feel comfortable pursuing connections with you.

Personal Photos

I always perk up when a well-designed site with interesting content treats me to photos and profiles of the folks behind it. Not only do photos provide a fascinating window on the personality, experience, and lifestyle of those pictured (see Figures 5.13), they almost always increase trust. After all, some nefarious criminal trying to earn money from a Web business while in hiding wouldn't post his picture, would he?

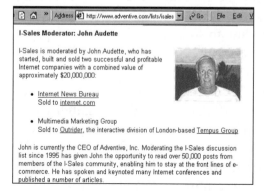

Figure 5.13: The photo that John Audette, moderator of the I-Sales Discussion List (http://www.adventive.com/lists/isales/), chose reveals that he's an informal guy of a certain age who feels at home at the beach.

Where's Your Privacy Policy?

If you collect e-mail addresses at your site, invite e-mail inquiries, solicit online orders, or set cookies, you must post a statement explaining what you do with users' information or risk losing the trust of those who visit your site. In one *Business 2.0* survey, more than half the respondents said that at least once in a while they read the site's privacy policy before making a purchase. Keep in mind the specific user fears assuaged by a privacy policy:

- They worry about being inundated with e-mail advertising.
- If they've visited, say, a sado-masochism portal or a herpes or debt information site, they fear being publicly identified in the future as a user with certain interests.
- They wonder whether their credit-card information might go astray.
- They don't want their purchasing history or browsing habits to be sold to third parties.

The seriousness of those fears carries implications for both the placement and the wording of your privacy policy. At a minimum, *Privacy Policy* should be a link on every page, so that no matter when visitors begin to wonder whether they're being tracked and what would happen if they registered, they can find where to get such questions answered. In addition, you're wise to insert privacy information or links to it at the precise locations where the fears listed previously would most likely arise, such as when you're asking for the user's e-mail address or when the shopper is proceeding to final checkout. Since my own privacy policy was so simple, I decided to place it at the bottom of every page at my site. (See Figure 5.14.)

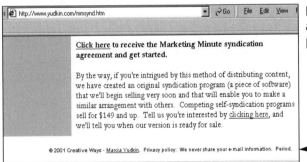

Figure 5.14: My privacy policy, appearing at the bottom of every page at my Web site.

As for the wording, if you hand this responsibility over to your lawyers, you'll end up with a legally dense statement incomprehensible to the average reader. That won't earn you much confidence. On the other hand, a simple blanket statement may not have enough "whereas"s and "just in case"s to protect you legally. A solution that strengthens your trust score with users and keeps your legal eagles happy is to present an easy-to-understand version linked to a detailed statement containing all the fine print. See Figure 5.15 for a privacy policy that strikes a happy medium between careful wording and comprehensibility.

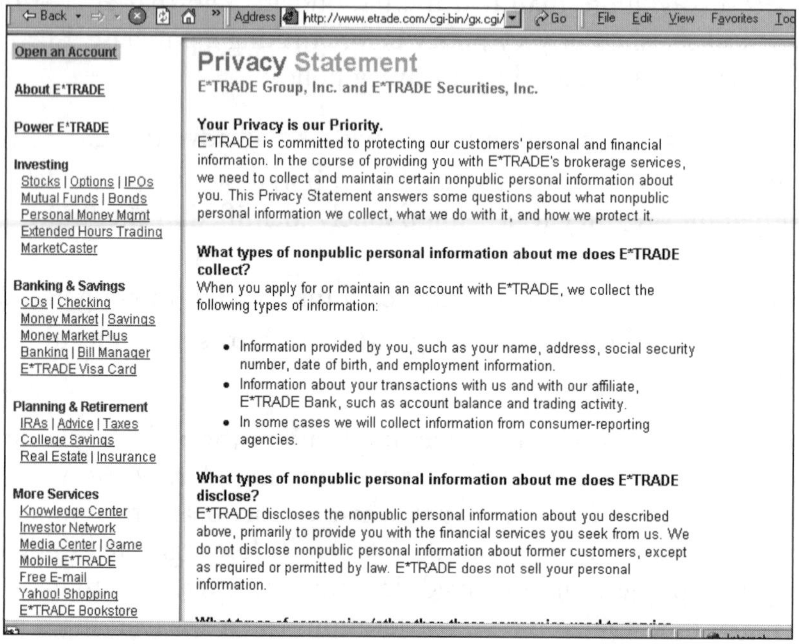

Figure 5.15: The privacy policy for the online brokerage E*TRADE (http://www.etrade.com/) is understandable, informative, and reassuring.

Action Steps:

• Imagine visiting your site as a skeptic afraid of being ripped off. Find and fix the weak spots in your marketing presentation.

• Correct all the typos, mistakes, and out-of-date information at your site and create a process for catching such problems in the future.

• Set your browser to reject cookies and see what happens when you visit your site.

• If you don't have any customer testimonials, get some and post them.

• Do you have media coverage, awards, industry memberships, certifications or other credibility boosters that you haven't used at your site? If so, add them.

• Make certain that photos you've used are clear and attractive.

• Post an understandable privacy policy if you haven't yet done so.

CHAPTER SIX

Content as Bait

I now tell people to stop calling themselves *freelance writers*. Where the Internet-savvy are concerned, at least, they are *content providers*. Content actually encompasses more than articles and other material supplied by paid, professional writers, however. *Content* includes any nonpromotional text or pictures having value for a target audience. Content is something that Web visitors enjoy or find useful whether they have gone online specifically to find information or are shopping for products or services on the Web. Content represents a prime way of attracting prospects to your Web site, getting them to come back, and inspiring them to recommend your site to others.

For instance, suppose you work for a community bank or credit union trying to increase loyalty among current customers and to attract more accounts from those living in your service area. You could run an interactive feature called *Should You Refinance?* with current mortgage rates and blanks where homeowners could plug in their loan information and learn whether and how much they'd save by refinancing. You could start a *Children's Corner* with kid-friendly pieces on banking that local teachers could use in lessons about money. You might invite a local financial planner to answer customers' questions about money management at the site, and so on. Clearly such content would increase traffic from both current and prospective account holders and encourage greater patronage of the bank or credit union's services.

In this chapter:
- *Which kinds of content lure visitors to your site?*
- *Who might be willing to contribute free, relevant content?*
- *How to feature and use content effectively*
- *What pitfalls to avoid in using content*

Varieties of Content

Let's look at varieties of Web content, from the obvious and common to the farfetched and creative.

Articles and Tip Sheets

Most companies have good stuff hidden away in their file cabinets that would work as bait at their Web site if revised and updated. Were you asked once to write an article for your Chamber of Commerce newsletter? Didn't you create a useful handout for a panel discussion last year? Following are some types of businesses and examples of this variety of content that you could modify or create for your Web site:

> **Printer**—What You Should Know About Digital Printing
> **Investment advisor**—Myths and Realities About Retirement Portfolios
> **Car dealer or mechanic**—Keep Your Family Safe: Tips About Tires
> **Women's boutique**—Seven Steps to a Wardrobe That Works
> **Architectural firm**—Office Renovation Checklist
> **Flying school**—Frequently Asked Questions About Flying Lessons
> **Software company**—Distributed Computing Options: A White Paper

Events

Unlike articles and tip sheets, which retain their value for a long time, events listings have a now-ness that makes them a lure for repeat traffic. The events you post needn't be your own, so long as the information is up to date and accurate. (See Figure 6.1.)

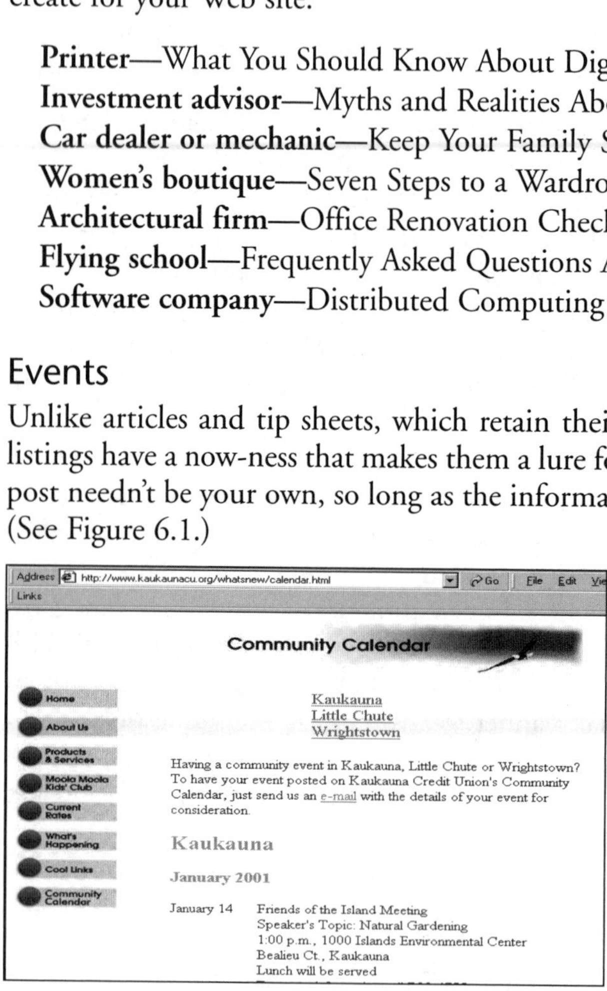

Figure 6.1: A Wisconsin credit union posts area events as a community service to its members and the public.

A locally owned furniture store trying to differentiate itself from the chains might offer listings of community events like concerts, whereas a church might feature the week's Bible groups, tag sales, sports meets, and singles' gatherings. Your community calendar of course can extend far beyond your locality. If you serve, say, whale lovers, your calendar might consist of whale-watching tours around the world.

News, Weather, Sports Scores, Etc.

You can get general, local, or topical news installed and kept up to date automatically at your site through various Internet services such as **iSyndicate** (http://www.isyndicate.com/) and **Moreover** (http://www.moreover.com/). The same goes for weather reports, ski reports, either general or specialized sports scores, and so on. (See Figure 6.2.) Such content turns your site into a valuable destination, particularly when paired with material visitors can't find anywhere else on the Net. Certainly, you can also post original news and commentary, such as a law firm providing notice of recent legislation and court rulings and their implications.

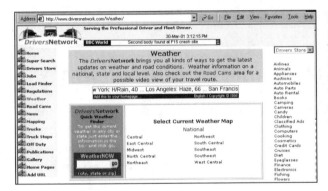

Figure 6.2: DriversNetwork (http://www.driversnetwork.com/) features a box for an up-to-the-minute weather report for anywhere in the United States, which is provided by arrangement with Weather24 (http://www.weather24.com/).

Links

This option takes concerted effort, but if you want targeted traffic to your Web site that you don't have to pay for, it's hard to beat a top-notch collection of Web links that exactly meets the needs of your clientele. For instance, a spa might assemble links on everything from meditation to seaweed wraps to the history of rest cures. A speech coach could provide links to audio files or texts of famous speeches, to medical information on voice care, and to online humor banks. With a great set of links, people recommend it and link to it in turn, thus attracting people who get hooked by the content into exploring what your organization can do for them. (See Figure 6.3.) Finding useful links relevant to your target market and updating your previously compiled list of links are terrific tasks for summer interns. According to Internet law professor Jonathan Bick, if you link to someone's home page and do not cast a bad light on the linked site, there's little need to ask permission for the link. However, if you're linking to a specific page deep within someone else's site, it might be prudent to request permission of the site owner for the link.

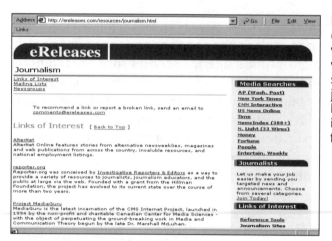

Figure 6.3: eReleases (http://www.ereleases.com/), which sells press-release writing and distribution services, offers links to journalism sites. Annotating links with editorial comments is a terrific way to add value for site visitors.

Reviews

When you can go beyond collecting links to evaluating them, providing a blurb on what makes a particular site valuable, you are edging into the territory of reviews. Reviews might be of restaurants, cities, movies, products, politicians, or other public figures, or just about anything else on which people have opinions. To ensure that your reviews engage readers, don't be bland or monotonously enthusiastic. Opinionated reviews, grounded in a consistent sensibility or perspective, help you attract a following for your content.

Pictures

So far we've looked at content as though it must be verbal, which of course it does not have to be. It could also consist of cartoons, snapshots, fine photos, historical images, drawings, diagrams, and so on. (See Figure 6.4.) Just be sure to remember that for many visitors, images take a long time to load, and they'll stick around and wait only if you've given them strong reason to believe they'll be glad they stayed.

Figure 6.4: For someone interested in history, historical photos represent appealing content equal in value to the articles.

Data

Sometimes sheer facts serve as a draw. For example, you're an Internet security firm and have kept tabs on how often the Web's top 10 sites have been hacked. Put that on a Web page! Or you're a marital therapist and follow divorce statistics and studies on what keeps couples together: Add summaries to your site and tell colleagues and the media about your research digest. Or you produce low-calorie snacks: Supply calorie counts for junk food and anything people might be tempted to eat instead of your products. In a convenient format, figures like these have wide appeal for your target market. Perhaps someone in your industry provides data free for the taking in an attractive graphical format, as shown in Figure 6.5.

Figure 6.5: Adventive (http://www.adventive.com/), a company offering Internet-related discussion lists, offers sites a free graphical counter that registers the current estimated value of e-commerce so far during the year.

Stories

Whether true or fictional, narratives have beguiled human beings since the invention of campfires and cave paintings. They retain their appeal in the Internet age, but few nonliterary sites take advantage of the widespread desire to find out what happened next, and next. Consider either fiction or nonfiction serials—stories delivered in installments over time—as an attraction for repeat traffic. For instance, the **Massachusetts Wedding Guide** site (http://massweddingguide.com/) had a bride and groom periodically share their perspectives during the nine months of preparation for their wedding. (See Figure 6.6.) A sports site could commission a daily or weekly story from someone training for a marathon or recovering from an injury. A consultant specializing in helping merged companies adjust to one another could construct a fictional serial on the trials and tribulations typically involved.

Quizzes and Contests

Riddles and puzzles are irresistible tempters to settle down and stay for a while, and while you might expect them mainly at sites for young people or adult leisure pursuits, plenty of serious grownup businesses use them successfully. A

Figure 6.6: Few can resist the lure of "What happened next?" Consider true or fictional stories, like this story in installments of an engaged couple, to get readers emotionally involved.

car site addresses the question of should you buy or lease with a quiz. A foot health association gets people thinking about stresses and strains on their feet through a quiz. A personal coach asks questions that the visitor can answer privately to illustrate the types of issues she explores with clients. (See Figure 6.7.) Interactive tests of knowledge or needs make magnificent use of the online medium, and you can build traffic to your site by promoting such features in print or broadcast ads and direct mail.

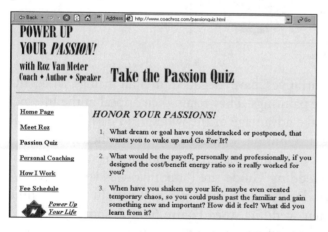

Figure 6.7: This self-awareness quiz subtly illustrates the kinds of issues personal coach Roz Van Meter of Dallas explores with her clients.

Stay Out of Jail, Free—Do you know the crucial differences between a lottery and a sweepstakes? Do you know why asking people to fill out a long survey to become eligible to enter your contest can land you in trouble? Do you realize how specific you must be about the closing date of the contest? These and other important questions about contests, games, and sweepstakes are addressed in plain English by Chuck Kish, Esq., at Law for Internet (http://www.lawforinternet.com/pages9.php3?asktype=mainorganizesweepstakes.html).

Humor

Todd Raphael, editor of **Workforce.com** (http://www.workforce.com/), says that two of the most popular areas of the site are their *Funny Management Word Problems* and *Top E-mail Addresses of Frustrated HR Professionals*, both of which invite input from creative readers as well as spark laughs. Just make sure that your humor won't offend certain groups among your target audience. One humor piece at **Workforce.com** might have been interpreted as making fun of Senator Hillary Clinton and therefore put off fans of hers.

Sources for Free Content—The following sites provide content—jokes, cartoons, articles, tips—you can freely use at your Web site, so long as you retain the byline and copyright notice of the author.

Ara Content, http://aracopy.com/

Click for Content, http://www.clickforcontent.com/

Ezine Articles, http://ezinearticles.com/

Find Sticky, http://www.findsticky.com/

Find Your Dream, http://www.findyourdream.com/

FreeSticky, http://www.freesticky.com/

Idea Marketers, http://www.ideamarketers.com/

Marketing-Seek, http://www.marketing-seek.com/

Solnet.net, http://www.solnet.net/webmasters.htm

Top7Business, http://top7business.com/

World Wide Information Outlet, http://certificate.net/

WriteBusiness, http://www.writebusiness.com/

User-Generated Content

Who creates content for your site? Besides the two most obvious sources—you and people you hire—your visitors can be a fertile source of content if you take measures to solicit, select, and edit their contributions. A site that does this brilliantly is **Car Talk** (http://cartalk.cars.com/), the Web home for the popular National Public Radio show by that name. You won't dare visit it often because it will be several hours until you are able to tear yourself away. Its user-generated content includes hilarious letters about car problems, heated debate over controversies like the use of car phones, customer reviews of more than 15,000 garages and mechanics all over the United States, owner comments about the quirks of specific car makes, models, and years, and survey results on the psychological characteristics of people who own a car like yours. (See Figure 6.8.)

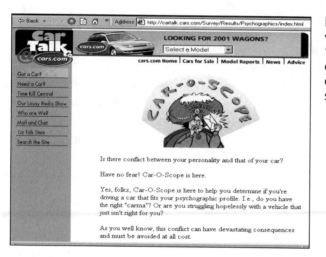

Figure 6.8: Do you and your vehicle share the same "carma"? This irresistible questionnaire makes use of data contributed by previous site visitors.

According to Doug Mayer, senior Web lackey for the site, they receive about 3,000 e-mails a week, from which interns select the items worth adding to the site. Besides taking the burden for content creation off the site managers, user-generated content inspires community, Mayer says. "We all like to share our thoughts, participate, and feel helpful. Many of our features enable listeners to share funny stories or to provide actual, useful help to others."

So consider setting up options for reader reaction and participation, such as a tell-us-what-you-think Web forum or something more structured and selective. (See Figure 6.9.) Interactive user contributions might consist of polls or surveys, letters, an essay contest, or visitor ratings of products, services, or people in the news. A hybrid of owner-generated and user-generated content would be to invite questions from users and have an outside expert post answers to those questions, the expert either being paid to do so or doing it for the publicity value.

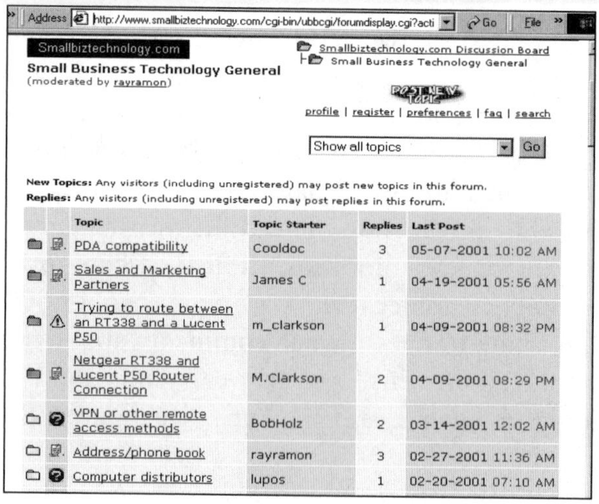

Figure 6.9:
Smallbiztechnology.com (http://www.smallbiztechnology.com/) includes a forum where people can share technology tips and get advice.

Topic	Topic Starter	Replies	Last Post
PDA compatibility	Cooldoc	3	05-07-2001 10:02 AM
Sales and Marketing Partners	James C	1	04-19-2001 05:56 AM
Trying to route between an RT338 and a Lucent P50	m_clarkson	1	04-09-2001 08:32 PM
Netgear RT338 and Lucent P50 Router Connection	M.Clarkson	2	04-09-2001 08:29 PM
VPN or other remote access methods	BobHolz	2	03-14-2001 12:02 AM
Address/phone book	rayramon	3	02-27-2001 11:36 AM
Computer distributors	lupos	1	02-20-2001 07:10 AM

Want a Free Discussion Forum?—*These sites provide either free scripts with which you can offer a discussion forum at your site or free hosting for one.*

Anyboard, http://netbula.com/anyboard/

Backpack, http://www.conferenceroom.com/backpack.shtml

Coolboard, http://www.coolboard.com

Forum Company, http://www.forumco.com/

Plug-in-Community, http://www.everyone.net/main/html/community_tour.html

---

How Best to Feature and Use Content

Whatever the source of the content, you need to highlight your offerings so that first-time visitors won't have to find their way accidentally to the good stuff. Many sites accomplish this by offering a *What's New* section on their home page. Others set up their list of content with the newest material first, recent material next, and then a link to older items accessible from a separate archive page. Both of these solutions ease the way for repeat visitors to zero in on features they haven't yet seen. You might consider drawing attention to "oldie but goodie" favorites on the home page as well.

The more content you provide, the more you need to have categories for the content as well as a way to search according to a visitor's interests. Online publishers, whose very business is their site's content, may also want to differentiate the availability of material by kinds of customers. Some content, for instance, is there for everyone to read, while other content is for registered users only. (See Figure 6.10.) Naturally the more you tell unregistered visitors about what lies beyond the registration barrier, the more disposed they are to part with their personal information to gain access to it.

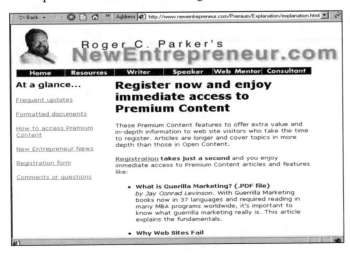

Figure 6.10: Roger Parker offers some articles for casual visitors and premium content only for those who register, which is free.

Some online publishers make their distinction between free content and for-fee content, the latter usually on the basis of a monthly or annual subscription. For example, Dr. Ralph Wilson of **Wilson Internet Services** (http://www.wilsonweb.com/) makes thousands of links and articles available to all visitors, but how-to material on e-commerce requires an annual subscription fee of $49.95. His on-site search engine marks which articles are free and which require the subscription. (See Figure 6.11.) With the subscription, he says that people can do research in a few hours that would take days and days if they were just searching on the Web.

Figure 6.11:
Wilson Internet Services (http://www.wilsonweb.com/) offers thousands of pages of free material along with, as shown here, many articles that require a subscription to access.

A different and interesting way of making such a divide is at Randy Cassingham's humor site, **This is True** (http://www.thisistrue.com/). Cassingham does not allow any archiving of his columns but instead provides access to back issues of his material in a series of bound books available for sale. Likewise, some publishers of expensive reports for the corporate market offer the summary free to one and all and the details only to those who shell out several hundred dollars per report. For instance, **eMarketer** (http://www.emarketer.com/) releases general conclusions and some tantalizing statistics to the public and reserves the rest of its research for its $795 reports.

Content Cautions

A full briefing on copyright do's and don'ts is beyond the scope of this book, but let me offer a few guidelines here. There can be serious legal and financial ramifications if you use other people's intellectual property without permission. Cartoons, puzzles, recipes, logos, photos, jokes, articles, and other kinds of content normally belong to somebody, requiring explicit permission and sometimes a fee before you can use them. And as for content you commission from freelancers, paying a fee alone does not transfer ownership of that property to you. You also need a signed document transferring certain rights over the content to you. Consult an intellectual property attorney for help.

Feel free to set whatever ground rules you like about the proper use of your material, from "feel free to forward this to friends" to "All rights reserved" or some other permutation of permission, so long as you announce those rules explicitly at your site. Figure 6.11 shows how Randy Cassingham posts and explains his restrictions at his **This is True** site.

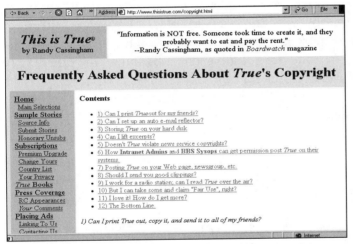

Figure 6.11: Randy Cassingham explains explicitly what you can and can't do with his content.

If you decide to commission content from writers or solicit content from practitioners outside your organization, beware of the temptation to save money by choosing low-paid or unpaid contributors. Amy Gahran, vice-president of **Content Exchange** (http://www.contentexchange.com/), a site that helps match content providers with purchasers, points out, "A writer who can't deliver exactly what you need, on time, all the time, is no bargain. The trouble is that usually you don't find out who is going to be a problem until you're depending on them."

Writer, Writer, Who's Got a Writer?—*Numerous newsletters and specialized job boards will be happy to pass along your specifications at no cost if you are looking for a writer to create customized content. These reach serious, experienced writers:*

American Journalism Review , http://ajr.newslink.org/joblink

Content Exchange, http://www.content-exchange.com

Inscriptions, http://www.inscriptionsmagazine.com

Sunoasis Jobs, http://www.sunoasis.com

User-generated content brings with it the danger that you might inadvertently publish something defaming a company or an individual. Yet, paradoxically, the more you winnow user contributions, rejecting some and posting others, the more vulnerable you become if you miss a smear that upsets its target. According to Lance Rose, an intellectual property attorney, "The more editorial control a system operator or owner wields over the messages and materials on an online system, the greater the responsibility for the damage those messages and materials may cause to others." You wouldn't want to open yourself up to libel charges, so get legal advice before publishing highly charged opinions on your site.

Finally, make sure that the content you publish is truly geared to your audience, and not merely what you happen to be able to round up. *Inc.* magazine once reported the abysmal ratings a panel of CEOs gave to the content posted at 10 small-business portals trying to appeal to such executives. On the sophistication of the content, one site got a B+, one a B, and all the others C or D+. No wonder that the overall comment for 3 of the 10 was "I'd never go back" and for the other 7 just "I'd go back occasionally." Relevant content earns you return visits, word of mouth, links, leads, and sales.

Action Steps:

- Go through your files for content that would have value to your site visitors.
- Investigate newsfeeds, event listings, lists of links and reviews that might be of interest to your audience.
- Ponder whether user-contributed opinions, questions, data, etc. would meaningfully beef up your offerings.
- Check whether you have adequately informed your visitors about the contents of each article or feature at your site.
- Make sure that you have the legal right to post your content and that you've alerted visitors to any restrictions on its use.
- Assess the level of sophistication of your content and its appropriateness for your target audiences.

CHAPTER SEVEN

Gathering Leads, Members, and Subscribers

In the 1990s, the request for buyers' telephone numbers at Radio Shack cash registers, even when buying batteries with cash, became notorious in the United States. On the other hand, who hasn't experienced the frustration of clicking a Tell Me More link and then never hearing back? These two examples illustrate twin dangers lying in wait for Web site owners attempting to rake in leads, members, or subscribers through a sign-up box or Web form. One guiding principle is that you must demonstrate respect for visitors' privacy. As well, you need to carefully match promise and fulfillment as you use your Web site to grow your business.

In this chapter:
- *Why getting permission to send e-mail is essential*
- *Which subscription sign-up practices can endanger your reputation*
- *What to avoid in the site registration process*
- *How to encourage leads from your Web site*

Why Opt-In Marketing Reigns

Before we discuss the best ways to collect visitor information, you must understand how to use the data you collect responsibly, so that you maintain a spotless reputation with your target market and with certain behind-the-scenes entities that have the power to disrupt communication with your customers and prospects. The safest policy is to send broadcast e-mails only to people who have knowingly signed up to receive them from you and to guard your list of customer e-mail addresses zealously from abuse.

Trouble with mass e-mail arises because so-called *spam*—unrequested bulk e-mail—has become a tremendous economic burden for Internet service providers (ISPs) and an aggravation for many recipients who regard it as a plague. ISP employees spend a considerable portion of their time fighting and filtering out spam, which constantly threatens to overwhelm their capacity to process wanted e-mail. Hence, if someone complains to your ISP that you are perpetrating spam, the ISP may terminate your account without warning. Cutting you off without the right to appeal is perfectly legal when the ISP has included this possibility in its terms of service.

If the original complainant or the ISP names you as a spammer to an organization called the **Mail Abuse Prevention System**, or MAPS (http://maps.vix.com/), you might end up being included in The Realtime Blackhole List. This honor you most definitely do not want, because inclusion may mean that hundreds of ISPs that subscribe to this list refuse to deliver any of your mail to their customers. That's right: Their customers may want to receive your e-mail, but if you're on the Realtime Blackhole List, these ISPs may reject it. In addition, people who know the Internet backwards and forwards and believe you are a spammer sometimes take it upon themselves to sabotage your Web site or overwhelm your e-mail address with more volume than it can handle.

While the debate over spam and the Realtime Blackhole List is beyond the scope of this book, emotions run sky-high on this topic. When an article defending one type of spam appeared on an Internet marketing Web site, both the author and the site received a flood of e-mail that included death threats. While some recipients simply delete spam without making a fuss and others delete and complain, those who object sometimes take matters into their own hands to make sure culprits are punished. You do not want this to happen to you.

Your online survival and success require that you avoid even the perception of spam. As MAPS puts it, the fundamental principle is that "all communications must be consensual." One thing they don't make clear is that perception plays a great role in consent, and the following procedures put you at great risk of complaints from people who, for good reason, don't believe they consented to your communications:

- Prechecked signup boxes, as in Figure 7.1.
- A company name or identification on an impersonal commercial e-mail different from the one they subscribed to. (For instance, users sign up with Kmart but get mail from Martha Stewart.)
- Mailing to someone else's list under your auspices, not theirs. (For example, you rent a list from Thor.com, but you mail your promotion so that it comes from you, not from Thor.com.)

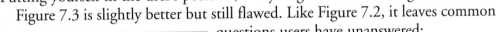

Figure 7.1 form (iGrandparents registration):

| Address | https://www.igrandparents.com/Registration/regpage1.asp |

Please complete the following form below to become an iGrandparents member. Items marked in red with an "*" are required to become a member. Check out the left side of the page for help with registering.

* First Name:
* Last Name:
* Screen Name:
* Password:
* Retype Password:
* Email Address:
* Retype Email Address:
* Zip Code/Postal Code:
* Select Country: Select a Country
* Gender: ◉ Female ○ Male
* Birthday (MM/DD/YYYY):
Weekly Email Newsletter: ☑ I would like to receive the iGrandparents Weekly Email Newsletter and occasional promotional newsletters from iGrandparents.

Figure 7.1: With prechecked subscription boxes, people who didn't read carefully may believe you are sending them something they did not choose to receive, and in a sense they would be right.

Prechecked boxes for online subscriptions or registrations are sometimes put under the heading of *opt-out* marketing—the user has to make a deliberate click to avoid receiving e-mail from the site. This contrasts with *opt-in* marketing, where the box starts off unchecked. People don't always notice prechecked boxes or read captions carefully. Thus, an opt-out procedure greatly heightens the risk that recipients of your e-mail complain that they never gave you consent to contact them. The same snafu is likely to occur when people registered with boo.com and later ghostscarers.com (which doesn't say it bought out boo.com) sends them marketing e-mail. Even riskier is sending e-mail to some other company's list; subscribers may recall that they gave the other firm permission to send them e-mail, but may not link your name to that permission.

It's safest to stay in the good graces of e-mail recipients by requiring them to take some positive, self-initiated action to get onto a list. Let's now look at standard and better sign-up procedures.

The Treacherous Subscription Box

Figure 7.2 shows a sign-up box similar to those you'll find all over the Web. Putting yourself in the user's position, can you guess what's wrong with it?

Figure 7.3 is slightly better but still flawed. Like Figure 7.2, it leaves common questions users have unanswered:

• What is this Streetmail exactly—a pure promotion for your company or news that has unmistakable value for me? May I see a sample?

• How often will I receive it? (The Weekly Newsletter option addresses that question.)

• Will you sell, rent, or give away my e-mail address to other companies?

Figure 7.2: Here is a typical bare-bones subscription sign-up box. What would one be signing up for? Not one clue is provided.

• Will I be able to unsubscribe easily if I don't like it?

Figure 7.3: In the upper-right corner, this sign-up box is slightly more informative, specifying it's for a Weekly Newsletter.

- Is it in text or HTML format—that is, in just plain characters or looking like a Web page? And if the latter, is it compatible with America Online? Is it something I can read offline or only while connected to the Internet?

Now look at an excellent sign-up invitation, for **Search Engine Watch** (http://www.searchenginewatch.com/). In Figure 7.4, you'll see the omnipresent blank box and Subscribe button in the lower-right corner. Just above that it says the newsletter comes monthly and covers search engines—implicitly, full of content rather than special sales offers.

Figure 7.4: This excellent sign-up box states the frequency, topic, and nature of the subscription, along with a link to learn more.

Just below the Subscribe button is a Learn More link that leads to Figure 7.5, which enables readers to unsubscribe, look at the current issue or past issues, and understand how their e-mail addresses will be handled. Now go back to Figure 7.4 and look at the bottom of the center column, where you'll find a boxless description of the newsletter with links, plus the number of subscribers, adding whopping credibility. Smart!

Figure 7.5: The link from Figure 7.4 leads here, with information that enables readers to unsubscribe, see the current issue or past ones, and understand what the site does with e-mail addresses.

Figure 7.6, for another newsletter, also includes the most crucial facts potential subscribers want to know, in a different tone than Search Engine Watch. As with any other kind of marketing information, you can fulfill users' expectations in just about any personality you can dream up, from crisp and authoritative to edgy and dark, to light and humorous.

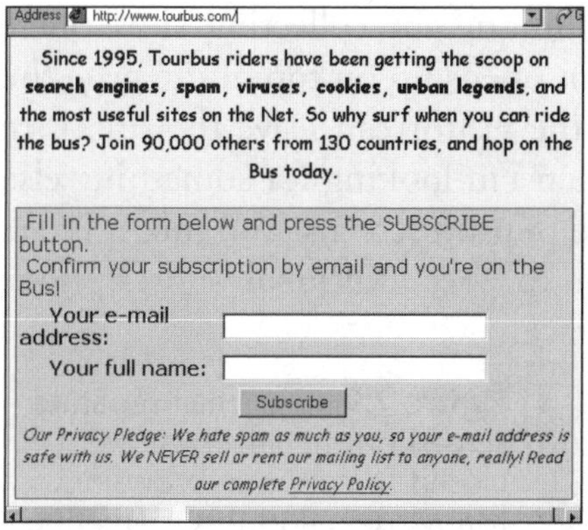

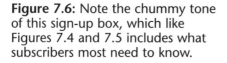

Figure 7.6: Note the chummy tone of this sign-up box, which like Figures 7.4 and 7.5 includes what subscribers most need to know.

A question not addressed by Figures 7.2 through 7.6 is what format the e-mail newsletter arrives in. This question arises more and more with the growing popularity of prettily laid out, full-color e-mail with live links and content perhaps partially stored back on the originating Web site. Advertisers love this style of e-mail, because it enables them to present their message imaginatively and attractively and to know how many recipients opened the e-mail and how many deleted it without opening. Yet people who use old e-mail systems, who pay by the minute for e-mail access, who are apprehensive about being tracked, or who just prefer something plain do not want HTML e-mail, as it's called. Unless you're absolutely certain of potential subscribers' preferences, the safest course of action is offering a choice of formats. See Figure 7.7 for a signup system that offers a choice of format and Figure 7.8 for what HTML e-mail looks like to someone who is not equipped to receive it.

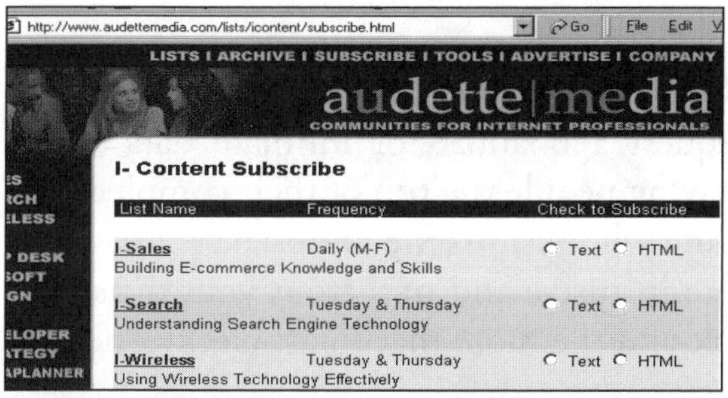

Figure 7.7: Most of Audette Media's e-mail discussion lists (http://www.audettemedia.com/) are available either in plain text or in HTML. The subscriber chooses here.

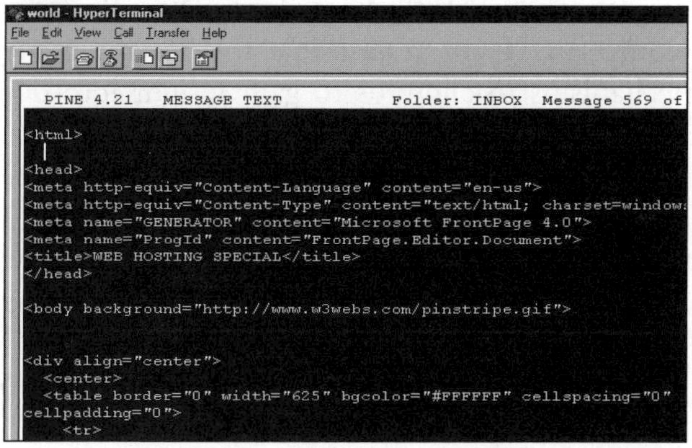

Figure 7.8: HTML e-mail looks like this—unreadable—in a plain-text-only e-mail system.

I'm not a big fan of a relatively new technique for collecting subscribers through a pop-up screen. Here a smaller screen opens up on top of the page the visitor is reading and must be closed before the visitor can leave the site. (See Figure 7.9.) I find it obnoxious, especially when I'm looking for something else at the site and have to keep swatting down the pop-up screens. You might judge the annoyance factor minor in comparison to the additional subscriptions gained by jumping repeatedly into the user's face.

Figure 7.9: The small separate screen on the left must be closed to continue browsing. Many users find this marketing technique annoying.

Member Registrations

Hardly anyone asks for personal information to subscribe visitors to an e-mail newsletter. However, many sites request a boatload of intimate data before dispensing a membership password giving people the run of their complete site. The collected information helps define who visitors are and makes it easier to attract advertisers. However, the more intrusive and numerous your questions, the more that skittish visitors will bolt and the more that smart-alecky ones will input absurd, wildly false data.

Rob Emerick, director of **Internet Marketing for iWorldLottery** (http://www.iworldlottery.com/), confesses, "I am responsible for designing my company's Web site tracking mechanisms to allow us to gain insight into our customers. Personally, however, I do not trust any Web site with my personal information. When I register, I lie about everything: My name is something I make up on the fly. I put down my residence as some mideast country unless I have to put someplace in the U.S. Then I always put Beverly Hills because I know the ZIP code. I am a male, but I list as female. I lie about my age, my likes and dislikes, and every single thing they ask for. I don't care how they reward me—I will not be truthful."

Can anything be done to minimize backlash against collecting personal data and drop-offs for other reasons during the site registration process? Certainly. Empathize as much as you can with the paranoid, the impatient, and the two-fingered typists, and follow these suggestions:

- Don't request off-topic personal information. For instance, if you offer business-to-business services, there's no reason to ask the registrant's gender, household income, or age. For a matchmaking site, however, some of those questions would be essential.

- If you need information that some might not eagerly divulge, explain why you need it and what you'll do with it. Look back at Figure 7.1 for an explanation in the left panel of why the site requests the user's birthday on its registration form. However, make certain that your explanation makes sense. **iGrandparents.com** (http://www.igrandparents.com/) says it's asking for one's birthday to be certain site registrants are over 13. However, birth year only would suffice for that, as would options like Before 1987 and After 1987, or whatever year may be applicable.

- Consider a Prefer Not to Say option to heighten the odds that registrants tell you the truth (see Figure 7.10). You can also position intrusive questions in an optional section of the registration form, as **women.com** (http://www.women.com/) does.

- Tell users what's behind the curtain—what benefits and features they'll have access to after they register.

- Instead of burdening your registration process with an interminable number of questions, think about the possibility of doing a member survey later, when you've built a bond of trust with regulars.

- Offer a bonus for registrants who provide detailed information. (See Figure 7.11.) A really smart company understanding the value of communicating with its clientele in more than one medium makes the bonus something that can only be sent by mail, maximizing the chances of getting accurate postal addresses from registrants.

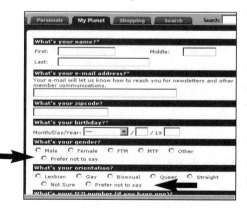

Figure 7.10: When it asks the user's sexual orientation, PlanetOut (http://www.planetout.com/) includes the option, *Prefer not to say.*

All told, the registration process shouldn't last more than one screen, and you should provide some mechanism for members who have forgotten passwords to have them (or

Figure 7.11: Offering a registration bonus that is appealing to your desired clientele increases your sign-up rate.

their previously provided password clue) sent to the e-mail address they previously registered. Usually sites do this by adding "Forgot your password? Click here." to the log-in form.

Collecting Leads Online

Controlling your greed for information in designing registration forms applies equally to forms inviting people to inquire about becoming a client. Ask for too many details and interested parties will bail out of the process. Don't require nonessential or nonuniversal information. And don't waste your prospects' patience on details that have nothing to do with providing good service to them, such how they heard about you. Save questions like that for later in the getting-to-know-you process, such as when you've already built up rapport with them.

I've looked at dozens of leads forms from one industry that uses them extensively—speaker's bureaus—organizations that secure celebrities, entertainers, or professional speakers for meetings and events. Their most common weakness, besides those previously mentioned, was that hardly any of them said anything about how long they would take to reply to the form submission. Of the speaker's bureau sites I've looked at, only 20% went so far as to say that one should hear back "shortly." Only one bureau was reassuringly more specific. (See Figure 7.12.)

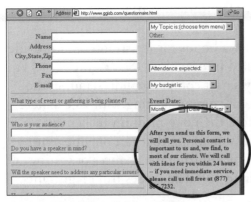

Figure 7.12: The Golden Gate International Speaker's Bureau (http://www.ggisb.com/) gains an edge by promising to follow up on inquiries within a specific time frame.

Keep in mind that in this competitive industry, as in many others, bureaus want to minimize the tendency of meeting planners to solicit information from many bureaus at once. Naming a period of time within which you'll respond to a lead increases the chances that a visitor who liked your site will submit a request for information and wait for your reply. And considering the number of sites that don't say this, adding this little bit of balm to a leads form gives you a competitive edge. Naturally, you then have to fulfill your promise.

Another thing that I would have thought goes without saying is that a form for collecting leads should have a positive tone. But Figure 7.13 was just the most extreme example of a negative, antagonistic tone in intake forms. In its follow-up page, **Barber & Associates** (http://www.barberusa.com/) explains that it receives over 1,000 requests a month from fans to forward information to celebrities, which it cannot do.

I don't believe this justifies their stop sign and two *nots* preceding the form (along with four more *nots* below the form), which together make them appear beleaguered and out of control. Instead, they can arrange to reply to all inquiries with an automated message like this:

If you've submitted a speaker request, we welcome your inquiry and will get back to you within 48 hours with suggestions. If you've asked us to forward a message to your favorite artist, or asked us for their contact information, we're sorry, but this is beyond the scope of our business and we're unable to help you.

Figure 7.13: The flashing red stop sign here and the *nots* may help screen out some unwanted e-mail, but they also set the wrong tone for legitimate business inquiries.

The same applies to a statement like "We will not respond to inquiries unless a telephone and fax number are included." As explained in the *Member Registrations* section earlier in this chapter, it helps if you provide a plausible reason for needing them and word your requirement positively. For instance: "To provide you with appropriate follow-up information, we need both your telephone and fax numbers." Another solution would be to insert that statement in an error message programmed to pop up when a user has omitted the required information.

The most creative leads form I've seen online appears on the site of **WF Meyers** (http://www.wfmeyers.com/), which produces various kinds of saws for industrial use. The Web site invites visitors into a Product Design Room, which gets them started collaborating on custom-made saws or tools by specifying the type of stone to be cut, the RPMs and horsepower of the cutting machine, the number of segments desired on the saw, their spacing, and much more. (See

Figure 7.16.) The "Design Your Own..." idea is uncommonly friendly and enticing and an ingenious way to put a smile on prospects' faces while asking for their business.

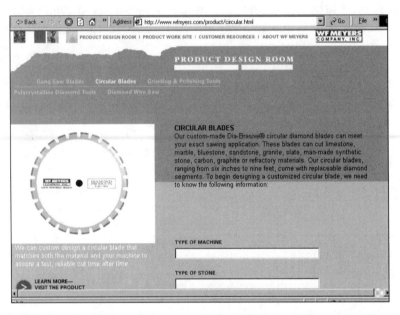

Figure 7.14: This site contains the most inviting leads form I've seen online. Even if you have no use for industrial saws, the idea of designing your own is appealing.

Action Steps:

• Determine whether your site uses opt-out or opt-in techniques for collecting subscribers or leads and ponder what you can do to move toward the latter policy.

• If you currently have a bare-bones sign-up box, add text or links explaining what subscribers will get, how often, and in what format.

• Wherever you've requested personal information from subscribers or registrants, explain why you need it and what you'll do with it.

• Let people know (truthfully) how long it will take you to respond to an inquiry.

• Where possible, reword negative, warning, or scolding statements more positively.

CHAPTER EIGHT

Order Forms and Customer Service

When the secure-server shopping-cart service I relied on for my site's online orders for more than two years went from free to fee, I received an overdue kick-in-the-pants lesson. My husband had agreed to program our own shopping-cart system and wanted to see how others were constructed. To dissect the process step by step, we placed a pretend order through the system I'd been using. Surprise! Even before asking me which items I wanted, the shopping-cart system asked for my e-mail address and required me to choose a password! How dare they presume I would want to buy more than once? What business of theirs was that? A bit later, the system asked me to check which payment option I preferred: credit card, check, or money order, even though my own copy stated clearly that I accepted only Visa and MasterCard!

When setting up my online catalog through the shopping-cart service, I had assumed that the content and options I had chosen would be presented to the customer exactly as I saw them when I surfed to the ordering pages I had constructed. It hadn't occurred to me that the service could have built in additional choice points. No wonder our orders took a sharp jump upward after we installed an ordering system fully under our control.

The lesson: What matters most in online ordering is how customers experience the process, which includes factors that you may not have introduced deliberately, such as error messages and the system blocking the way to the next step. In addition, the order in which you present various elements to customers has a dramatic influence on the rate at which they complete their shopping or bail out in the middle of placing an order. Don't make the mistake of looking at the order pages as static content. Place test orders and watch others do it so that you can understand and improve the process from the customer's point of view.

In this chapter:
- *Why creating order forms that work is so difficult*
- *Which pitfalls can afflict the ordering process*
- *What to ask for and how on the order form*
- *How time-saving robots can do more harm than good*

Misunderstandings Are Your Problem

Rule Number One in designing effective order forms is that if people can misunderstand something, they will. And as challenging as it is to make instructions unambiguous and the process mistake-proof, that's your goal. The least confusion or doubt evoked by order forms can sabotage the eagerness to buy that your first-rate marketing copy produced.

For instance, an order form once asked, among the usual questions about name, address, etc., "Do you mind if we send you occasional e-mail about our new products and services?" I did mind, but I had an inkling that if I checked Yes they'd interpret that as "sure, go ahead," and if I checked No, they'd draw the conclusion that I didn't mind. Forced to choose Yes or No without a human being to tell me what the ambiguous options really meant, I backed out of the sale. Likewise, looking at the screen in Figure 8.1, what would you have to do to discontinue a subscription at the one-month point? Regardless of where else a guarantee may be stated, a skittish buyer needs reassurance about the ease of cancellation here.

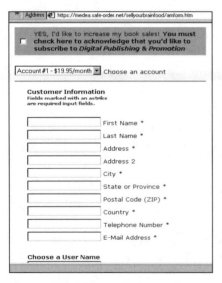

Figure 8.1: This order form does not contain any information about cancellation or guarantees.

Home-grown usability testing with as few as five people can uncover most of the problems with your order process. Recruit testers who have never seen your site before and who resemble in demographics and Internet experience the users you expect as shoppers. Have them speak their thoughts aloud as they order items at your site, and don't give them any tips or guidance if they get stuck. Simply watch and listen. It's common for site owners watching testers to wonder where such stupid people came from, but it's more productive simply to observe and take down or reduce the barriers. In one study of online shopping procedures, Jakob Nielsen and his team had several participants who were asked for a password assume that they were being asked for their e-mail account's password, and they either acquiescently typed it in or took umbrage at being asked to reveal it. In a case like that, the site should request explicitly that the user invent a password for shopping there.

Besides testing, e-mail feedback from shoppers provides a vital source of intelligence for improving your order forms. The questions and complaints you receive often point the way toward revisions and explanations that would boost your rate of completed orders. For instance, at **Amazon.com** (http://www.amazon.com/), people kept asking how they were supposed to indicate which books should be shipped to each of multiple addresses. Amazon eliminated that obstacle by modifying its forms. One book buyer complained that returning customers who were asked their e-mail address were then presented with the options, "Forgot your password? Click here" and "Sign in using our secure server." This customer said that time after time he would mistakenly click the first option even though he meant to sign in. Amazon flipped the order of the options, not only to solve this particular guy's headache, but because the more common situation— signing in—should have been presented first.

Nailing Down the Order

People don't like filling out forms in the real world, points out usability expert Adam Baker, and unlike tax forms, your Web site order form is optional. You can minimize buyers' discomfort and maximize your rate of completed purchases by understanding users' expectations of the purchasing process, eliminating unnecessary and repetitive steps during the order process, and providing reassurance after the sale. Although some of the following guidelines may sound painfully obvious, many million-dollar sites fail to heed them.

First, it should be clear that a first-time shopper is welcome to look around anonymously at your site. At **JCrew.com** (http://www.jcrew.com/), even this fundamental fact comes into question. In Figure 8.2, the message "Welcome! Click here to register, or if you are already registered, click here to log in" gives the impression that you have to register to shop—which might send you packing. However, by clicking a link such as Women, you can get started shopping without registering. The misleading text needs rewording to present registration as just an option.

Figure 8.2: The home page for JCrew (http://www.jcrew.com/) implies that registration is necessary to shop there.

Once they begin to shop, people expect that before handing over their credit card they can easily learn all the store's policies about privacy, returns, taxes, international delivery, and shipping methods, speed, and cost. However, as shown in Figure 8.3, coffee merchant **Gevalia** (http://www.gevalia.com/) fails to divulge shipping charges and taxes until you enter credit-card information. You're turned back when you try to proceed without giving credit-card information, and shipping costs and taxes are not revealed under Customer Service. Only a small, easy-to-miss Store Policies link explains shipping charges and taxes.

Figure 8.3: Taxes and shipping costs for your purchase "are to be computed" after you submit credit-card information. For many shoppers, this arrangement doesn't wash.

A much more user-friendly place to put that link would be below "to be computed," worded "Shipping, Taxes, Returns information." Compare the way electronics dealer **Outpost.com** (http://www.outpost.com/) announces its shipping policy for items over $500 right on the home page, offers a Returns link in the main navigation bar, and offers an International Orders link almost as prominently. (See Figure 8.4.)

Figure 8.4: The central welcome message here includes the shipping cost for items over $500. The return policy is accessible from the main navigation bar, and international shoppers can find relevant policies from a link below the company's phone numbers—all very shopper-friendly.

At the **Dun & Bradstreet** site (http://www.dnb.com/), when I tried to purchase a report on a company, the obstacle was not failing to find out the total price of the purchase. Worse, I could not find any price listed at all. One screen allows only subscribers to continue, but it doesn't say how to become a subscriber. Ten minutes into my search, long after the typical shopper would have given up, I found I could order a report by credit card, but I still could not find a price.

Users also expect that they'll be able to put things in and out of their shopping cart and assess what they've chosen before committing themselves to buy. This too was a problem at **Gevalia**. When you click Add to Shopping Cart, it looks like something is happening, but the site returns to the very same page. If you click again, have you ordered, one, two, or no gift baskets? After clicking twice in this way, you might notice a "1" up by "Items in cart," leading you to conclude that you'd ordered just one gift basket. In fact, you'd ordered two. Practically everyone would consider that they had two items in their cart at that point, rather than two instances of one item, so the site's logic needed adjustment.

At anti-virus software site **McAfee.com** (http://www.mcafee.com/), I couldn't get anywhere trying to order a copy of its Personal Firewall product. The only thing resembling an order button was "Current users, click here to start." (See Figure 8.5.) But I wasn't a current user and didn't see how to become one. I clicked the Shopping button and that took me around in a circle to Figure 8.5 again. At the bottom of the page, below a dotted line, was this: "Stop hackers—subscribe now. Haven't subscribed yet? Buy a 1-year subscription now for only $29.95 (USD)." Subscribe to what? It crossed my mind that maybe this was the way to place an order for Personal Firewall, but it seemed far-fetched to me for a software product to be delivered by "subscription." More likely, this referred to a newsletter on how to stop hackers. This site completely stumped me, but the problem could be fixed by changing the "Current users" invitation to "Click here to order" and

Figure 8.5: If you're not a current user and don't wish to subscribe to the "Stop Hackers" publication, how do you order Personal Firewall from this page of the McAfee site (http://www.mcafee.com/)?

then sending current and new users on two separate paths. If Personal Firewall was a service and not a product, the marketing copy had to make that clear.

Shoppers dread placing an order online and not learning until days or weeks later that the company couldn't and didn't ship it, as happened to hundreds of thousands of people during the Christmas season of 1999. They hope to know when they place an order that the item is in stock, which **Tower Records** (http://www.towerrecords.com/; see Figure 8.6) made clear, but other sites such as **CDNOW** (http://www.cdnow.com/) did not. Guess where most people would prefer to order.

If your site can't indicate the actual availability of items, you should promise to let people know the status of their order within 24 hours, and do so. Jitters about availability led my husband to place his order for a new laptop with **Outpost.com** (http://www.outpost.com/) by phone, after selecting what he wanted from the Web site. Shoppers hate surprises, especially when ordering gifts, emergency replacements, or expensive things.

Figure 8.6: Tower Records (http://www.towerrecords.com/) shows that an item searched for is in stock.

Because you won't be able to foresee every kind of uncertainty a buyer might have, you should offer at least one course of action for questions that arise during the ordering procedure, such as an e-mail, telephone, or live chat link to customer service. For instance, someone might want to know whether he could order a gift for his wife without any e-mails coming to their shared e-mail address. Or someone might want to specify delivery instructions, like "Leave it on the back porch" or "Deliver on Thursday, not Wednesday."

Live Chat Can Save the Sale—*Enabling customers to click and open up a chat link, whereby they can type questions and receive prompt, one-on-one answers, prevents shoppers from clicking away in frustration. A variety of Internet companies either provide chat boxes for your representatives or answer the questions for you, the way a telephone call center would. The following companies do the former for free:*

Get1on1, http://www.get1on1.com/

HumanClick, http://www.humanclick.com/

Livehelper, http://www.livehelper.com/

Designing the Order Form

When it finally comes time for shoppers to fill in personal information, they won't want to type the same data more than once. Order forms that verify the credit-card holder's address should therefore allow shoppers to type their name and address as it appears on their credit-card account and then, as in Figure 8.7, click a box to indicate that their "ship-to" information is the same. Shoppers also expect that if they type in some or all of their information and then decide to change their order, they won't have to re-enter their data on the order form.

Figure 8.7: After you fill out the billing address for your credit card, you can just click the top option on the right if that's also your shipping address.

In constructing your order form, be careful which data fields you specify as required, meaning that if they aren't filled out, the order can't go through. Some customers get spooked when they can't leave off their telephone number from an Internet order. They fear—in some cases for good reason—having that phone number handed off or sold to telemarketers. I once received an order with an obviously fake phone number. Worried that the credit card might be fraudulent as well, I e-mailed the customer asking for her telephone number, which I explained I needed in case there was a problem with her credit card. Oh, she replied, in that case here it is. That incident taught me to add, not only at my Web site but also on my voice-mail order system and my printed order forms, every time I ask for a customer's phone number, "in case there's a question." A prominent link to a readable privacy policy can help assuage such fears as well.

For an example of an information demand that goes way beyond what's necessary, see Figure 8.8, where financial software company **Intuit** (http://www.intuit.com/) requires a telephone number for the order to go through and reveals that the number may be used for telemarketing. Intuit then forces visitors who want to opt out of being contacted in the future to re-enter all their

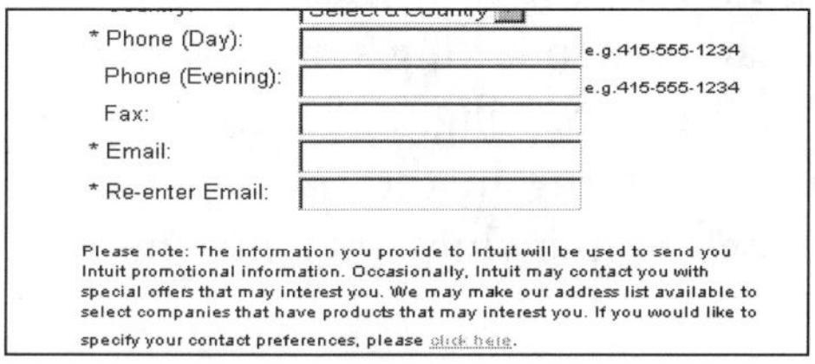

Figure 8.8: Intuit (http://www.intuit.com/) forces shoppers to provide a phone number and then fill out another form if they prefer not to be contacted by telemarketers.

data on a separate form, which they will attempt to correlate with the first form in order to remove them from the contact list. That killed my interest in ordering TurboTax from their Web site, and I'm sure sabotaged other sales as well.

If you fulfill international orders, be careful that you don't unintentionally shut them out of your ordering process by requiring certain fields that don't universally apply on your order form. For instance, you might insist on a ZIP or postal code without realizing that some countries, such as Denmark, don't have one. Not every country has states or provinces, either—witness Israel and Singapore. Likewise, requiring a three-digit telephone area code can prevent some Europeans and Asians from ordering.

Informative error messages when someone has skipped essential information or entered it incorrectly help save the sale. Merely telling the shopper something was omitted or not filled out correctly doesn't provide enough guidance. For instance, when I was trying to buy an airline ticket from Boston to San Francisco through **Expedia** (http://www.expedia.com/), the site asked me to choose an airport for San Francisco. The official name of Boston's airport, Logan, I knew, but I didn't have a clue about the name of San Francisco's airport. I clicked again, and a more specific error message appeared, offering choices. (See Figure 8.9.)

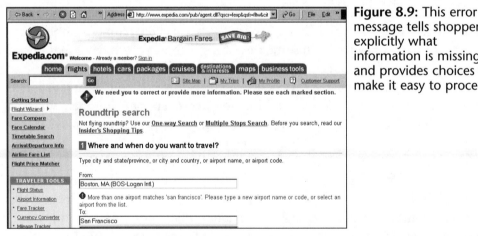

Figure 8.9: This error message tells shoppers explicitly what information is missing, and provides choices that make it easy to proceed.

From the beginning of the ordering process, shoppers should always know whether they have reached the point of no return—in other words, whether the sale has been officially recorded. Unless you explicitly state otherwise, users expect that once they enter their credit-card number, the next click transmits the order. Better shopping sites spell this out clearly when asking someone to click to the next screen with the order not yet finalized. (See Figure 8.10.) Shoppers should have one screen where they can see everything in their shopping cart, along with the total cost of their purchase, before knowingly making the click that sends in their data.

Figure 8.10: Amazon.com (http://www.amazon.com/) tells you that if you go to the next screen, you still have a chance to bail out of the order.

Let's suppose most customers sail smoothly through your order forms. For satisfactory shopping, they must also learn as soon as possible that their order was actually processed. Nothing sours people on e-commerce more than thinking that their order went through and finding out otherwise two weeks later, when the merchandise does not arrive. The best practice includes the following steps, in this sequence:

- Immediately after transmitting an order, a screen at the Web site should thank the shopper for the order and say what will happen next.
- An immediate e-mail should confirm receipt of the order, listing the items and quantities ordered and estimated delivery time.
- A subsequent e-mail should state that the order has been shipped, along with the predicted arrival date and a tracking number from the shipping company.

Another e-mail should state when the merchandise was delivered.

Free Shopping Carts for Your Site*—Instead of creating a shopping cart from scratch, check out the following sources for free shopping carts that you can customize for your products or services and add to your site. Most include third-party banner ads that disappear when you upgrade to the paid version of the shopping cart:*

Free JavaScript Shopping Cart, http://www.nopdesign.com/freecart/

Marketers Choice, http://www.1shoppingcart.com/

ShopSite SC Lite, http://www.redwoodinternet.com/lite.html

Steve's Free Shopping Cart, http://www.stevespages.f2s.com/

WebContactPro,
http://www.webcontactpro.com/freelshoppinglcartlsoftwaremi.htm

---

You might assume that of course the customer would know when the merchandise arrived. The last step provides reassurance when the order represents a gift, and it helps prevent misunderstandings about the details of actual delivery. "We had a big problem with customers calling weeks after we shipped a product to inquire why they never received it," says Glen Roberts of **Office1000.com** (http://www.office1000.com/). "In fact, UPS showed that it had been left on a porch, delivered to the mail room, loading dock, etc. We upgraded our system to notify customers by e-mail when their package has been delivered, providing the UPS tracking details. That almost completely eliminated those calls."

Providing Customer Service Options

You'll achieve more completed sales if you have one or more support services to help shoppers who get stuck technically or mentally while attempting to place an order. Such support services include live customer service by phone or live on-screen chat, FAQ files accessible from shopping-cart screens, and a Web forum (also known as a discussion board) where visitors can see answers to other users' questions about buying or using the product or service. (See Figure 8.11.)

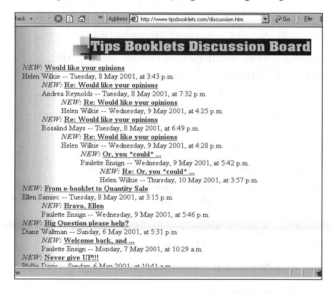

Figure 8.11: This is a public discussion board for Tips Booklets International (http://www.tipsbooklets.com/), a site selling e-booklets and advice on marketing printed and electronic booklets.

Beware, though: Appearing to offer a live help option that doesn't work as expected gets you no further than offering nothing at all along those lines. For instance, when I became stuck trying to order a software program, I clicked a picture of a woman wearing a headset alongside the legend, "May I help you?" At first, I assumed this was connecting me with a real person working for the software company. The following dialog (with the identity of the culprit masked) ensued:

Software Site: Hello, my name is Lori. I am the zzz.com Web Site Assistant. How may I help you?

Me: Where do I click to buy the Personal Productivity Program?

Software Site: Please look below for more information about our *Personal Productivity* online service. If you have already subscribed to this service and would like to run it, please click START.

Me: But I'm not a subscriber... I want to buy your software.

Software Site: Good.

Me: Are you stupid or what?

Software Site: Sorry, I'm trying to understand though. Maybe if you change the subject to our online organizational, storage, and backup services, that's my job, I can help you.

Needless to say, this dialog with a robot left me more frustrated than ever.

Action Steps:

- Place a complicated order, such as for multiple items shipped to two addresses or to an overseas country without ZIP codes, through your site to see what happens. Make any procedural changes necessary to accommodate more customers.
- Ask someone who has very little experience buying things online to place an order through your site, and watch and listen to his or her comments.
- Check the order page to determine whether it offers information or obvious links to your information on return policies, guarantees, shipping charges, and estimated delivery times. Even if such data is offered elsewhere, add it to the order page also.
- Is the price of every product or service crystal clear and explicit? Reword where necessary so that shoppers don't have to be mind readers.
- Make sure you have revealed shipping information and taxes before asking for credit card information.
- Add a confirmation screen and e-mail telling buyers you have received their order and explaining when they can expect delivery.

CHAPTER NINE

Graphics and Layout

Throughout this book, I've assumed that a great-looking Web site is nice, but not an end in itself for a site that you hope will boost your sales and heighten your influence. From that point of view this chapter clues you in on visual howlers to avoid and choices of placement and presentation that detract from the results you would like from your site. This chapter offers ways to make sure your design serves your marketing goals.

In this chapter:
- *Why you must coordinate your Web site's look with your desired business image*
- *What to place above the fold on your home page*
- *Why icons can't substitute for words*
- *How to format text for readability*

Your Site's Overall Look

As with any sort of marketing or sales piece, your site should have a distinctive look that at a glance conveys the sort of organization it represents, suits how you wish to be perceived, and remains recognizable on every page of the site. Colors, fonts, and density of information each play a part in determining a match or a clash here. If you sell $400 Italian loafers, you need a chic, airy look with curvy lettering rather than a screen teeming with small words and phrases. If your service is founded on comfort and care, you'd be better off with soft colors and whispery art work than a brisk, institutional look. (See Figure 9.1.)

Once a business consultant asked me to help rewrite her business bio, citing her Web site as background information. Because the site used bright colors in kindergartenish fonts, I assumed that she had a rather low-end practice and was surprised to learn that her annual revenues were upwards of $200,000. I mentioned that her design had thrown me off, and within a couple of months, she had a completely new site using maroon and dark blue stripes, reminiscent of banks and financial service providers instead of a day care center.

Figure 9.1: A soft blue and curves help set the tone for this patient-care site.

Most people know that colors have emotional connotations, with red linked to danger and love, yellow to cheeriness, purple to royalty, green to money and the outdoors, and so on. But color combinations also have implications for accessibility. While reviewing sites for the Webby awards, I encountered several home pages whose color choices had me marveling, "Whatever were they thinking?" Olive green letters on a black background, orange letters on dark blue, tiny light gray text against white, and faint white on lime green—the designers involved had slapped up an instantaneous and in some cases unbridgeable barrier for me. I simply could not read the words there. Maybe twenty-year-olds wouldn't have a problem with it, or maybe the designers had created their color palette without thinking about readability. It's hard to imagine how any site could accomplish its goals if most of the words on it can't be deciphered.

Another thing that annoyed me repeatedly while touring sites as a Webby reviewer was having to explore with my mouse to identify the location of hyperlinks. Designers who think blue underlining is ugly have a point, but forcing your visitors to play hide and seek to improve aesthetics has a cost. According to usability researcher Jared Spool, experienced Web users find blue underlined links in less than one second when a new site comes up on their screen, which enables them to get right down to the business they're trying to transact there. Invisible links slow down visitors set on a purpose, which would almost always contradict the goals of your site. For the same reason, avoid slow-loading graphics on a home page, reserving them for situations where visitors choose to view them (see Figure 9.2).

Figure 9.2: Ofoto (http://www.ofoto.com/), which uses photographic quality as a selling point, nevertheless does not load up its home page with huge or multiple photos.

Color Resources—How best to use color is a complicated topic when it comes to the Web. You'll find help at the following Web sites:

All About Color—Which colors mean what? What colors are in this year and why? What are the most popular colors? How do colors affect us? Pantone has some fascinating stuff.
http://www.pantone.com/allaboutcolor/allaboutcolor.asp

Boogie Jack's Color Schemer—Choose any of 216 colors from a chart and get its equivalent code in the red/green/blue system (255,0,214) or the hexadecimal code (#FF00CC), so that it will show up that way in any browser.
http://www.boogiejack.com/colormach2.html

Color Center—Quickly test color combinations to see how well they work together.
http://www.hidaho.com/colorcenter/cc.html

Using Color on the Web—Get up to speed on color theory, color wheels, and the difference between complementary, split-complementary, triad, and analogous colors so that you can more choose more harmonious and interesting color combinations.
http://www.projectcool.com/developer/gzone/color/index.html

The World of Color—Designer Dmitry Kirsanov offers tips for combining colors in original, striking ways on the Web.
http://www.webreference.com/dlab/9704/index.html

Page Layout

Designers and technical staff tend to have much larger monitors than people accessing the Web at home or on older computers at work. What looks great on a large screen may lose quite a lot when viewed on a smaller one. A solution that accommodates everyone is designing so that the most important elements appear in the reduced window and relegating elements less central to the site's existence to outlying, optional areas. For instance, **Ford's** home page (http://www.ford.com/) stretches wider than would fit on a smaller monitor, but the design includes a break to the right of "Breaking News," "Our Services," and "Our Company." (See Figures 9.3 and 9.4.) Except for the Welcome line and tag line, this makes the smaller rectangle seem like a self-sufficient site. Yet the larger layout works too. Other sites use the same strategy for a home page that looks like the length fits within a smaller window but actually extends far below.

Figure 9.3: Ford's home page (http://www.ford.com/), as seen on a small screen. It sort of fits, but also lets you know there's more over to the right.

Figure 9.4: This shows the entire width of Ford's home page (http://www.ford.com/).

The terminology for this two-faced design evokes a long-established reality in the newspaper business. *Above the fold* signifies the top half of the front page of a traditional-sized newspaper, and for the home page of a Web site it similarly means the portion of the home page visible to the viewer upon arriving at the site without scrolling. Just as the major stories and most gripping photos always begin above the fold of the newspaper, everything that the first-time visitor needs to navigate around your site should sit within the site's initial rectangle that appears before any clicking or scrolling.

When creating a site or working on a makeover, estimate how much of that initially visible area—called *prime real estate* in another common metaphor—consists of information truly relevant to the purpose in the mind of the visitor. Jakob Nielsen's analysis of space usage of home pages shows that on some well-financed sites, as little as 14% relates to the content that the user came there to find. The rest is devoted to "distracting machinery" such as internal navigation paraphernalia, external links, ads, and blank space. Nielsen says the percentage should be at least 50% and ideally more like 80%.

Four Elements of Professional Design—Robin Williams, author of more than a dozen books on design, singles out these four aesthetic principles as responsible for the difference between dorky and delightful looking:

Alignment—Line up items on a page along the left side, the right side, or centered. Don't mix alignments, which looks confusing and messy.

Proximity—Place items that are related to one another in close proximity. For instance, after a subhead, use the Break command instead of the Paragraph command so that the subhead appears related to what follows. Group bits of information so that white space indicates a separation before an unrelated unit of meaning.

Repetition—Create unity by repeating colors, backgrounds, images, formats, layouts, fonts, and so on from page to page and within a page.

Contrast—When two visual features are different, make them very different, not almost the same. Help the reader find what's important by making key elements more prominent and de-emphasizing less important elements.

In the struggle to make the most of prime real estate on the home page, some sites have tried replacing navigational words and phrases with small icons. As someone who's tried to work unfamiliar dashboard accessories that have no words usually finds, though, most icons are not universally intuitive. One site uses space-saving images such as a question mark and a shopping cart, which appear to have clear meanings, but don't. You might think the question mark would lead to Frequently Asked Questions, but instead it leads to a Customer Care page. You might assume the shopping cart icon would link to a shopping cart, but instead it leads to the site's store. Verbal equivalents of those pictures don't appear anywhere else on the home page, putting too great a communication burden on the icons. A good rule of thumb on the Web is that *whatever you think is obvious probably isn't*. Redundancy and multiple routes to important inside pages help your site function better.

In laying out pages, occasionally juggle the locations of various crucial items, like important news or special offers, looking for the sweet spots that attract the most attention and response. I found that information in the center left and bull's-eye center of the above-the-fold portion of my home page got vastly more clicks than features or offers in any other locations. (See Figure 9.5.) "By putting our offer at the top of the page on the right, we pulled about 14 times (1,400%) more giveaway entries as we received on the side columns, even though the side column description is on many more pages of the site," says Audri Lanford, head wizard of **wz.com** (http://www.wz.com/). "Elsewhere, tiny changes in wording and placement have made huge differences in results—often 300% to 500%. If you don't test, at best you are wasting you're money. More likely, you'll become another dot bomb."

Figure 9.5: The "sweet spots" on my home page are dead center (*Eye-Opening New Book*) and the top of the left column (*In a rush?*).

Tips on Using Photos—Nothing adds authenticity and immediacy to a Web site like photographs. However, pitfalls abound. Enhance rather than burden your site with photos by following the advice in these articles.

Clean Up Those Digital Photos!,
http://www.webreference.com/graphics/column11/

Creating Digital Images,
http://kodak.com/US/en/digital/dlc/book1/chapter1/

Image Editors,
http://www.gif.com/WebDesign/Tools/Windows/Image_Editors/

Photography in Web Design, http://www.webreference.com/dlab/9708/

Treatment of Text

Whereas anyone laying out words to appear on paper has collective wisdom of several hundred years to draw upon, our knowledge of the psychology and physiology of absorbing words from monitors is still evolving. However, some seemingly reliable principles have emerged. In some respects, the optimum treatment of type resembles guidelines for text on paper, but in other respects, recommendations are the opposite.

The standard size for readable text online is the same as for words in print—12-point type. Long passages of 10-point type cause eyestrain in many readers, so I don't recommend it for anything longer than a paragraph or two. When it comes to which fonts are most readable online, the findings contradict what we know works best in print. On paper, so-called *serif fonts*, where letters have little feet and tops that draw the eye horizontally along a line of type, speed up reading, while plainer, more modern-looking *sans serif* fonts slow reading down. On a screen, serif fonts don't appear as sharp as sans serif, particularly at 10 points or smaller. Even so, because we're accustomed to reading text with serifs in books and magazines, at 12 points serif text is about as readable as sans serif. (See Figure 9.6.) Thus, for small lettering, stick to sans serif fonts, while for body text and headlines you can choose according to the image you prefer to project.

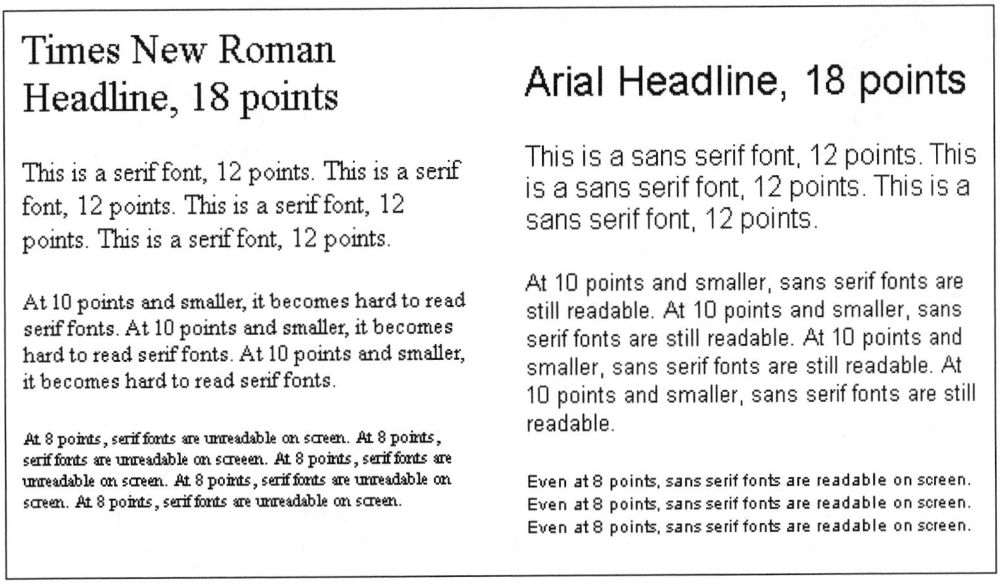

Times New Roman Headline, 18 points

This is a serif font, 12 points. This is a serif font, 12 points. This is a serif font, 12 points. This is a serif font, 12 points.

At 10 points and smaller, it becomes hard to read serif fonts. At 10 points and smaller, it becomes hard to read serif fonts. At 10 points and smaller, it becomes hard to read serif fonts.

At 8 points, serif fonts are unreadable on screen. At 8 points, serif fonts are unreadable on screeen. At 8 points, serif fonts are unreadable on screen. At 8 points, serif fonts are unreadable on screen. At 8 points, serif fonts are unreadable on screen.

Arial Headline, 18 points

This is a sans serif font, 12 points. This is a sans serif font, 12 points. This is a sans serif font, 12 points.

At 10 points and smaller, sans serif fonts are still readable. At 10 points and smaller, sans serif fonts are still readable. At 10 points and smaller, sans serif fonts are still readable. At 10 points and smaller, sans serif fonts are still readable.

Even at 8 points, sans serif fonts are readable on screen. Even at 8 points, sans serif fonts are readable on screen. Even at 8 points, sans serif fonts are readable on screen.

Figure 9.6: Compare the looks and readability of a serif font, on the left, and a sans serif font, on the right.

When it comes to emphasis, forget about underlining except to indicate hyperlinks, and use italic type sparingly, only for book titles and such, never for more than four or five words at a stretch. The curlicues and slanting added in italic type disrupt readability considerably more on screen than on paper. On the

Web, bold works better for emphasis. Forget about extended uses of all-capital letters, too. Lots of people have gotten the message that in e-mail, all-caps comes across as shouting. Fewer know that in headlines, capitalizing only the initial letters of words—mixing upper- and lower-case letters—makes lines easier to absorb quickly than capitalizing everything.

Choosing fonts only for their aesthetic characteristics can land you in dilemmas that require adjustments. For example, in Figure 9.7, the rounded letters of the primary font chosen for this e-commerce consultant's Web site convey friendly femininity. Designer Robin Williams calls this kind of font a "pudgy space hog." That otherwise desirable roundness makes one of the link titles along the left spill over onto two lines, in turn requiring line breaks between separate labels or a less pudgy font for clarity. Some fonts have versions especially designed for efficient use of space, often labeled "(Font name) Narrow."

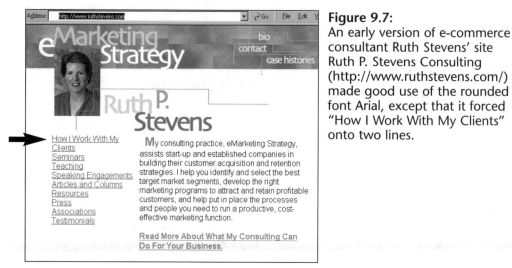

Figure 9.7:
An early version of e-commerce consultant Ruth Stevens' site Ruth P. Stevens Consulting (http://www.ruthstevens.com/) made good use of the rounded font Arial, except that it forced "How I Work With My Clients" onto two lines.

Is Your Design Fast Loading?—*Graphics, photos, fancy fonts, and other special effects can slow access to your site. Use these resources to time and adjust the loading time of your site.*

    Bandwidth Conservation Society, http://www.infohiway.com/faster/

    Dr. Html, http://www.drhtml.com

    Web Site Garage, http://websitegarage.netscape.com/

For the sake of readability, avoid centering more than one line or two, and stick to aligning type along the left-hand side of a column, reserving alignment along the right margin for headings and subheads rather than running type. Any time the reader has to think about where exactly to look from the end of one line to the start of the next, reading speed and comfort suffer. This principle also applies to column width, which should never fill the user's screen all the way from left to right. (See Figure 9.8.) Inserting a colored stripe down the left or right side of the page not only provides space for links and promotions, but also ensures that columns stay within a readable breadth.

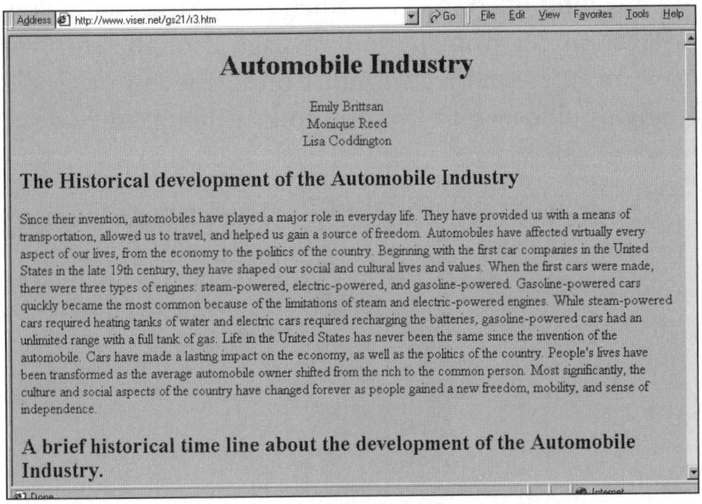

Figure 9.8: Stretching text all the way from left to right of the screen makes it hard to read. Compare the much more readable column width in Figure 9.9.

Although many of us spend hours every day viewing words on computer screens, we don't read online the way we do curled up with a book, magazine, or newspaper. We're much more likely to skip around on the surface and skim, looking for main points to take away, rather than consume the text completely and consecutively, sentence by sentence. Therefore, bullet points, numbered lists, and short paragraphs (seven lines or fewer) enhance the chances of getting your message across online. In one study, Jakob Nielsen found that converting regular paragraphs to bullet points improved readability 47%. Use subheads to break up text on the Web much more than you might elsewhere, too.

Long Pages Rule!—*According to information architect Michael Hoffman, long pages—even very long ones—have important advantages over short, granular snippets on separate pages:*
- *A visually obvious, scannable structure*
- *Faster reading*
- *Faster searching for content within a document*
- *Easier printing*

Read the complete 13,000-word article, "Enabling Extremely Rapid Navigation in Your Web or Document" at http://www.pdrinterleaf.com/infoaxcs.htm.

Some Internet commentators believe that because the essence of the Web is the ease with which we can jump around from page to page, we should inject

Web text with as many hyperlinks as possible. (See Figure 9.9.) I disagree. Finding links that don't add anything useful to the original text is the online equivalent of a storyteller who can't keep to the point. I also take issue with the practice—less common now than a few years ago, thank heavens—of dividing a long article or sales pitch into brief sections on separate pages. On dial-up Internet connections, or on any kind of connection when the Web server is slow to respond, it can take forever to get from page 1 to page 2 of the story or explanation. When you have an interested reader, don't break the visitor's spell! On the Web, people willingly scroll down to keep reading, although they don't appreciate being forced to scroll sideways.

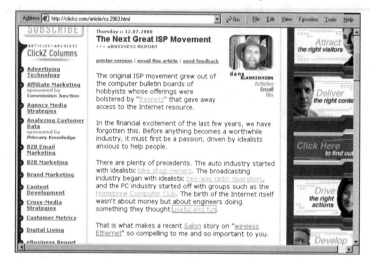

Figure 9.9: An average of two links per paragraph is too many for me, making me dizzy.

Working with a Designer

If you're not a trained, experienced designer and want a radically different look in a Web site makeover, you'll probably be working with someone who has a knack for translating business concepts into creative visual elements. The better you communicate with your designer, the more likely you are to end up with a site that pleases you and your target market. Yet, if you don't naturally think visually, you may find it hard to provide meaningful guidance. Minimize your own and the designer's frustration by using this checklist for information on what you'd like the site to be like.

- Find three Web sites, not necessarily in your industry, that you like a lot and explain what you like about them.
- Describe the age, gender, income, occupations, nationalities, and other demographic characteristics of your desired visitors.

- If you have a logo, provide it. Are you satisfied with it? If not, explain what you don't like about it.
- What clichés and taboos for your industry should the designer avoid? For instance, in the legal field, the scales of justice are overused, as is the mortar and pestle for drugstores.
- Choose at least three or four adjectives that describe how you want your business to be perceived. The following list shows some examples:
  - Classic or contemporary?
  - Sophisticated or simple?
  - Exclusive or popular?
  - Emotional or intellectual?
  - Opinionated or neutral?
  - Precise or creative?
  - Expensive or affordable?
  - Wild or stable?
  - Formal or informal?
  - Fun or serious?
  - Verbal or nonverbal?
  - Predictable or challenging?
- Describe the kind of emotional response you would like visitors to have at your site. For instance, comfort, surprise, fascination, envy, pity, camaraderie, outrage, or trust.

If the designer's first draft isn't what you're expecting, run through this checklist again for help in putting into words the ways in which it doesn't match what you're looking for. However, also be open to the designer's justification of the design. After all, as an expert in visual communication, he or she knows how to get across intangible qualities nonverbally.

Action Steps:

- Assess your color scheme and text size to make sure it can be read by practically all visitors to your site.
- Can someone see at a glance, with their hands off the mouse, which areas of your site serve as links? If not, consider the cost of forcing visitors to poke around with their mouse.
- If you normally surf the Web using a large monitor, make your

browser window smaller to determine whether the main portions of your home page appear "above the fold."

• Try juggling the location of key items on your home page to determine the optimal placement of information.

• Have you used bullet points and subheads to help those skimming your page? Reformat your content to facilitate fast reading and absorption.

PART II

Putting it All Together

CHAPTER TEN

Single-Product Sales

Let's start our before-and-after makeovers with the simplest kind of sales site, one page promoting a single product. Such a page has much to achieve: It must attract the attention of the target market, intensify interest into a desire to buy, dispel any doubts or confusions of potential buyers, and channel the intention to buy into an actual purchase—all before visitors click away to continue their Internet travels elsewhere. While pictures may help seal the sale, the greatest burden falls on the page's words, which have to tantalize the visitor with something not available elsewhere, explain the offering thoroughly, and persuade the reader to take action.

This makeover discusses:
- *How to increase the drama of your marketing copy*
- *What to do when you have your choice of spellings*
- *The powerful value of testimonials for sales*
- *How to head off shoppers' doubts and questions*

Capturing Attention

Nancy Hendrickson, co-author of an e-book on genealogy, felt her Web copy could be stronger, but she wasn't sure how to improve it. Since it's a long page, let's begin with what the user sees first at her site (see Figure 10.1).

Since this site doesn't have multiple pages, it doesn't need a name plate to maintain a stable identity for the site from page to page. Nevertheless, it is important to begin with a marketing message orienting the reader and stating the benefit of spending time reading the Web copy. Leading off with the title of the product doesn't accomplish that goal. After all, people landing at this site probably arrived looking for information on using the Internet to track down family connections, not specifically seeking a book on the topic. Hence, I added an introductory line worded as an invitation to the population the site was geared toward. (See Figure 10.2.)

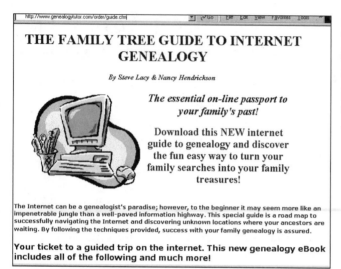

Figure 10.1: This is what visitors originally saw first at Steve Lacy and Nancy Hendrickson's Web page, The Family Tree Guide to Internet Genealogy (http://www.genealogytutor .com/order/guide.cfm).

If you compare Figures 10.1 and 10.2 closely, you'll discover three other kinds of changes made above the fold of this Web page—that is, in the portion immediately visible to the visitor. First, the "before" version asks visitors to download the product before it explains what it is and why it's valuable. This element belongs later in the Web copy. Second, the "information highway" metaphor was overused and dated, so I took it out. Third, the description of what genealogy enthusiasts are typically trying to accomplish was a bit dry in the initial paragraphs. Note the more dramatic language in the "after" version. Note too that the original sometimes had *Internet* capitalized and sometimes in lower case. Where usage hasn't yet become standardized, as with *Web site* (or is it *website?*) and *on-line* (or is it *online?*), you need to choose one spelling or treatment and stick to it.

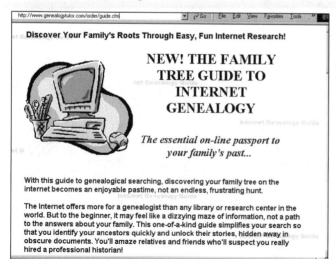

Figure 10.2: In this "after" version of Figure 10.1, note the invitational line inserted above the title of the e-book.

In the next section of the Web page, Steve and Nancy's original version makes excellent use of informative bullets, detailing selling point after selling point in digestible nuggets. (See Figure 10.3.)

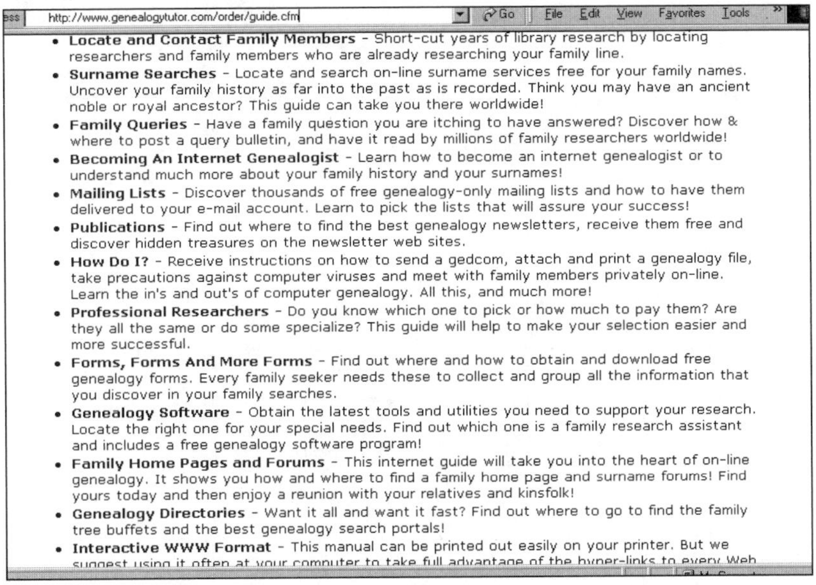
http://www.genealogytutor.com/order/guide.cfm Go File Edit View Favorites Tools

- **Locate and Contact Family Members** - Short-cut years of library research by locating researchers and family members who are already researching your family line.
- **Surname Searches** - Locate and search on-line surname services free for your family names. Uncover your family history as far into the past as is recorded. Think you may have an ancient noble or royal ancestor? This guide can take you there worldwide!
- **Family Queries** - Have a family question you are itching to have answered? Discover how & where to post a query bulletin, and have it read by millions of family researchers worldwide!
- **Becoming An Internet Genealogist** - Learn how to become an internet genealogist or to understand much more about your family history and your surnames!
- **Mailing Lists** - Discover thousands of free genealogy-only mailing lists and how to have them delivered to your e-mail account. Learn to pick the lists that will assure your success!
- **Publications** - Find out where to find the best genealogy newsletters, receive them free and discover hidden treasures on the newsletter web sites.
- **How Do I?** - Receive instructions on how to send a gedcom, attach and print a genealogy file, take precautions against computer viruses and meet with family members privately on-line. Learn the in's and out's of computer genealogy. All this, and much more!
- **Professional Researchers** - Do you know which one to pick or how much to pay them? Are they all the same or do some specialize? This guide will help to make your selection easier and more successful.
- **Forms, Forms And More Forms** - Find out where and how to obtain and download free genealogy forms. Every family seeker needs these to collect and group all the information that you discover in your family searches.
- **Genealogy Software** - Obtain the latest tools and utilities you need to support your research. Locate the right one for your special needs. Find out which one is a family research assistant and includes a free genealogy software program!
- **Family Home Pages and Forums** - This internet guide will take you into the heart of on-line genealogy. It shows you how and where to find a family home page and surname forums! Find yours today and then enjoy a reunion with your relatives and kinsfolk!
- **Genealogy Directories** - Want it all and want it fast? Find out where to go to find the family tree buffets and the best genealogy search portals!
- **Interactive WWW Format** - This manual can be printed out easily on your printer. But we suggest using it often at your computer to take full advantage of the hyper-links to every Web

Figure 10.3: Here's a good use of bullet points to move the reader closer to buying. This appeared just below Figure 10.1 in the original version of the genealogy site.

While most of the copy required only minor changes, the following four factors, changed in my new version, shown in Figure 10.4, needed attention:

- It's always important to envision what doubts or objections Web visitors may have about your offering, and to forestall them. The market for this guide includes people who are a bit intimidated by the word *download* and may not be sure what an *eBook* is. Assurances that the product is easy to use help solve this problem.
- Another possible concern is that the guide might be overly focused on certain geographical areas or ethnic groups, shortchanging the ancestry of a particular user. The new text, "whatever part of the world your forbearers came from," addresses this concern.
- As mentioned in Part I, *Crucial Web Site Elements*, insider jargon must be handled with great care. Steve and Nancy used the term "gedcom," which I'd never heard of, so I inserted reassurance that it would be explained in the guide.
- Since professional researchers should be the last resort for most amateur

genealogists, I moved that bullet item to the end. (This didn't quite fit in Figure 10.4.) The general principle is to lead with the most important and most universally applicable features and benefits.

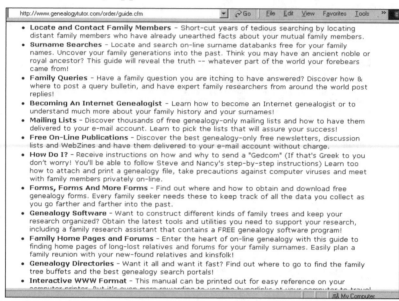

Figure 10.4: My revision of Figure 10.3 incorporates changes designed to head off readers' concerns.

Clinching the Sale

Steve and Nancy were smart to include a signed reader testimonial, which increases credibility for potential buyers, especially when the person behind the blurb holds relevant credentials. (See Figure 10.5.)

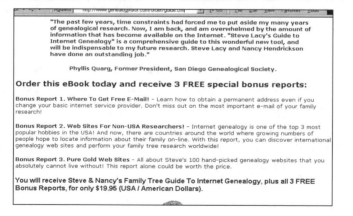

Figure 10.5: Testimonials increase credibility. This appears just below Figure 10.3 in the original version of the genealogy site.

However, the quote needed editing, and three testimonials would be even more persuasive than one. We selected two of the more powerful additional blurbs for the site revision, as shown in Figure 10.6.

Editing Testimonials—*Can you edit someone else's testimonial (or other quotation)? The general answer is a qualified "yes." In this murky niche of law and ethics, the main concern is that you fairly retain the original meaning of the writer.*

Kudos to Steve and Nancy also for sweetening the sale with three bonus reports. (See Figure 10.5.) However, as with the bullets, the bonus reports should appear with the most appealing one first—the one most relevant to genealogy. Therefore, we switched the order of Report 3 and Report 1.

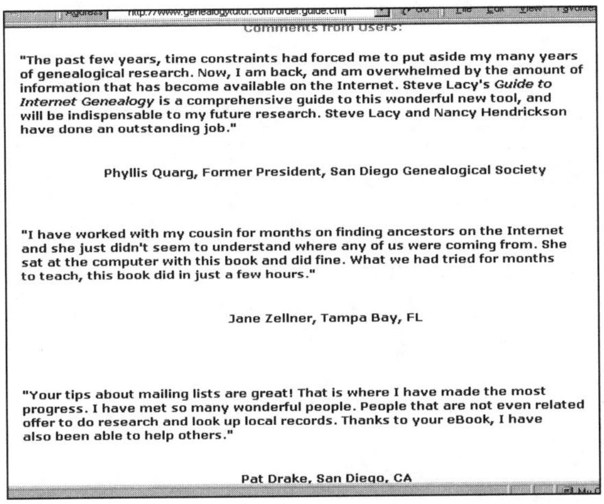

Figure 10.6: Figure 10.5 after editing the orignal testimonial and adding two more.

When asking people to order, always repeat the benefit of the product, as shown in the copy added in Figure 10.7. Also it is essential to specify what kind of file they would be downloading. I had assumed it was in PDF format for Adobe Reader, like most e-books, but Nancy said it was a self-executing file, so we added that. She wasn't sure whether the file was accessible to Mac users, a question that would surely come up and that would be smart to head off by adding something to the copy there. Finally, a guarantee would help take away the feeling of risk when people aren't sure whether they really want something and would increase orders by much more than it would cost in returned items. Note that the wording of the guarantee in Figure 10.7 restates the benefit of the product one more time. It's hard to overdo hammering home what buyers enjoy with their purchase!

Still missing from the "after" version are a few elements that would further reassure genealogy enthusiasts skittish about ordering online: an e-mail address shoppers could use if they had question. (For example, how could one buy it as a gift for a family member? Suppose one is surfing the Net at a public library; how could the user e-mail the product home?) Steve and Nancy's physical or postal address would calm buyers' fears of dealing with a fly-by-night operation and a telephone number for placing an off-the-Net order or asking questions,

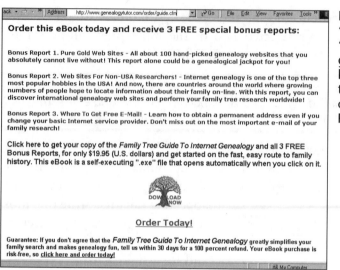

Figure 10.7: Never say just "click here to order." Say "click here to order and get this benefit." Add the benefit to the guarantee too. This shows the revision of the bottom portion of Figure 10.5.

would likewise reassure nervous shoppers. The site also doesn't say how many pages are in the e-book. Three credible testimonials might still leave shoppers wondering what kind of value they're getting for their money. They wouldn't know whether for $19.95 they're receiving 75 or 400 pages.

Taking the Order

Now let's look at the process of placing the order for Steve and Nancy's e-book. Clicking the *Download Now* or *Order Today!* links, which are just off the screen of Figure 10.5, brings visitors to Figure 10.8.

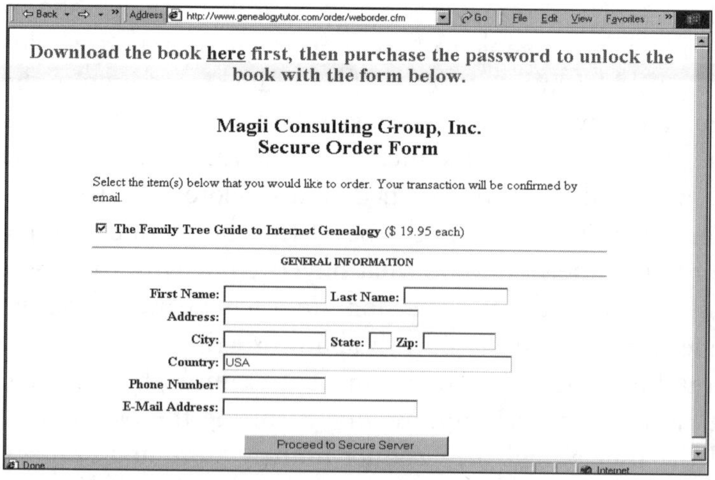

Figure 10.8: The original order form for The Family Tree Guide to Internet Genealogy.

It's good that this page tells buyers they will be proceeding to a secure server. But does the site accept American Express and Discover cards? Suppose a buyer wants to pay by money order—could one? Clicking the *Proceed to Secure Server* link reveals the forms of payment accepted, including—surprise!—checks.

Based on the information on the order page and the desirability of reminding the shopper of your guarantee at the decision-making moment, I revised the page where the buyer enters her or his ordering information in Figure 10.9. Note that I also changed "General Information" to "Billing Information." Even if their credit-card processing service does not match addresses entered here with those on the credit-card account, it's wise to imply that it does, to discourage cheaters.

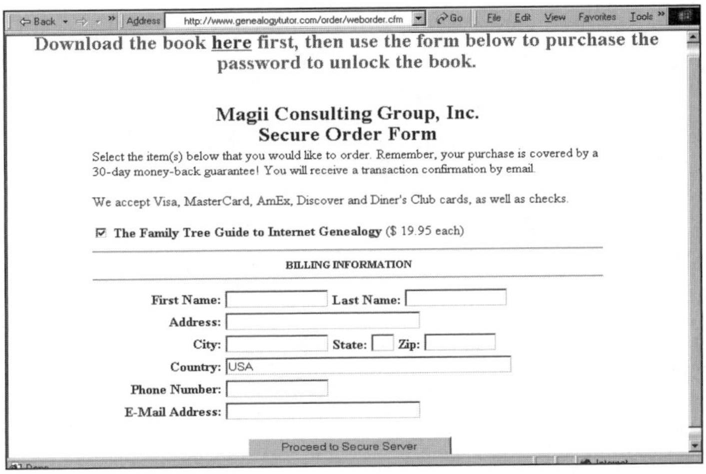

Figure 10.9: The revision of Figure 10.8 adds information shoppers need when asked to enter their credit-card information.

CHAPTER ELEVEN

Multiproduct Sales

From a single-product site to a multiproduct site, the copywriting and design challenges multiply, but not only due to the greater number of products for sale at the latter. Problems of organization and navigation arise for the first time, because marketers must not only arouse interest in their online visitors and persuade them to buy. They also have to steer shoppers to the right products and explain how items differ from one another. In addition, the site may have multiple audiences, which poses questions about how to present material for Audience A without confusing Audiences B and C and vice versa. All of these challenges and more cropped up in this chapter's makeover.

This makeover discusses:
- *How to engage multiple audiences without alienating any of them*
- *What to write to convey benefits*
- *Why and how to create at-a-glance markers for different types of products*
- *How to attract the right kinds of business partners*

The Company's Situation and Goals

This site, for **Magnet Media** (http://www.digitalmediatraining.com/) in New York City, describes and sells training videos on digital media. (See Figure 11.1.) They have several divergent audiences for their product line, called the Digital Media Training Series or DMTS, and for the Web site:

End users—This group purchases the videotapes and comprises those purchasing the videos for themselves and those purchasing for their organization. (The latter probably constitute the majority of this group.)

Distributors, resellers, and dealers—These entities are wholesalers who sell training videos to their customers or to yet other dealers. They need to be motivated to add the DMTS videos to their product line.

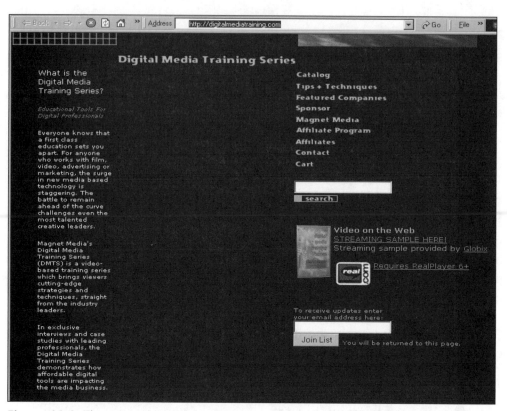

Figure 11.1: The original DMTS home page appeals almost entirely to end users.

Software manufacturers—Members of this group need information about how and why they should engage this company to produce videos on their product. Magnet Media often works with the software manufacturer behind the product on which a video series focuses, giving them some input on content, attractive price breaks on bulk purchases, and other benefits for videos that will also be distributed to the target market at large.

Those in the first audience, end users, need to be convinced that these training videos have distinct advantages over other modes of training, such as in-person training classes, Web-based training, printed manuals, technical help lines, in-house mentoring, and so on. They must also be convinced that the DMTS videos will meet their needs better than videos from other vendors. In addition, they should be able to complete a purchase easily at the site.

Those in the second audience, distributors, resellers, and dealers, need to find information that explains why becoming a reseller, dealer, or distributor of these videos would benefit them and information describing how to sign up for the reseller program.

Those in the third audience, software manufacturers, need to become interested—right from the home page—in Magnet Media as a training-video producer they might want to do business with and to find enough information about how such a relationship might work to contact the company for in-depth discussions.

Navigation Improvements

The original home page of this site—nicely designed, like the rest of the site—appeals almost exclusively to end users. With *Catalog* as the first navigation link in the right column in Figure 11.1, it is clear that the videos can be purchased at the site. Distributors and dealers would know to click the *Affiliate Program* link to learn more. For software manufacturers, the word *Sponsor* isn't a clear enough signal of the sort of partnership Magnet Media forms with software manufacturers, although since it is the nearest equivalent, it might provoke a click.

My solution for addressing the needs of all three audiences was to include in the introductory copy descriptions of what's at the site for each of the three groups, rather than depend completely on the navigation labels to catch and channel their attention appropriately. Since the majority of site visitors fall into the end-user group, the home page should continue to appeal mainly to them but clearly mention the other two purposes in ways that draw them to pages that explain what they need to know in detail. Before showing you my solution, we need to consider other changes recommended for the text on the home page.

Name Plate and Home Page Marketing Copy

Prior to revamping the site, I had extensive discussions with a Magnet Media principal, Megan Cunningham, about the advantages of the DMTS videos over other training options, including classroom training, printed manuals, and other training videos. We agreed that it was important to stress the distinctive use of industry professionals as trainers in these videos and the cost effectiveness and convenience of video training in general. The videos' high production quality also was a key selling point. Accordingly, I came up with two tag lines: "Learn from the pros" and "Broadcast-quality software training videos featuring digital-media professionals." The latter didn't fit, so Magnet Media substituted a shorter headline that originally appeared as a subtitle in the left column, "Educational Tools for Digital Professionals." See the top of Figure 11.2 for the revised name plate, which makes a much more effective marketing pitch than the video series title alone.

The left column of the revised home page (shown in Figure 11.2) begins by stating the problem that this product line solves, moves on to its primary

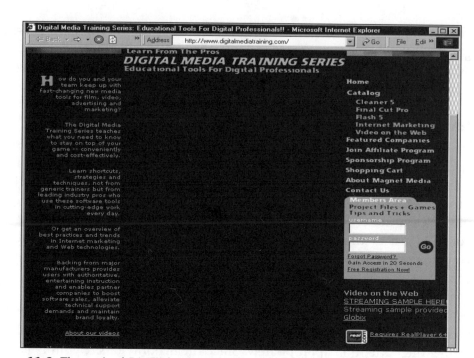

Figure 11.2: The revised DMTS home page is a more effective marketing tool.

advantages over competing training products, and mentions how Magnet Media's alliance with major software manufacturers benefits both software makers and video users. This change engages software manufacturers as well as end users. Then below the introductory marketing copy, a link is inserted for each of those three target audiences to find out more. Some of the links in the right column duplicate these three links, but the differences in wording should help ensure that distributors and software manufacturers understand what's in the site for them.

You'll notice several significant differences between the "before" and "after" versions of the major links in Figures 11.1 and 11.2. Under *Catalog* the major products in the training series are newly listed, with titles like "Cleaner 5" corresponding to the software packages that the videos train viewers in. *Sponsorship Program* is clearer than the original label *Sponsor*. The *Tips + Techniques* link previously led to a page containing two links for downloading files of tips related to the video topics, and Magnet Media wisely moved that into a members-only section accessible after registration with the site. On the original home page, it wasn't clear what kind of update subscribers would receive. Now they know they can immediately access "project files, and games, tips, and tricks" upon registering.

I recommended dropping the Search box because their entire product catalog fits on one page, which people who felt lost or impatient could search using their browser. Since it is difficult to tell that the upright rectangle on Figure 11.1, to the left of the invitation to view a streaming sample, is a video cover, that image could be dropped. It's gone in Figure 11.2. Finally, a list of the advantages of DMTS videos over training alternatives, in the revised site, appears in a pop-up screen accessible by clicking *Why Buy?* in the lower-right corner of Figure 11.2. See Figure 11.3 for the pop-up screen, whose advantages read as follows:

- Compared to classroom training, the videos are cheaper, more cost-effective, and are constantly available, irrespective of geographical location and scheduling constraints.
- They facilitate on-demand learning, with students able to rewind and rewatch problematical techniques, as well as to find solutions for a specific need through the use of a time code card keying an index of topics to the VCR's time clock.
- Video training involves more senses and thus promotes higher retention than printed manuals or classroom training.

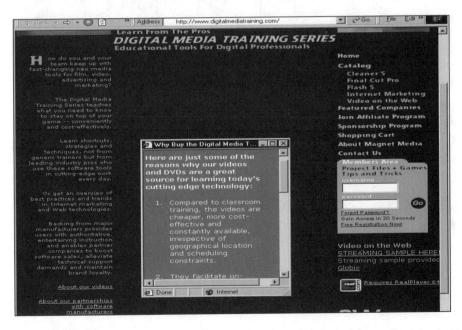

Figure 11.3: Magnet Media displays the advantages of their videos over training alternatives in a pop-up screen that appears when users click *Why Buy?*

- Unlike other training vehicles, these feature, as teachers, working professionals, who use the software programs in their everyday work and share tips and tricks from the front lines.
- Compared to competing training videos, these are broadcast quality in a more entertaining format.

Reorganizing the Catalog

Magnet Media's Catalog page (shown in Figure 11.4) had several problems. First, it should be clear at a glance that the company is selling two distinct kinds of videos: instructional training and overviews of a certain new media topic. The differences could be distinguished by color, with subheads, or through some other visual cue. The company also sells printed reference guides, both bundled with the videos and separately, which should be more clearly identified and set apart as well. Also, because some people might click straight to the catalog, the videos need a general introduction on the Catalog page.

Figure 11.4: Magnet Media's original main Catalog page contained several weaknesses.

First, Figure 11.5 shows the new copy written to convey the general benefits of the videos on the page where shoppers would actively consider buying. The company also added two more links leading to the *Why Buy?* pop-up screen: one visible in Figure 11.5, and another farther down the page. Note that the toll-free number appears twice in the upper right of the Catalog page. It also appears at the end of the pop-up screen.

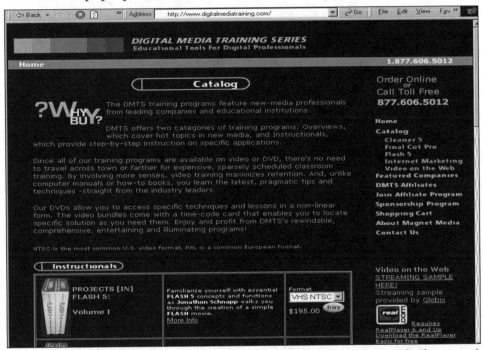

Figure 11.5: The new Catalog page begins with introductory copy to clarify general points about the products featured there.

Second, as you can see in Figure 11.6, the company decided to use both subheads and boxes to identify the different product types. If you look closely, you'll see that they also use boxes to separate the sets of videos for different software programs.

Third, the inconsistent presentation of the products was a problem—some sections included a photo of the product, while others didn't. Magnet Media fixed this variability in the new version of the Catalog page.

Fourth, the product descriptions benefited from featuring more about the credentials of the instructors and the content, while remaining concise. Changing the future tense ("will bring you up to speed") to present tense ("brings you up to speed"), as in any kind of marketing copy, adds immediacy and punch. In both versions, shoppers can click *More info* to view additional information about each product, including an outline of the topics covered and a fuller bio of the instructor. (Figure 11.7.)

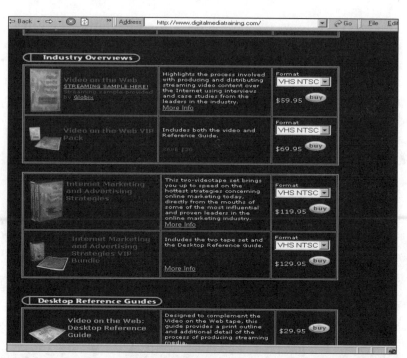

Figure 11.6: A lower portion of the new Catalog page uses subheads and boxes to indicate separate sets of videos and related products.

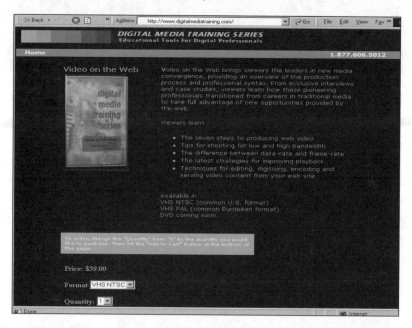

Figure 11.7: Clicking *More info* on the Catalog page opens a page, such as this one, with Add to cart, Shop More, View Cart, and Checkout buttons just out of view.

Attracting Sponsors

The original Sponsor page was confusing. (See Figure 11.8, continued in Figure 11.9.) It isn't clear whether the company is seeking advertisers who would get exposure on or in the videos, or companies who would subsidize the production costs of a training video on that company's product—or some other kind of commercial relationship entirely.

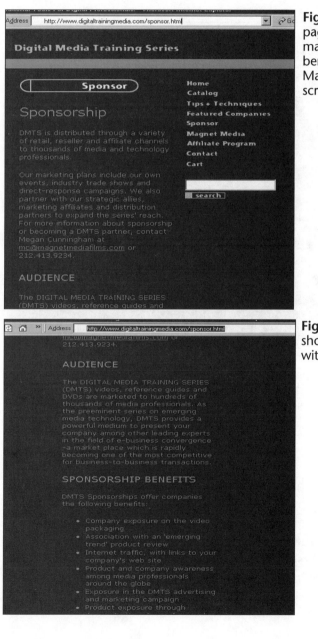

Figure 11.8: The original Sponsor page invites software manufacturers to form mutually beneficial partnerships with Magnet Media. This browser screen is continued in Figure 11.8.

Figure 11.9: The Web page shown in Figure 11.8 continues with this material.

After a long discussion with Magnet Media principal, Megan Cunningham, about what the sponsorship program involves and its benefits for participating companies, I wrote a new page. (See Figure 11.10). This page switched the order of the elements so that they fit how most people need to be persuaded. Manufacturers need to learn the benefits of sponsorship first. If these benefits are compelling enough, manufacturers can call or e-mail for details about how the program works.

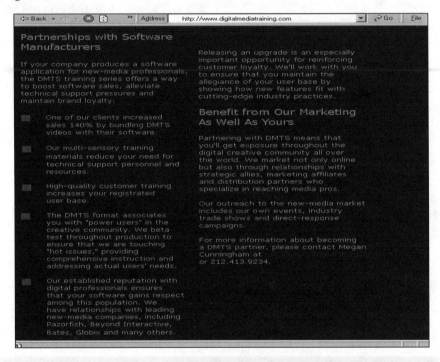

Figure 11.10: This new copy for the "after" version of the page for software manufacturers depicted in Figures 11.8 and 11.9, which will be formatted in the same way as the original page, positions material in the order that will persuade most people.

Attracting Affiliates

On the Web, many companies have programs enabling other entities to provide sales leads or funnel sales inquiries to the first company's order page in such a way that the second company gets a commission on those sales. Such programs usually go by the name of "affiliate programs," with the secondary companies considered "affiliates" of the first. Magnet Media had a page describing such a program whereby third parties in the new media industry could present DMTS

Figure 11.11: The top portion of the original affiliates page invites third parties to sign up as affiliates.

training products to their Web site visitors in exchange for commissions on any resulting sales. (See Figure 11.11.)

In the original version, it isn't clear exactly who would benefit from being an affiliate. After all, Magnet Media wouldn't want get-rich-quick types to waste Magnet Media's time and perhaps even put a dent in its reputation by trying to sell these high-priced videos to an inappropriate market. Also, the various elements in the appeal to affiliates aren't arranged in the most persuasive order. See the rewrite in Figure 11.12.

Note too that the makeover of the affiliate page removes the justification from the paragraphs, which had made the right margins line up evenly by creating uneven spacing between words. Except in print laid out with high-quality typesetting programs, justified copy is always harder and more tiring to read than unjustified—so-called "ragged right"—margins.

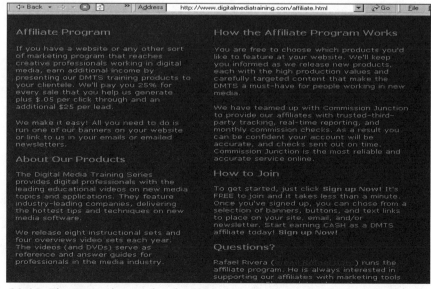

Figure 11.12: The revised copy for the Web page in Figure 11.11 is to be inserted in the original format.

CHAPTER TWELVE

Solo Service Provider

W e now consider a type of site with quite different goals to accomplish than a sales site. A professional service provider isn't angling for the Web visitor to plunk credit-card numbers into an order form or to call a toll-free order number. Instead, attorneys, accountants, dog groomers, or plumbers hope their Web sites will attract client leads or bolster their marketing appeal for those who heard about them elsewhere and want more information. When they include subscriptions to some sort of e-mail list, such sites also function as a funnel for continued contact that in the long run leads to business. Even though this kind of site isn't going for the immediate sale, it still must include carefully crafted marketing messages tailored for the target audience.

This makeover discusses:
- *How to create a consistent professional image*
- *Why a solo practitioner shouldn't talk about a firm*
- *What steps encourage site visitors to subscribe to a newsletter*
- *How to come across as friendly and accessible*

Introducing Jean Sifleet and SmartFast.com

Jean Sifleet is a Massachusetts attorney and accountant with an untraditional approach to business and the law. Instead of helping businesses initiate or defend against lawsuits, she helps clients understand the legal and financial implications of day-to-day business decisions and navigate past various pitfalls to business growth and higher profits. Her clients include entrepreneurs and business owners around the country and indeed in other parts of the world.

To attract potential clients and help answer the questions of those checking her out, her Web site should clearly explain how her approach is distinctive, what kinds of matters she handles and for whom, and her background and qualifications. It should also provide general guidance on topics relevant to her target market and evidence of her character and responsiveness in the form of testimonials. In short, it needs a clear focus, relevant content, credentials, contact information, and all of that in a smoothly flowing site that encourages a response.

Her **SmartFast.com** site (http://www.smartfast.com/) was already accomplishing many of its goals when I looked at it. Unlike many other solo practitioner sites, it transcended "brochureware" by using a brand name with some marketing appeal, by publishing a biweekly newsletter that addressed topics of great concern to her clientele, and by using ordinary language instead of stuffy "firm-speak." However, it needed to get its message across in a more internally consistent manner. The site also needed a refined marketing pitch and required a few aesthetic changes that would reinforce her professionalism.

Design, Slogans, and Image

The first noteworthy points on the home page (shown in Figure 12.1) were two

Figure 12.1: The top portion of Jean Sifleet's original home page at SmartFast.com.

design elements that interfered with the impression of trustworthiness and reliability Jean undoubtedly wanted to convey. First, the background to the name plate consisted of a spread of green paper money, a genre of illustration that is more often associated with get-rich-quick schemes and work-at-home scams than with respectable professional services.

Second, the bright red used for the navigation buttons was an unfortunate color choice. Red carries associations of danger, while Jean's services are designed to steer clients around perils. Along with the green of the cash along the top, the red created a Christmas-tree color scheme, which also didn't fit her professional profile. Although blue is the traditional color for inspiring trust, maroon or dark green would achieve a similar effect consistent with her image of being an alternative to corporate lawyers and accountants.

Next, the wording at the top of the home page was less than ideal. The slogan "Level the Playing Field" doesn't make sense in relation to legal or consulting services. Also, the meaning of the word "level" in that phrase and in "Take your business to the next level" stood in direct conflict with each other. (If you're leveling something, there can't be a next level.) And because **SmartFast.com** is a solo operation, not an organization of entrepreneurs, the phrase "by tapping into a network of experienced entrepreneurs" is misleading. The tag line should include the following concepts:

- Services that integrate legal and business advice in a preventive approach
- Benefit: **SmartFast.com** helps the client's company grow
- Something that explains the "smart fast" moniker
- A statement that business owners are the intended clients

After trying many synonyms and combinations of words, I came up with: "Secure your company's growth the smart, fast way." As explained in Chapter 1, *The Name Plate*, a site's title belongs in the background and the marketing message in the foreground, so "SmartFast.com" should be smaller and the tag line bigger in a visually distinctive logo that could appear at the top of every page on

the site. See Figure 12.2 for a rough draft of how that could look. Also, sometimes the original site spelled "SmartFast" in that way and sometimes "Smartfast" or "Smart Fast." Consistency reinforces professionalism—particularly for an attorney and accountant—so it was important to standardize usage.

Figure 12.2: A rough revision of the top section of Jean Sifleet's home page, with the name plate to be spiffed up by a designer.

Home Page Marketing Copy

The **SmartFast.com** home page continues with marketing copy and testimonials, as shown in Figure 12.3.

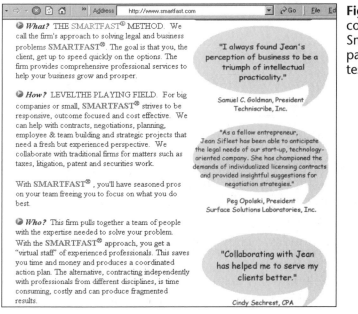

Figure 12.3: The continuation of the SmartFast.com home page includes testimonials.

The quote snippets in the right column of the home page are excellent—well-chosen and nicely worded, exactly the right length, and from people who sound like they have credibility in the business world. As for the "What? How? Who?" copy in the left column, some changes were in order. (See Figure 12.4.) In the original text, the reader got mixed signals as to whether this "firm" is really a firm or just Jean Sifleet. One situation or the other must be true. On the one hand, the single photo, the wording of the testimonials, and a separate bio page all clearly convey that Jean is a solo practitioner. On the other hand, talk of "the firm" and "this firm" imply that Jean has associates. Saying that Jean calls upon other professionals is perfectly fine and appropriate, as is reference to a "virtual team." The copy could sidestep confusion by sticking with this description and avoiding references to a "firm." The word "we" can stay where it refers to the team.

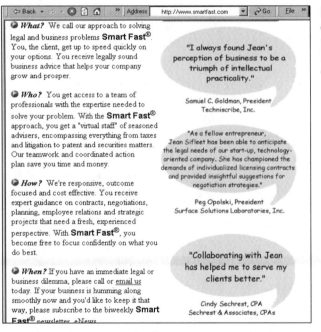

Figure 12.4: The next section of Jean Sifleet's revised home page now has reworded and rearranged copy in the left column.

Other changes in the home page marketing copy involve these principles:

- Phrases like "the goal is" and "strives to" subtly undermine professional credibility because they imply that you only try and do not necessarily succeed at the goal. Eliminating such phrases helps you come across as more confident and polished.

- Always look for ways to condense copy. When a point comes across in fewer words, more people read it.

- It's been proven repeatedly in political and business marketing that an explicit call to action—asking people to vote for you, place an order, or get in touch—always produces better results than leaving the point unsaid. Giving people a reason to take that action *now* is even more powerful.

• Always use *you* more than *we*.

Finally, let's look at the links at the bottom of the page (see Figure 12.5). I kept the "Smart Fast" theme going by changing *Services* to *Smart Fast Services*. Also, the *More Testimonials* link was confusing. More than what? It implied a nonexistent link for *Testimonials*. After thinking about it, I realized that "more" meant more than the three testimonial quotes on the home page. Even so, just *Testimonials* is clearer. Then the Testimonial page needed a note reminding the reader that the home page included three more client quotes.

Figure 12.5: On top, the original links for the SmartFast.com site; on the bottom, the links are revised to boost the Smart Fast branding and to be more logical.

Signing Up Subscribers

A big component of Jean's Internet marketing strategy consists of publishing a biweekly newsletter, *eNews*, that discusses, in lay terms, common business and legal decisions facing business owners and entrepreneurs. Like some online publishers, Jean makes her entire archives available online, amounting to a storehouse of readable advice accessible from the page depicted in Figure 12.6. So the page serving as a gateway to the newsletter has several purposes:

• It should encourage people to find, read, and recommend articles pertaining to their business dilemmas, in the long run increasing Jean's reputation as an expert and her appeal as an attorney and business adviser.

• It should encourage casual visitors to sign up for *eNews*, thus boosting Jean's opportunities for new clients and referrals.

• Since visitors may arrive here from a search engine or other link without having seen the home page, this page should orient readers about the kind of information they'll find in the newsletter archives, so that the right people know immediately that they've come to the right place.

The recommended revision of this page added the Smart Fast name plate, a précis of how *eNews* fits with the whole Smart Fast approach, an additional

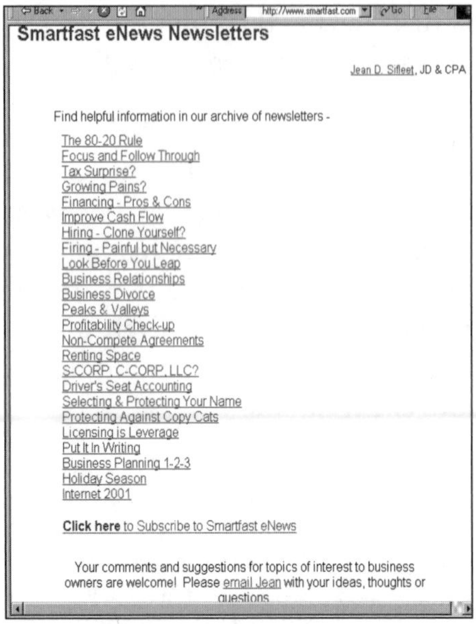

Figure 12.6: The "before" version of Jean Sifleet's newsletter page.

Figure 12.7: On this "after" version of Jean Sifleet's newsletter page several of the issue topics are omitted. Topics are now listed with the newest one first.

invitation to subscribe, and the facts that it's biweekly and free. (See Figure 12.7.) The list of topics within *eNews* began with the first issue and placed the most recent topic at the bottom. Reversing this order is better, with the most recent topic at the top, partly because leading sites do it this way and partly because inevitably some topics go out of date. At the top, the freshest material would be read first. Also, people arriving at this page might not realize Jean is an active attorney and business adviser, so adding explicit links to her bio and services pages is a good idea.

While Jean's newsletter titles do a good job of indicating what readers could expect in a particular issue, the longer this list gets, the more it calls for an on-site Search box or some other searchable method of indexing available content. This was a feature to consider for the future. (See Chapter 2, *Navigation Labels and On-Site Searches*, for a discussion of options.)

Since the free *eNews* was not an end in itself, but a marketing tool, I also thought about ways to increase the chances that each archived newsletter might attract inquiries from potential clients and persuade readers to subscribe, especially if a stranger discovered that page from a search engine or outside link. As you'll see in Figure 12.8, the brief explanation of *eNews'* purpose is repeated on top of each archived article and a clear byline inserted below the title of each article rather than a link in the upper-right corner. Each article ended with a "send this to a friend or colleague" link at the bottom.

Figure 12.8: Originally, "Jean D. Sifleet, JD & CPA" was in the upper-right corner. The explanation of *eNews'* purpose and the invitation to subscribe are new.

The *Who* and *What* Pages

Jean Sifleet's bio on the Who is Smart Fast? page was already excellent in tone—friendly and accessible. Well-organized too, it can serve as a structural model for the bio of practically anyone else who has been working for some time and changed directions in ways that benefit current clients. It leads with an overview statement and contains the necessary credentials at the end, where they do not overshadow the more important points about Jean's background and approach. See Figure 12.9 for the "after" version, changed only in minor ways from the original.

In a relapse to the traditional legal marketing approach, the page describing Jean's services was originally headed "Practice Areas." This page also needed only minor revisions, including changing "the client" to *you* and "can help" to *help*. (See Figure 12.10.) When people are looking through Web pages trying to choose a professional service provider, a detailed rundown of services helps them determine whether the practitioner is accustomed to handling situations like theirs. Most readers understand that such a Web page can't list everything the professional has ever done or could do, so they get in touch to find out more as long as what they see listed seems in the same ball park as their current predicament. The "before" version of both this page and the bio page left out any Smart Fast logo, which after revision added a consistent look throughout the site.

Offering Workshops

As discussed in Part I, *Crucial Web Site Elements*, concepts that may, to the site owner, seem too obvious to mention often do bear explaining to people who

Address http://www.smartfast.com Go File Edit View Favorites Tools

SmartFast.com

Secure Your Company's Growth the Smart, Fast Way!

Who is Smart Fast?

Smart Fast® is a distinctive approach to business and legal issues developed by Jean Sifleet, based on her experiences as an entrepreneur and from working with companies large and small.

Jean's career spans many years in large multi-national corporations and includes two successful entrepreneurial ventures. Along the way, Jean learned that the essence of effective management is the ability to gather and distill important information and make decisions quickly.

Jean began her career in the traditional way, with big law and accounting firms. She did a stint in state government, and then moved to the computer and communications industry. Frustrated with bureaucracy, Jean co-founded and sold two successful companies.

Today, Jean practices business law. She enjoys working with people who are starting a company, or who want to grow their company and stay out of trouble. Her advice is grounded in her first-hand experience as an entrepreneur as well as her knowledge of law, finance and management.

Calling herself a nontraditional lawyer, Jean uses **Smart Fast®**, a practical and systematic approach to evaluating options and making informed decisions. In contrast to many traditional lawyers, Jean avoids litigation and expensive procedures, striving always to anticipate and resolve business issues.

Jean works collaboratively with other professionals to get the information and expertise needed for sound decisions.

Jean holds a BBA (cum laude) from Ohio University and a Juris Doctorate from Boston University School of Law. She is a Certified Public Accountant and a member of the Bar in Massachusetts. She is also active on many public interest issues.

Internet

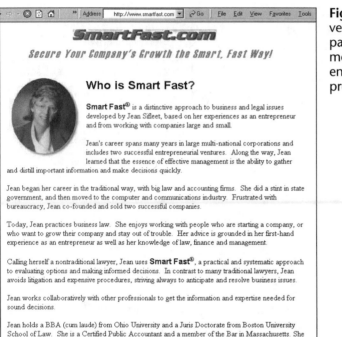

Figure 12.9: In the "after" version of Jean Sifleet's bio page, this bio can serve as a model for a well-written, engaging, and persuasive professional profile.

Figure 12.10: The "after" version of Jean Sifleet's services page, minus the sections on Business Planning and Employment Issues, now appropriately ends with a call to action.

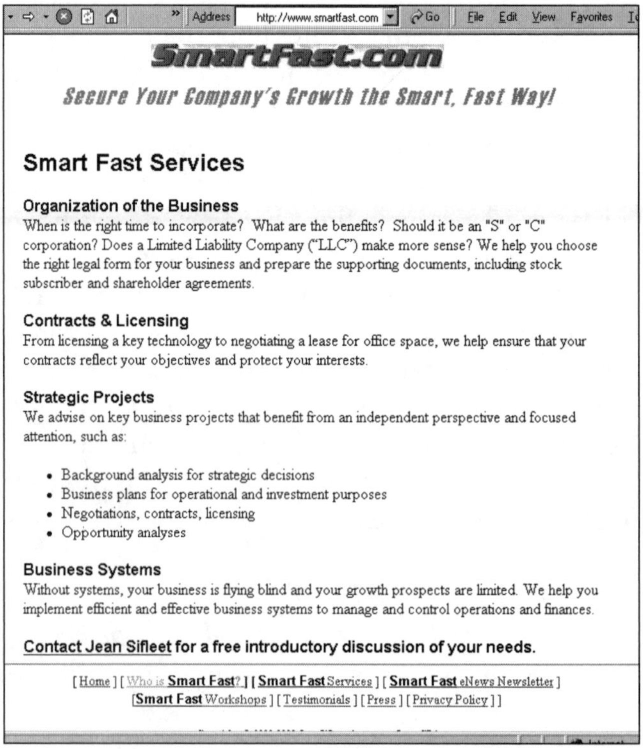
Address http://www.smartfast.com Go File Edit View Favorites

SmartFast.com

Secure Your Company's Growth the Smart, Fast Way!

Smart Fast Services

Organization of the Business
When is the right time to incorporate? What are the benefits? Should it be an "S" or "C" corporation? Does a Limited Liability Company ("LLC") make more sense? We help you choose the right legal form for your business and prepare the supporting documents, including stock subscriber and shareholder agreements.

Contracts & Licensing
From licensing a key technology to negotiating a lease for office space, we help ensure that your contracts reflect your objectives and protect your interests.

Strategic Projects
We advise on key business projects that benefit from an independent perspective and focused attention, such as:

- Background analysis for strategic decisions
- Business plans for operational and investment purposes
- Negotiations, contracts, licensing
- Opportunity analyses

Business Systems
Without systems, your business is flying blind and your growth prospects are limited. We help you implement efficient and effective business systems to manage and control operations and finances.

Contact Jean Sifleet for a free introductory discussion of your needs.

[Home] [Who is **Smart Fast**?] [**Smart Fast** Services] [**Smart Fast** eNews Newsletter]
[**Smart Fast** Workshops] [Testimonials] [Press] [Privacy Policy]]

have no background knowledge about that particular business. When first clicking Jean's workshop page, you might wonder where and when workshops take place. How would you sign up? (See Figure 12.11.) In fact, Jean presents workshops to organizations on request. To make that clear, she added, "Jean is available to speak to groups on these topics and develops customized programs for clients." To address the need for credibility as a speaker, Jean also added a testimonial from the Center for Women and Enterprise about the usefulness of her workshops.

Figure 12.11: The "before" version of the Workshop page needs to make it clear that these workshops are available for organizations upon request.

Other Issues

Jean had a clear and explicit privacy policy accessible from a main navigation link. However, since questions about her use of e-mail addresses would mostly arise when people were at the point of subscribing to *eNews*, she needed to add a more obvious link on the Sign-up page. (See Figure 12.12.) That same page also needed to tell people that the newsletter appears every other week and that it is free.

Throughout this site, a down-to-earth tone and reference to Jean by her first name conveys a friendly attitude that encourages potential clients to call or e-mail about their situation. Jean's decision to invite e-mail inquiries rather than force people interested in her services to fill out a Web form further reinforces that accessibility.

Figure 11.12: The "after" version of the *eNews* sign-up screen has an extra privacy policy link, along with clarification of how often *eNews* published and that it is free.

CHAPTER THIRTEEN

Professional Firm

The Web site for a professional firm usually has more in common with a solo service provider's site than with a multiproduct e-commerce site. The purpose is attracting, securing, and channeling leads from appropriate clients. To accomplish this, a firm or solo practitioner must provide background information that helps convince clients to choose this firm over the competition. While a solo service provider's site may reflect the personality, interests, and creativity of that particular practitioner, a professional firm's site normally places more emphasis on capabilities of the firm as a whole. The firm has an enduring identity apart from its current partners and employees. In addition, because professional firms often deal with much larger, more multilayered client organizations than do solo practitioners, the issue of whether firms can handle the scope of a need or problem is more likely to arise in the minds of those visiting the firm's Web site.

This makeover discusses:
- *How to bring out subtle promotional themes more clearly*
- *Why certain professional firms face special credibility challenges*
- *What kinds of content can increase trust*
- *Which kinds of repetition in promotional content are advisable*
- *How to identify and pull out hidden treasures*
- *What to do to encourage contact*

Computer Security Services

Founded in 1994, **Jerboa Inc.** (http://www.jerboa.com/) is a company based in Cambridge, Massachusetts that provides computer security services to organizations ranging from small startups through multinational giants. According to vice-president of business development, Jim Verzino, the firm's Web site was not a powerful business generator for the company. Although it received a decent amount of traffic, most new clients came to Jerboa through marketing efforts other than the Web site. Even so, the site had a vital role to play in acquiring new clients and new projects with existing clients: It ought to exude credibility to high-level executives who had to sign off on Jerboa's proposals. In addition, when prospective clients heard about Jerboa from the industry press or at a conference and checked the firm out on the Web, the site should intensify casual interest into a phone call or e-mail about a particular project. To accomplish those two results—as well as capture attention from those searching the Web for a computer security firm—the site required a clear explanation of what the firm does and how it does it distinctively.

The home page should set the stage for credibility and contact. (See Figure 14.1.) Jerboa's color scheme of medium blue and white against a gray background of heavy-looking, interlocked chain links does a good job of establishing the security theme. The design has a professional look, but the message is too subtle and static to arouse urgent interest in the reader. Phrased as a definition, the four lines of prose on Jerboa's home page contain many clues about why technology executives should favor this firm. Since I caught on to these hints only after exhaustive study of the site, however, these points should be much more explicit. Embedded in the definition are these points:

The overall safety of an enterprise—At stake is the well-being and perhaps even the survival of an organization.

Policies, practices, and tools—Security consists of behavior and rules as well as software.

Figure 13.1: The original home page of computer security firm, Jerboa, Inc. (http://www.jerboa.com/).

Unbiased thinking—Since Jerboa does not sell software, it approaches clients' situations with objectivity.

At all levels—Security can be compromised by shipping clerks and administrative assistants, not just by programming lapses.

Unlike some competitors, Jerboa uses a comprehensive approach to protect businesses against hackers, computer thieves, and industrial spies. The stakes are high and organizations need to understand that they can't turn their future over to security experts who don't use the broadest methodology to defend against all sources of threats. In keeping with the theme that ordinary, away-from-the-computer behavior, such as answering questions by phone or writing down passwords, can compromise a company's data, Jerboa practices not so much computer security as information security. The notion of high stakes became the focus of my revised home page copy for Jerboa. (See Figure 13.2.) After all, if potential clients are not worried about the consequences of security lapses, they won't feel motivated to spend anything at all on security, much less to spend time and energy seeking the firm that offers the soundest protection.

Trust, but Verify

In attempting to earn the trust of potential clients, Jerboa faces a formidable challenge shared by some other professionals, such as bankruptcy attorneys, substance abuse counselors, plastic surgeons, and hazardous-waste consultants. Clients of security firms do not want to go on the record as having been either

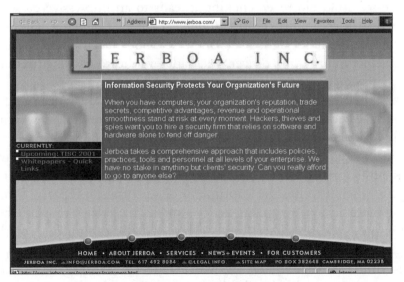

Figure 13.2: Jerboa's revised home page strengthens the message that was only hinted at in the original in Figure 13.1.

kept out of trouble or rescued from disaster. Two powerful tools for building trust with strangers—testimonials and a client list—are therefore out of the question. Jerboa's profiles of company principals make it clear that the firm's executives have impressive experience with information security. In addition, the white papers available at the site back up the executives' claim to expertise. A media page buried deep within the site also demonstrated recognition within the computer industry, with 17 media mentions in one year alone. Still, a possible gap remains between what these experts know and what they can actually do.

To help address that credibility gap, I asked Jim Verzino whether clients would feel comfortable with Jerboa posting unattributed case studies. He liked that solution and provided examples that we turned into stories about how the firm had helped a "large national bank," a "major pharmaceutical firm," and a "software development firm." Anonymous case studies work best when they're brief, contain credible though not recognizable detail, and use a problem-and-solution format.

Usability studies demonstrate that a site element can appear in plain sight on a page and yet because of its color, font, or proximity to something else never be noticed by users. On the Jerboa site, several nearly buried credibility boosters needed to be relocated or reorganized to become more conspicuous. For example, the main navigation link *News+Events* connects to a page that displays the company's most recent press release and makes accessible from the left frame six previous releases, in reverse chronological order. (See Figure 13.3.) Under *News*, the phrase "Jerboa in the Media" appears. It's not obvious at a glance that this phrase is a link. However, clicking it leads to an impressive page that lists and provides links to articles in *Computerworld, Computer Reseller News, Network World,* and other trade magazines. Reading a few of these articles would convince a chief information officer who had never heard of this firm that Jerboa is regarded as a major player in the security field.

Unfortunately, the Web site had hidden this jewel of a page and instead highlighted the company's own news in the form of its press releases. Remember, practically everyone regards media coverage as more credible than a company's promotional materials. Even when the article in a trade publication derives from the company's press release, the news takes on greater significance and believability when it carries the imprimatur of a neutral third party. Don't forget too that almost always, magazine articles make for livelier reading than do a company's press releases. Therefore, we reversed the prominence of the press releases and the links to media coverage by making Figure 13.4 display first when the visitor clicks *News+Events*, with Figure 13.3 accessible by clicking the *Press Releases* link under "Jerboa in the Media."

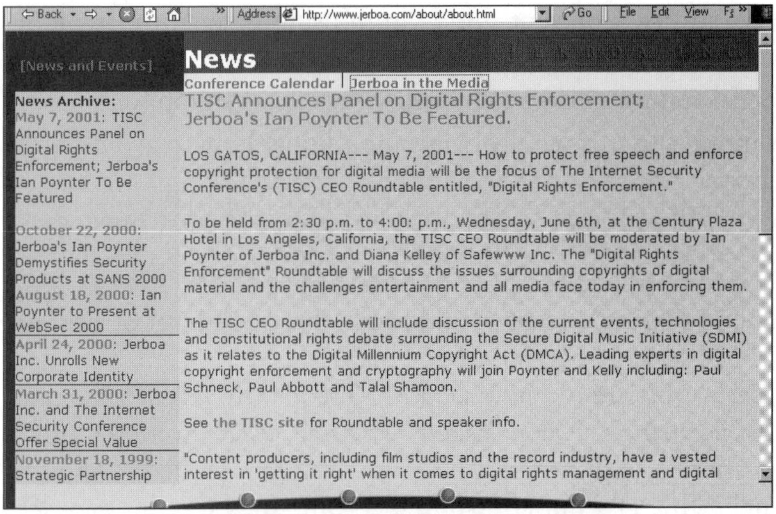

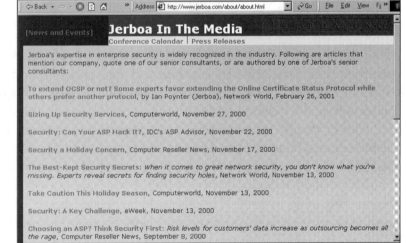

Figure 13.3: On Jerboa's News+Events page, the unobtrusive *Jerboa in the Media* link under the *News* heading leads to an impressive list of media citations.

Figure 13.4: Jerboa's impressive citations in the media, partially shown here, should come up prior to the company's own press releases.

After adding the case studies and bringing Jerboa's media coverage into a more prominent location, the site still didn't have quite enough trust-building features to entice newcomers to stop shopping for a security consulting firm and get in touch by e-mail or phone. We began working on an interactive quiz that would get executives visiting the site actively thinking about the weaknesses of their information security procedures and the strengths of Jerboa's comprehensive approach. Titled "How Protected Is Your Company Against Saboteurs, Thieves, and Spies?" this feature would be accessed from a link on the home page called "Take our security awareness quiz now" and include questions like these:

- Do you have computers in public areas, which remain on when their users go to lunch?

- Do you have systems that prevent people from using their birthday or pet's name as passwords?
- Could confidential company data be accessed if the CEO's laptop were stolen?
- Does every computer user in your organization know how to avoid spreading a virus?
- Have you trained all staff not to give out usernames and passwords over the phone?

The quiz's automatic scoring system would assess the user's level of risk and provide links to Jerboa's services page and white papers.

Another great asset to the site is a new section, "Frequently Asked Questions about Information Security." When asked whether there were common misunderstandings about computer security, Jim Verzino replied, "About a million. No kidding!" This FAQ briefly addresses some of the more prevalent myths and misconceptions.

Presenting the Firm's Services

Along the bottom of each page of the Jerboa site are the links *Home, About Jerboa, Services, News+Event,* and *For Customers,* in that order. It would be nice to feel confident that first-time visitors to the site would click the links in that sequence; but users have their own way of exploring sites. Because of the way search engines and word-of-mouth links function, we can't even be certain that visitors begin at the home page. Thus it's essential to hammer home on page after page the themes that have the best chance of captivating potential clients. Don't worry about appearing repetitive. So long as you vary the wording, readers will get the message without becoming irritated. The About Jerboa page (shown in Figure 13.5) thus needs to emphasize the high stakes of its work, its broad, comprehensive approach to information security, and its objective, no-commissions-on-products stance.

In addition, Jim Verzino explained a competitive advantage that made a positive impression during his sales presentations but wasn't mentioned at the Web site. Unlike some of its competitors, Jerboa's security work was carried out by seasoned professionals with 10 or more years of experience, not by 20-something whiz kids who understand technology but not business. Such kids have been known to pull off cool stunts not in their work orders and put clients' networks at risk. Jim said, "We often tell our prospects, 'No kids with clipboards!' But I haven't found a way to translate this to Web or print." If something puts a smile on prospects' faces in person, it usually works on the page too with minimal changes. Figure 13.6 shows the revised About Jerboa page. Note that it eliminates the bulleted list of services and instead ends with invitations to find out more on the Services and Media pages, or to get in touch now.

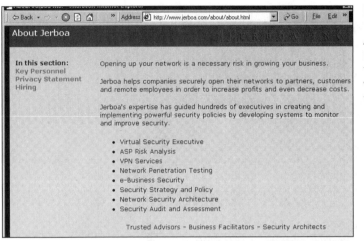

Figure 13.5: The "before" version of the About Jerboa page needed to emphasize the high stakes of its work and its approach to a solution.

Figure 13.6: This revision of the About Jerboa page in Figure 13.5 emphasizes the main themes from the new home page and encourages further exploration and contact.

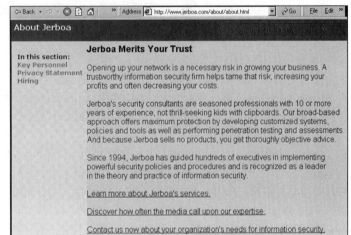

There's an inevitable and completely acceptable overlap between the About Jerboa page, which provides an overview to the firm's work, and the Services page, which lists its variety of service offerings, along with a mini-profile of each service. (See Figure 13.7.) Jerboa's list of services on the original About Jerboa page included several categories of services not mentioned or profiled on the Services page. The revision of the Services page added a needed headline and included a brief summary of each service the firm currently offers, with those it wanted to emphasize higher up in the list.

Hidden Treasures

Jerboa's spectacular page of media citations, discussed in the "Trust, but Verify" section earlier in this chapter, wasn't the only gem hidden deep in its Web site. Six informative and illuminating white papers written by Jerboa principals were

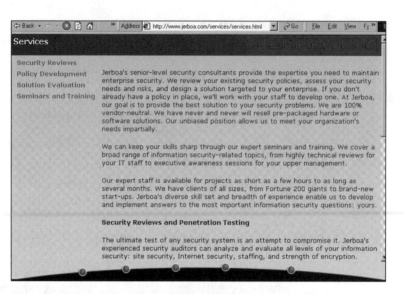

Figure 13.7: Jerboa's original *Services* page continues with brief explanations of policy development, solution evaluation, and seminars and training.

announced on a page accessible from the home page (in Figure 13.1 on the left, in hard-to-read blue letters on a black background it says, "Whitepapers – Quick Links") and through the *For Customers* link. "White paper" signifies a nonpromotional article issued by a company, which provides an overview of an industry issue and evaluates a range of solutions. White papers, common in high-tech circles, strive for authoritativeness and neutrality. In high-tech, they are generally educational efforts that subtly but dispassionately demonstrate the superiority of a class of products or services.

As shown in Figure 13.8, Jerboa's White papers page provided the titles and authors of the papers along with links enabling readers to download them in Adobe Acrobat (.pdf) format. Jim Verzino explained why these were set up to be downloaded rather than simply posted at the site. It wasn't just because this was the way so many companies presented white papers on the Internet. The reason had more to do with the fact that Adobe Acrobat files couldn't be hacked. He explained that people can hack or change content fairly easily with MS Word or HTML files, but not with Acrobat.

This made little sense. First, people determined to change content maliciously at the Jerboa Web site already had plenty of raw material to work with. Why would they prefer to do this on white papers rather than on the firm's Services page? Second, for some Web users, the process of downloading files and reading them offline is more cumbersome than clicking and reading immediately. Third, four of the six Adobe Acrobat files do not even mention Jerboa. This

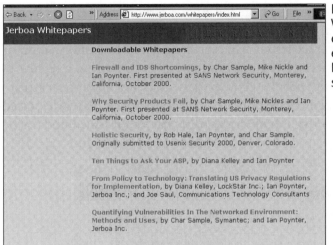

Figure 13.8: The Whitepapers page offers documents by Jerboa executives for downloading. Note that the proper spelling is "White Papers."

meant that if an employee at a potential client company printed the files and sent them to a superior, Jerboa might never get credit for being the source of the wise advice.

Jerboa needed to perform one of two revisions in its method of making these files available. Converting these files to HTML would be best, so that someone interested could read them immediately online, surrounded by Jerboa's branded identity or print them on pages that would make Jerboa visible as the source. On the other hand, if the security risk had ramifications that I hadn't appreciated, the firm should redo the Adobe Acrobat files, adding Jerboa's branding, contact information, and copyright notice on every page. This would not detract from the neutrality customary for white papers, but it would help ensure that readers recognize the source of the advice.

Encouraging Contact

How could Jerboa do a better job of encouraging Web visitors who found something of value at the site to begin to become clients? The original site did not include any call to action, any encouragement to visitors to send an e-mail inquiry, or to call about a need or an upcoming project—or so I thought. However, with a closer look at Jerboa's site map, accessible only from the fine print in the site's footer, I noticed an entry called *Contact Form,* which provided phone, fax, and address information for the firm as well as fields to fill in to send an inquiry via the Internet. This page was doing the company no good, since it was not accessible from anywhere else at the site. To encourage people to use it, Jerboa's Web designer just had to add one more major option—*Contact Us*—to the five buttons currently on the bottom of all the pages. In addition, the invitation to get in touch at the close of the copy on the About Jerboa and Services pages, linking to the contact form, would increase its use.

Another mystery was whether Jerboa had a practice of sending information or updates to clients and prospects. Even if it didn't want to commit to a regular e-mail newsletter, it could notify people who'd expressed interest about new articles quoting Jerboa, upcoming conference or trade show appearances, or newly posted white papers. The *For Customers* link opened a page that said it issued updates by e-mail, and it referred people to a Privacy Statement page. (See Figure 13.9.)

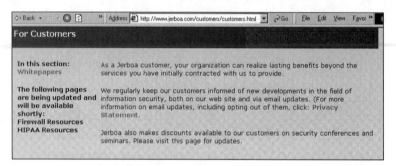

Figure 13.9: This page should invite interested site visitors, not only clients, to sign up for its Industry Update list and link directly and obviously to the contact form.

In twelve paragraphs, the Privacy page made four references to opting out of Jerboa's updates, but it said nothing about how to opt in. The only thing anywhere on how to opt in was a prechecked box, "Join the Jerboa Announcements list?" on the bottom of the near-orphan Contact Form. After the Contact Us button was installed among the main navigation links, it would land more visitors on the update list. However, to avoid implying that the list was only for Jerboa clients, I advised changing the *For Customers* link to *Industry Updates*.

The revised For Customers page in Figure 13.10 omits references to material that is not posted at the site. There's no reason to call attention to something Web visitors can't access.

Figure 13.10: This revision of Figure 13.9 encourages anyone interested in Jerboa's area of expertise to subscribe to its Industry Update list.

Chapter Fourteen

Advocacy Organization

For nonprofit groups focused on a cause, Web sites can be powerful marketing tools. Whether the mission is environmental, medical, religious, social, or political, the site can attract the attention of like-minded people, distribute information to the public, mobilize action, coordinate meetings and campaigns, and raise funds. As with corporate sites, effective marketing must proceed from the purposes of the organization and the desired results from the Web site. On the other hand, unlike for-profit operations, most nonprofit organizations have next to no budgets and depend on the energy of volunteers for the completion and maintenance of their Web sites. If that energy has dips and spurts, the organization should plan accordingly when designing and creating content for the Web site.

This makeover discusses:
- *What works better than a mission statement for a cause*
- *How to keep a site timely without regular updates*
- *How to encourage donations and volunteers*
- *What to say to get visitors involved in discussion groups*

Health Awareness and Outreach

With today's ultra-specialization in the labor force and poorly designed tools, millions of people suffer from repetitive-motion injuries that conventional medicine cannot readily cure. Trina Dunbar of San Diego, California, was a technical trainer for a software company when she experienced severe pain in her neck that would not go away. The company declared her disabled and retrained her to work in sales and marketing; but after more than five years of unrelenting daily pain, she quit her job to hunt full-time for a cure. One hour of treatment by a practitioner of myofascial therapy sent Trina's pain packing for good. Mindful that she had to change some habits that had contributed to her injury and knowing how hard it was to find treatment and prevention information, she founded an organization and a Web site, **ComputerAthlete.org** (http://www.computerathlete.org/), to help gather treatment information and disseminate awareness of repetitive motion risks.

As you can see from its home page, shown in Figure 14.1, the organization has a three-fold mission: spreading awareness of Repetitive Strain Injury (RSI); educating those vulnerable to RSI about injury prevention; and extending to those injured support through information, resources, and meetings. The page clarifies its mission further with a broad and inclusive definition of RSI—encompassing more than computer-related injuries—as well as with its current geographical scope. Then comes a wonderful graphic illustrating the ill-fated evolution of *Homo sapiens* from a hunched-over ape to a hunter standing tall to a hunched-over computer user. Although no glaring blunders jump off this page, the approach is overly intellectual. Raising the emotional temperature of the home page would generate more of a bond with the target reader and more desire to respond.

Figure 14.2 shows the revised home page for **ComputerAthlete.org**, in which the programmatic mission statement is replaced with a headline that conveys the purpose at a glance. Note the eyebrow headline—the small underlined and italicized modification of the headline message, just above it. This layout technique, borrowed from magazines, works well for adding subsidiary information to a headline, making it clear which aspects are most important. The evolution picture and caption have a much greater impact between the headline and the text than near the bottom of the page. The text "knives and musical instruments" is added in the opening sentence to let readers know right away that despite the organization's name and the illustration, the group welcomes folks injured through use of tools other than computers. The tone is friendlier without getting gushy, and the links in the text tell readers, apart from the navigation links across the top and the left, where else they should go in the Web site to learn about treatment options, sign up for the group's newsletter, and find out about meetings. Three places evoke the theme that Trina Dunbar said was paramount in her vision of the organization: hope.

Visitors to the original site who clicked *Resources* would find a grab bag of resources that were not always clearly tagged or well classified. Figure 14.3 shows the original Resources page.

The revision of Figure 14.3, shown in Figure 14.4, phrases the categories of resources as questions, adds two links that Trina always recommends to people, corrects some typos, and clarifies the purpose of each grouping of resources. Originally the headline on the Resources page read "Resources." "Repetitive Strain Injury (RSI) Resources" makes the topic instantly clear to someone who happened to see this page first.

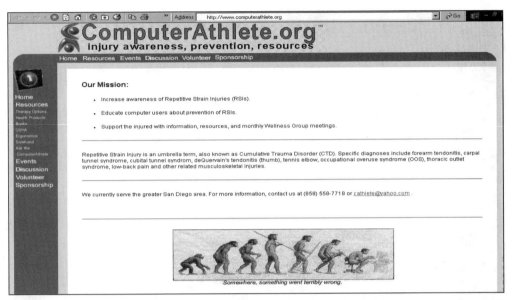

Figure 14.1: The home page of the San Diego, California-based health awareness and support organization ComputerAthlete.org contains a clear mission statement, but is weak on emotional appeal.

Figure 14.2: The revised home page for ComputerAthlete.org uses a friendlier tone and more directive calls to action.

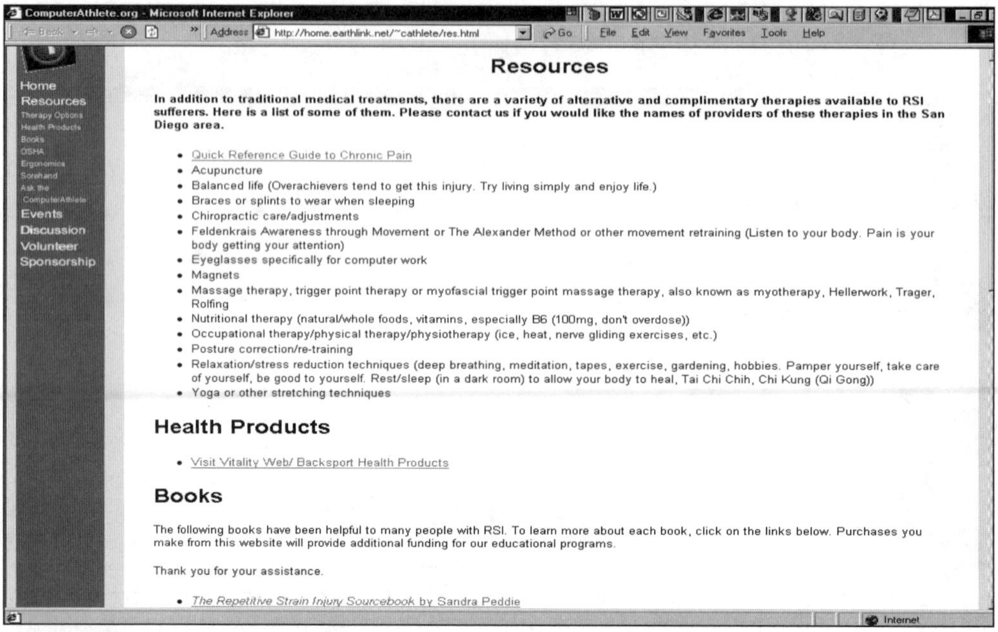

Figure 14.3: The original Resources page, shown here in part, provides a confusing list of resources that are hard for the visitor to interpret.

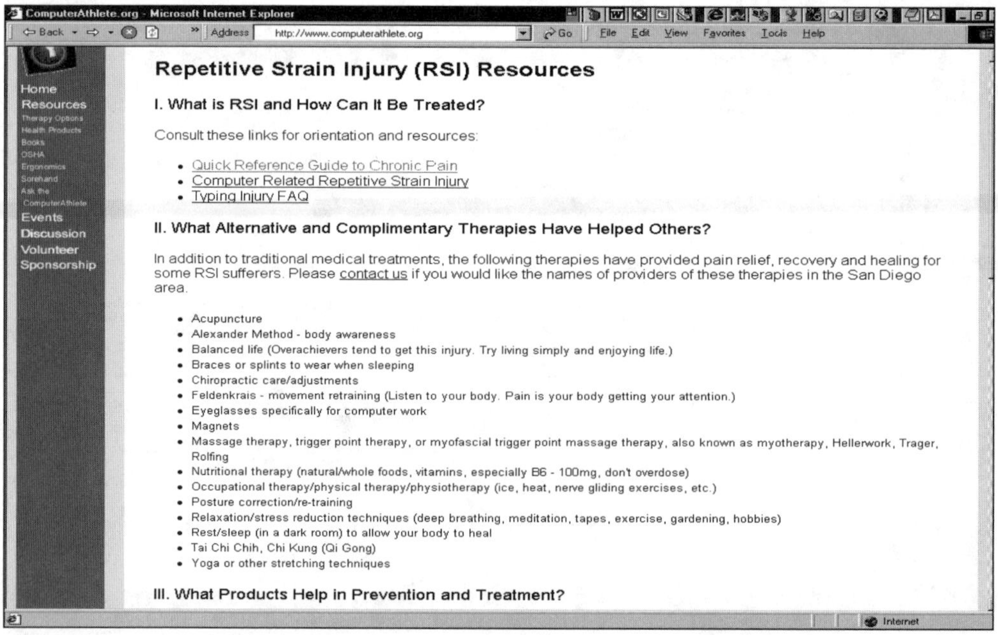

Figure 14.4: The revised and reorganized Resources page includes clearer headings and subheadings so that visitors can find their way around the list quickly.

The Timeliness Dilemma

The **ComputerAthlete.org** Events page, shown in Figure 14.5, was about one year out of date when I looked at it. In an ideal world I would simply remind Trina, the prime mover behind the site, that this gives the false impression that the group had fizzled and therefore prevents newcomers from showing up at meetings. However, it's not realistic to expect a volunteer-run organization, with no membership dues and members who are involved in working elsewhere to make a living, to turn over a new leaf and take care of regular Web updates. After all, that hadn't happened for some time. However, an alternative method of handling the Events page doesn't involve a detailed schedule of meetings.

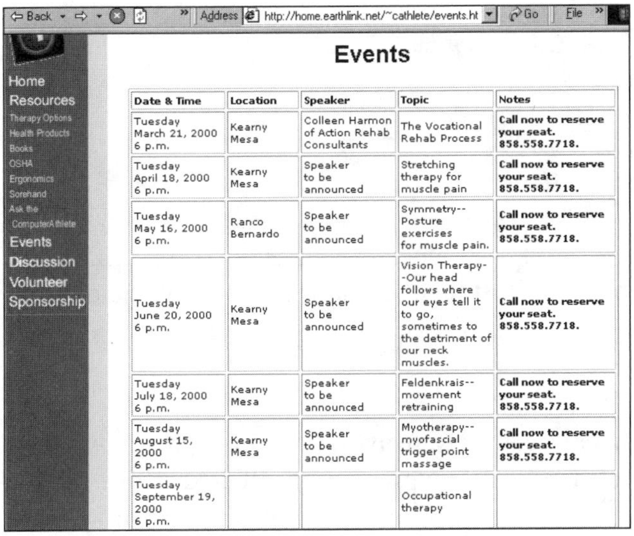

Figure 14.5: The original ComputerAthlete.org's Events page was set up as a specific monthly schedule, a format requiring continual updates.

As shown in Figure 14.6, instead of a bound-to-get-outdated schedule, the revised page contains a general description of the meetings and clarifies a few facts that had gotten lost in the details of the original. Knowing that meetings occur on the third Tuesday of the month makes this page informative even in the distant future without specific dates. Originally, the chart had enjoined readers to call to reserve a seat for upcoming meetings, and it's now explained that seating is limited. Also, the first version had not said that meetings are free. The main and eyebrow headlines now together announce the Who, What, When, Where, and Why of the page, in case someone searching for injury support groups in San Diego comes upon this page first. Note that the page repeats how to receive information on upcoming meetings. Some readers will arrive at this page wanting to know that, while others will have that question in mind when reaching the bottom of the page. Accommodating both needs will not irritate anyone.

Figure 14.6: The revised Events page is recast here so that it cannot easily go out of date.

Fundraising on the Web

Groups devoted to causes as diverse as saving wolves, preventing drunk-driving deaths, promoting political candidates, and helping those afflicted with a disease share an interest in using a Web site to attract donations. In deciding on ways to encourage contributions that are appropriate to a particular cause and clientele, consider that many marketing methods that increase people's willingness to buy equally improve the results of fundraising. Also, many of the techniques used successfully by off-line causes and charities translate well to the Web. Remember too that corporate sponsors typically receive so much visibility for contributions that it's almost a form of advertising for them. Thus, any roundup of effective online fundraising ideas would have to include these:

- Emotionally charged stories of people or animals helped by the organization
- The option to have one's name listed as a supporter and to have a building or event named after a big contributor
- Giveaway items (mugs, T-shirts, calendars) for contributors over a certain amount

- The opportunity to reach a specific target audience through Web links, banners, advertorial copy, printed programs, verbal recognition at events, and so on
- The chance to donate items for use by the organization (for example, furniture or food for a homeless shelter) or for a fundraising auction
- Explicit and repeated calls to action—requests for contributions
- Suggested donation amounts
- Explanations of how much money buys vaccines, pays for tutors, hires lobbyists, and so on

Figures 14.7 and 14.8 show how **ComputerAthlete.org** originally requested donations. On the positive side, this page catalogs three types of sponsors, suggests specific donation amounts for each, lists the benefits of sponsorship, and provides a form through which the public can contribute money. On the other hand, the headline needs more specificity and punch; the copy should make more of the visitor's opportunities to help than the group's needs, by using *you* rather than *our*; plans for what the group would do with money are wordy, and the nonword "verbage" has to go. Here too is another area where the lack of updating has an impact. Potential sponsors want to spend their outreach efforts on well-organized, active groups and on Web sites that attract the right traffic in significant volume. When the site becomes drastically out of date, sponsors may not even bother to investigate an organization further. And for corporate sponsors who may wish to contribute thousands of dollars, it should be clear that mailing a company check rather than plunking in a credit card number is an option.

Additionally, this organization was missing an opportunity to collect money that would make it easier to keep the Web site well stocked and up to date. **ComputerAthlete.org** had 65 members, but membership was free. People feel quite differently about payments presented as "dues" and those presented as "donations." Most people understand that organizations charge dues to defray their programming and publicity costs, and so long as it's clear that nonmembers are welcome at meetings and on the e-mail list, there shouldn't be a backlash from instituting annual dues of, say, $25. Some people would prefer to make a contribution of that amount or more rather than pay membership dues.

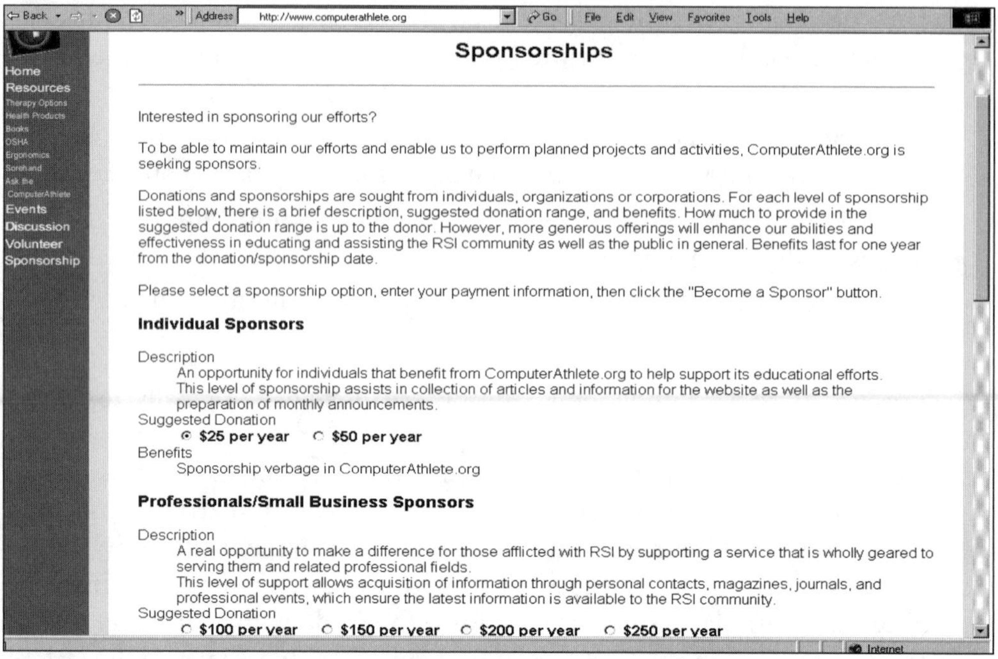

Figure 14.7: The original Sponsorship page, the top portion of which appears here, provides a contribution form, but needs to focus more on how visitors can help.

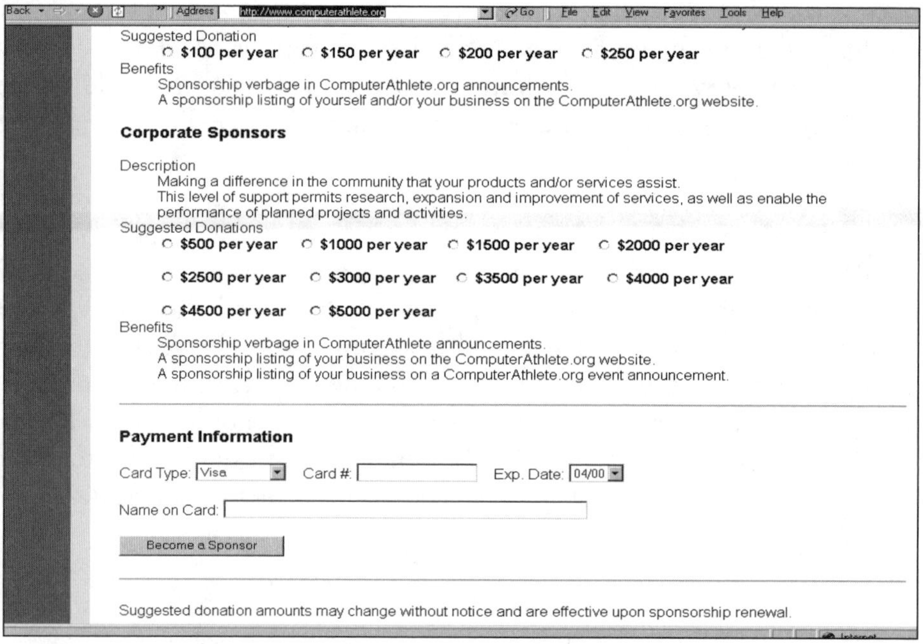

Figure 14.8: The original Sponsorship page, whose bottom portion appears here, missed the opportunity to collect dues and neglected to include a pay-by-check option.

Also, since some current members have had to stop working to devote energy to their recovery, an invitation to "adopt a member" could prompt some members who were financially better off to pay $50 a year instead of $25 to help support the involvement of others in the organization. Finally, when asking for dues and donations, it's often helpful to remind people of the tax benefits of shelling out money. While **ComputerAthlete.org** is not registered as a nonprofit organization and thus can't offer tax deductions for charitable contributions, some members might be able to deduct membership dues as a professional expense or sponsorships as an advertising expense. See the revised page in Figures 14.9 and 14.10.

Also new in Figure 14.10 is the online fundraising option, a contribution box for Amazon's Honor System, which collects micropayments for sites from just $1.00 up. This creates an option for collecting small donations from casual visitors who live outside of San Diego and who feel that the information presented at the site is valuable or the cause is worthy. Neither membership dues nor sponsorship would make sense for such visitors, but if they found a link pointing toward a cure for their RSI, they might wish to express their gratitude financially.

Figure 14.9: In a clear and friendly tone and with a stronger headline, the revised page for soliciting donations explains why readers should contribute money. This page continues in Figure 14.10.

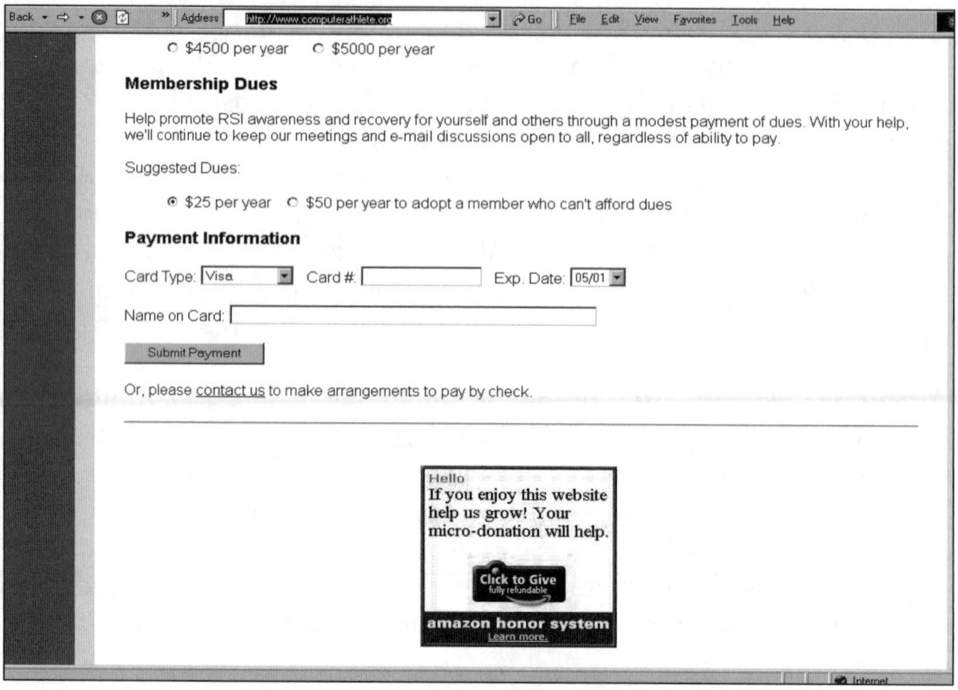

Figure 14.10: The revised Sponsorship page, continued from Figure 14.9, institutes a Membership Dues option, the opportunity to "adopt a member," and a way for casual site visitors to offer small donations. It also mentions the possibility of paying by check.

Getting People Involved

ComputerAthlete.org also resembles many other advocacy sites in explicitly asking for volunteer help. Its Volunteer page originally exhibited some of the same weaknesses we've seen on other pages at this site, such as skimpy headline (simply "Volunteer") and a vague list of three purposes with which volunteers might help—conducting public awareness and educational events and activities, designing and developing educational materials, and assisting RSI sufferers in finding relief from their injuries. More specific needs would do a better job of inspiring offers of help. Saying "We need someone to call the media or write news releases about our meetings" is more likely to rouse an RSI victim to volunteer than "We want to conduct public-awareness and educational events and activities." See Figure 14.11 for the revised page.

Finally, let's suppose that an RSI sufferer, a family member of one, or a practitioner who treats the condition happens upon this site, finds it illuminating and useful, doesn't want to become a member or donate money, but wants to network with other people interested in this malady. The Discussion page should entice such a person to say "Hello, here's who I am" or to simply listen in on the

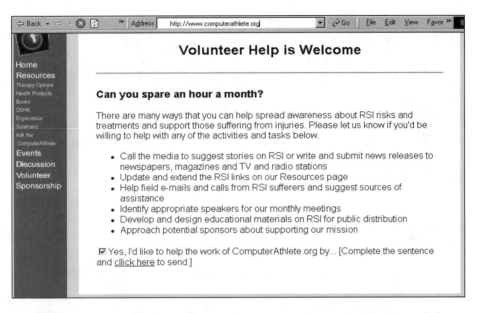

Figure 14.11: Just as with the suggested donation amounts, this revision of the original Volunteer page benefits from stronger, more specific descriptions of skills and effort that volunteers might offer.

group's exchanges. As explained in other contexts in this book, you get a great many more site visitors to sign up for your e-mail newsletter or discussion list when you paint a verbal picture of what they'll receive and how they'll benefit. Originally, **ComputerAthlete.org's** Discussion page invited people to sign up simply "to discuss RSI issues in San Diego." It also didn't explain the distinction between participating in e-mail discussions and receiving what was called a "monthly update."

Figure 14.12 represents the revision of the Discussion page. It clarifies that the site contains two lists with a great deal of overlap—one for discussion of RSI-related issues among members of this group and the other for receiving notices about upcoming meetings. Separating these two purposes is good, since some interested parties want to know about scheduled events but don't want their in-boxes clogged with group discussions, while others never go to events but love to exchange advice, support, and perspectives. On the original page, "listserv" is computer-speak for a participatory e-mail discussion list and a term newer computer users don't know, so the revised page adds a more commonly understood synonym. The revision also includes a sentence explaining the group's privacy policy and letting people know they can remove themselves from the list at any time.

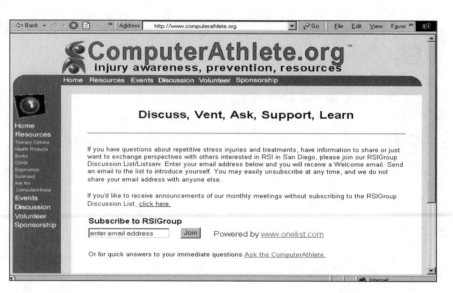

Figure 14.12: The revised Discussion page more completely outlines the purposes of participating in the RSIGroup list, more clearly explains the distinction between that and the "monthly update," and includes information about the organization's privacy and unsubscribe policies.

CHAPTER FIFTEEN

Event Reservations

Hotels, golf courses or tennis courts, airlines, concert venues, conference-call line rentals, and hair salons are just a few of the kinds of businesses that can use the Web for increased efficiency and 24-hour convenience for their customers—both first-timers and regulars. These sites need to address three major concerns. First, what is generally available? For example, for the hotel, that would involve its location and the type of rooms, rates, and facilities. A concert venue should list who's playing when and where. Hair salons need to list their open hours, the services they provide, and who their stylists are. The second concern is the availability and online booking for specific events, such as tee dates and times, flights, and haircuts. Third, users require reliable confirmation that they really did get that seat, room, ticket, or time slot that they booked.

Reservations sites are much more complicated technically than product sites, since in most cases events involve either unique booking—only one customer can get a haircut from David-Michael at 10 A.M. September 22—or a limited capacity—only 250 can attend the Koffee Klatchers awards dinner. With reservations sites, availability becomes a central issue. In addition, prices, features, dates, and content probably change much more frequently than with product sites. An out-of-date event reservations site won't do an organization much good, if any at all.

This makeover discusses:
- *Why acknowledging a lack of up-to-date information is essential*
- *How to clear up navigation confusions involving frames*
- *Which questions must be addressed at an events site*
- *How to confirm that the user did book the slot requested*

An Adult Education Center

The Boston Learning Society (BLS) in Needham, Massachusetts, offers life-enriching adult-education programs for upscale, educated adults in the suburban towns west of Boston. In the spring of 2001, the **BLS** Web site (http://www.bostonlearningsociety.com/) contained promotional copy that had apparently not been touched in at least four months, with courses listed for October through December 2000. Owner Kathy Brady-Romanelli said that a major overhaul of the site was in the works.

The first important point, then, was that if an event-focused site ever becomes out of date, this shortcoming must be explicitly acknowledged at the Web site. After all, dates always appear along with the descriptions of events. Someone who had heard of the BLS and found it online would have drawn the conclusion within a minute or two from the Web site that the center was out of business. Since that was hardly the case, with registration for scores of classes continuing through its mailed-out catalog, visitors to its Web site should encounter a prominent message on the home page explaining in an unapologetic tone that the Web site does not reflect current offerings and inviting people to e-mail or call for a printed catalog. For instance:

> *We're currently revamping our Web site to facilitate better customer service, and we expect to resume online registration in the summer of 2001. Please call 1-781-453-9800 or e-mail us at info@bostonlearningsociety.com for our catalog of upcoming classes and events. In the meantime, you can get a good idea of the types of seminars and workshops we offer by browsing our site.*

Another option is to remove links to the inner pages and meet visitors with only the first two sentences of that message. In that case, however, the BLS would have lost the opportunity to have some easily answered questions, such as for directions and membership fees, addressed at the Web site. It would also miss the chance to convey the general flavor of the center's classes.

Apart from the issue of the course listings being out of date, the first impression from the Web site was of a mismatch with this organization. (See Figure 15.1.) Besides the fact that it serves a more affluent clientele than many other adult-education centers, the BLS has a much higher percentage of well-known seminar leaders who have published books, own prominent restaurants, or have other distinguished credentials. The Web site should therefore exude exclusivity and quality. Two or three sets of clunky frame borders (depending on one's browser width) disrupt the classiness of the red, white, and blue color scheme. Someone with visual flair needed to redesign the site for more elegance and refinement.

Another change that would help make a more powerful first impression is a stronger, more eye-catching tag line. The idea of "inquisitive minds" is good and makes a fine slogan: "Where inquisitive minds get satisfied." That still left open how and where that satisfaction occurred, so one more line: "Seminars and workshops in Needham, Massachusetts" appears on the revised site. (See Figure 15.2.) To lessen how much the site's name plate resembled business stationery, the center's contact information is now at the foot of the page.

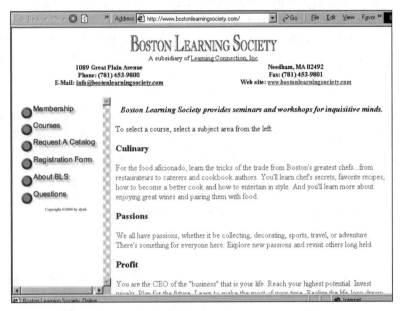

Figure 15.1: The home page of the BLS (http://www.bostonlearningsociety.com/) doesn't aesthetically match its high-quality offerings.

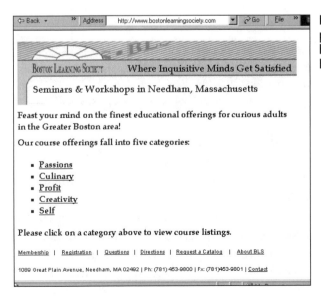

Figure 15.2: The revised name plate and copy enhance the BLS home page by clarifying the location.

Navigation Remedies

The BLS had a terrific set of five categories for its wide-ranging courses: culinary, passions, profit, creativity, and self. However, as you can see in Figure 15.1, the home page invited readers to "select a subject area from the left." Yet the five subject areas were listed below that sentence rather than on the left. You might get a sense of what was intended if you clicked *Courses* on the left, bringing up links for those five categories and many subcategories. (See Figure 15.3.) Clearly, the inconsistency of asking the user to do something impossible had to be fixed. The solution on the revised site involved making it more obvious how to get to the course descriptions, by turning a list of the five categories on the home page into links, as indicated by the underlining in Figure 15.2.

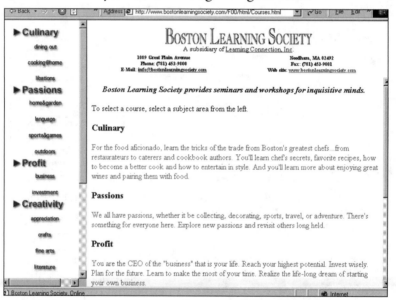

Figure 15.3: Clicking *Courses* in Figure 15.1 brings up this screen, from which visitors can select a category to see detailed course listings.

Ideally, the new site would not have frames, since frames multiply the opportunities for user confusion. If a site has to have frames, for instance because of the way the shopping cart and online catalog are programmed, the frames should be borderless for a cleaner look.

More navigation problems came to light when I pretended to select a course in which to register. When I clicked "non-members $195" under "Italian for Travelers" several times, for instance, there was a little twitch in the left frame each time, but nothing changed, which would lead a visitor to believe that the online ordering capacity had been disabled. Some time later, however, I happened to scroll down the left frame and discovered that I had signed up for the Italian class five times, owing $935! (See Figure 15.4.)

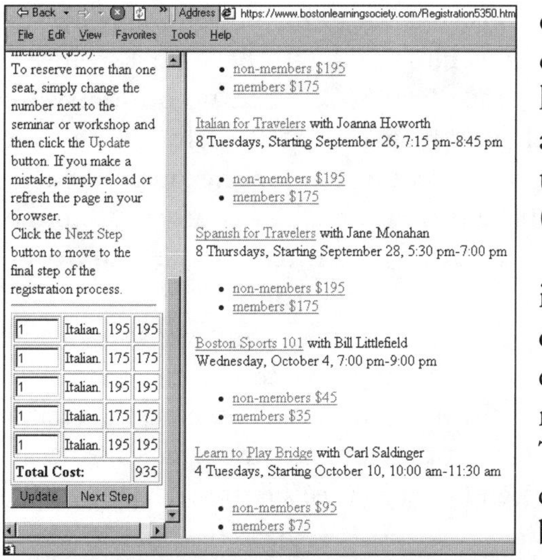

No matter what explanations appear in the left frame, shoppers will not detect a change when enrolling in a course and will believe that the registration mechanism is not working. The revision of the registration and checkout procedure places a quantity box beside the member and non-member prices. (See Figure 15.5.) This was essential because people fairly regularly sign up more than one person for a course, and one might be a member and the other a nonmember. In addition, the member price appears first, making it more obvious that nonmembers pay more (as opposed to members paying less), and an added button launches a pop-up window on the benefits and cost of membership. Also new is a Checkout button, so that visitors could either keep selecting courses or complete the registration process the same way they would check out their purchases at well-known e-commerce sites. Finally, the Questions button opens the Frequently Asked Questions page for anyone who is confused about how to register or about the BLS policies.

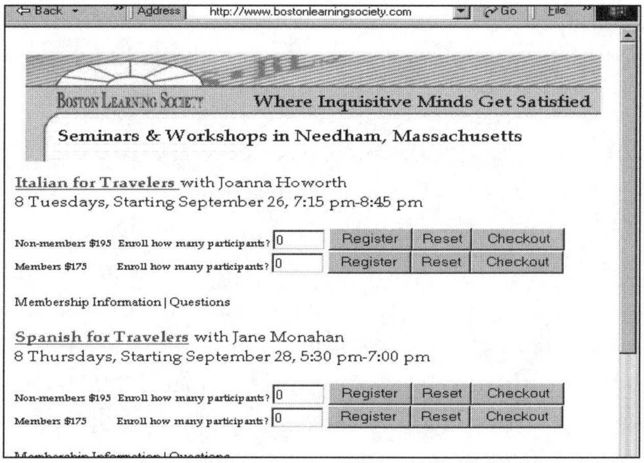

Figure 15.4: Scrolling down the left frame of this page revealed that I had signed up for the Italian class five times, owing $935.

Figure 15.5: A revision of the course listings makes it clearer how to sign up for courses.

The original version of the Web site wasn't clear about how to sign up for membership to get the lower price. The left frame said, "To become a member, click individual member ($39) or family member ($59)." Yet, no options were labeled "individual member ($39)" or "family member ($59)." After quite a bit of exploration, I discovered the links for becoming one or the other kind of member way up at the top of the long page listing the BLS's courses. Although Figure 15.6 shows the top of a page listing all of the center's courses, someone selecting courses doesn't usually arrive at this part of the page.

Clicking one of those links at the top of the Course page, one was able to add a membership of one type or the other to one's shopping cart. The revised site keeps those lines at the top of the course listings but doesn't assume the reader would find them. The Membership button on the new Catalog page calls up an explanation of the benefits and cost of membership. (See Figure 15.7.)

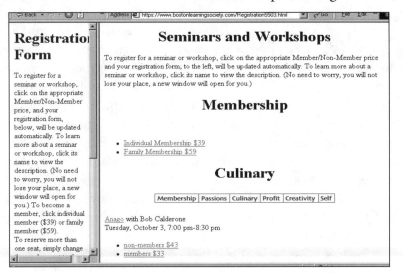

Figure 15.6: It took quite a bit of exploration to find the links for becoming an individual or family member of the BLS.

The bar of links below the "Culinary" heading also appeared below each of the four other major course headings. Although not always visible to someone browsing course listings, this was a good vehicle for making it possible for customers to continue browsing available courses. To put it to even better use, a version of it is now interspersed throughout the course listings so that it always appears somewhere within the browser window. (See Figure 15.7.) In a printed catalog, it is always clear how to continue looking around, and this device takes the place of that understanding for the online medium.

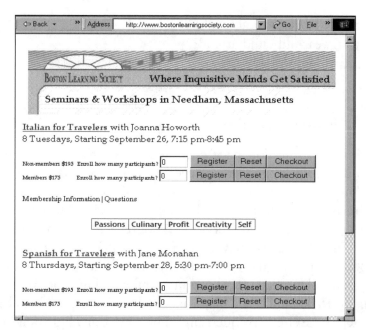

Figure 15.7: In the revised site, the bar of links for course categories is interspersed among the listings so that it will always be visible in the browser window enabling, people to keep shopping for courses.

As a final note in the category of navigation, clicking any of the underlined course titles called up an enticing description for that course that was several paragraphs long. These were generally well-written and complete.

Policies and Confirmations

In an online store selling tangible items, a variety of questions may require answers before someone takes the leap of placing an order, including "What's your return policy?" "Do you ship internationally?" and "How quickly will I receive what I ordered?" When booking events online, people may want to know "What if I buy a ticket and can't attend?" "What if it snows?" "Where do I park?" and "Is the facility wheelchair accessible?" For the BLS, frequently asked questions would include these:

1. What if I register and can't attend?
2. What if I attend and don't like the course?
3. What will happen with the class if it snows?
4. Where exactly are the classes?
5. Is there free parking nearby?

6. Is the facility wheelchair accessible?
7. Can my 16-year-old child attend?
8. Are scholarships available?
9. Is there a senior citizen discount?
10. How do I know if there is still space in a class?
11. How can someone teach there?

The BLS's existing question page answered questions 4 and 5, along with several other questions; the answers to several other questions were scattered on other pages. Answers to Questions 6–10 were nowhere at the site.

People who have questions for the BLS, such as those just listed, are probably serious about registering, so it is vital to make sure that they can easily find the answers. And since you can rarely predict who will have which questions at various locations at the site, it's best to consolidate all the questions and answers on one page, even if this creates duplication of information. The BLS home page (shown in Figure 15.1) included a major link called *Questions*, which helps serve those who entered the site with questions. The Questions button added to the Catalog shopping page helps direct those with queries while visitors are selecting courses. The other place requiring access to the site's bank of questions and answers is the page asking shoppers to enter their credit-card information. The BLS's "before" site placed a section "Things You Should Know" on the Registration page below the Send Registration button. The instinct was good, but the placement was unfortunate. Adding a Questions link or button that was visible while shoppers were being asked to enter credit-card information would address the needs of those who have questions that hold them back from completing their registration.

Next, let's consider the best way to present questions and answers. Apart from the issue of which questions it answered, the three-column format of the BLS's original Questions page made it difficult to see all the questions at once. To replace this overly wide presentation, we chose the traditional Frequently Asked Questions format of listing the questions first, with each question linked so that the user would go to the answer upon clicking the question. (See Figure 15.8.) Categories for questions also help the user to locate quickly the information sought.

A major concern with event bookings is users needing to know which dates, times, and events are available at the time of registration as well as whether or not they got the booking they desired. Depending on the kind of event, the lead time, and the population served, this can be handled online by visibly indicating availability at the site; disallowing registration for ineligible dates, times,

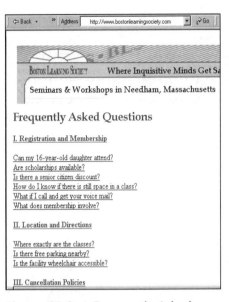

Figure 15.8: A Frequently Asked Questions page can be set up so that each question, when clicked, leads to the answer.

or events; telling users that they'll receive an e-mail confirmation of their booking within 24 hours; or advising users that their automatic e-mail confirmation means that space was available. No information at the BLS site clearly addressed space availability and how to know whether registration succeeded. Kathy Brady-Romanelli, the BLS's owner, said that only a few classes filled to capacity, and when that occurred, they would inform the registrant by phone and not process the credit-card payment. Kathy also said that the new online registration system would indicate within the database which classes, if any, were already filled. In that case, the new Questions page would explain this and the links to the FAQ that was previously described would take care of users' uncertainty on this matter.

Regardless of the chosen solution for indicating availability, registrants need explicit and unambiguous reassurance that the booking succeeded—not just that it was submitted. The BLS set users' expectations by saying this at the top of the Registration page: "You will receive a confirmation e-mail within one business day of the receipt of your registration at Boston Learning Society. If you do not receive any confirmation, please call us at (781) 453-9800. After processing your registration, we will send you a receipt-confirmation in the mail." The original BLS site also contained a wise advisory to registrants who got as far as submitting their credit card information: "Print this page for your records." Such a printout helps prevent a lot of problems, such as people wondering whether they signed up for the Cambodian cooking class or the Vietnamese one and whether they put it on their Visa or Discover card. Here as elsewhere on the Web, it's best to remind people to take simple steps that save everyone a lot of confusion later.

CHAPTER SIXTEEN

Local Business

Most of the makeovers in this book involve Web sites for companies that can do business with practically anyone anywhere in the world. The situation is different for an establishment providing goods or services that are normally delivered in person. For an auto body shop, a landscaping company, a restaurant, or a chiropractor, location and distances are as crucial as—or even more crucial than—credentials. People rarely get on a plane to go have their backs realigned, and a local landscaper would ordinarily take on clients only within a certain geographical radius.

This makeover discusses:
- *Why proper keywords are crucial for a local business*
- *How and why to keep reinforcing the location throughout the site of a local business*
- *How to assess the appropriateness of external links*
- *What to do with "under construction" pages*

Finding Flower Hill Farm

Carol Duke, a floral artist, owns a captivating farm on a hillside in western Massachusetts. In the warmer months, her 20 acres of perennials and rock gardens shower the visitor with color and scent. Carol provides gorgeous flower arrangements for weddings, special events, offices, shops, and homes. She also provides hospitality for bed-and-breakfast guests. For floral services, her primary delivery area ranges west to east from the Berkshire Hills to Amherst, Massachusetts and north to south from the Vermont border to Springfield and northern Connecticut. Her site notes that bouquets can be sent anywhere in the United States and to major European cities, but this would involve the work of other members of her floral association, not her arrangements.

This area includes several colleges whose chapels tend to be booked solid with weddings of couples who are not necessarily long-time residents and thus might

195

well be using the Internet to search for service providers. The bed-and-breakfast guests, of course, might come from anywhere, but often are parents or other visitors to the local colleges.

Accordingly, the first important consideration, even more critical than the content and presentation of Carol's home page, are the hidden keywords that search engines would use to bring her targeted traffic. Oops! Carol's Web designer had neglected to insert any keywords at all. Coded in HTML, a tentative list of keywords and a site description for her home page would look like this:

<meta name="KEYWORDS" content="Williamsburg, Northampton, Springfield, Amherst, Berkshire, Berkshires, Western, Massachusetts, Mass, Vermont, Connecticut, Smith, Mount Holyoke, Mt Holyoke, Hampshire, College, UMass, University, Five Colleges, 5 Colleges, Cummington, flowers, bed and breakfast, bed, breakfast, B&B, B and B, inn, wedding, floral, florist">

<meta name="DESCRIPTION" content="Flower Hill Farm: Floral Arrangements and Bed-and-Breakfast Retreat in Western Massachusetts">

For those not familiar with New England, Smith, Mount Holyoke, Hampshire, Amherst, and UMass (the University of Massachusetts) are the five colleges within an easy drive of Carol's farm. Cummington is a nearby town that has an arts colony and a state fair. The keywords ensure that if someone goes to a search engine and types in, say, "Vermont wedding flowers" or "Cummington Inn," Carol's home page will appear. The preceding description is what they would see in the search-engine report along with the title and URL of her site.

Because location is central to the success of this category of Web site, the locale must be prominently and specifically mentioned in the name plate or headline for the site. Visitors shouldn't have to hunt for the state, province, or country of the business behind the Web site. The original version of Carol's home page lacked any clue about where her business is located. The link on the left opens a page that does mention western Massachusetts in the first line of copy. The link on the right opens a page that does not mention Massachusetts at all until the bottom. This key omission is fixed in the revised page. (See Figure 16.1.)

Photos and Text

Two things about Carol's original version of the site that were crucial to keep intact were the warm color photos she'd selected to show off her work and the gracious tone of her text. Figure 16.2, the page accessed through the *Carol Duke Flowers* link on the home page, opened with a headline that nicely captured the aesthetic reward of her flower arrangements for the client.

Figure 16.1: This revision of Flower Hill Farm's home page adds geographical location and tag lines for Carol Duke's two businesses (http://www.caroldukeflowers.com/).

Figure 16.2: The original page describing Carol Duke's floral business already had an appealing headline but needed at-a-glance geographical grounding.

My minor revisions of the marketing copy below the headline on this page arose from the following concerns:

- The first paragraph didn't make it clear enough that Carol arranges the flowers that she grows on her land. In part, this fuzziness arose from the verb forms. Active voice ("Carol harvests") almost always works better than passive voice ("are harvested"), because the former makes explicit who is doing what.
- The original text used a lot of phrases—"is committed to," "will reflect," "to achieve," "is a promise," and "is available to"—that implied hesitancy and lack of confidence. Cutting unnecessary verb helpers and using present tense puts more conviction into descriptions of what a professional or business does.
- It doesn't work to mix references like "Ms. Duke" and "Carol" on the same page. The former puts the reader in a formal, distant mindset, and the latter presents Carol Duke in a friendlier, more casual close up. "Ms. Duke" and "Carol Duke" might have worked just as well as the "Carol" and "Carol Duke" in my revision. Consistency is what matters.
- As on the home page, it's essential to indicate the precise location of Carol's business early and prominently in the copy.

See Figure 16.3 for my revisions of the Carol Duke Flowers page. At the bottom, not shown in the screen shots here, the page already included a call to action and an explicit method of contacting Carol for more information.

Since weddings comprise one of the primary occasions for which people use flowers, it made sense that Carol included a *Wedding Flowers* photo and link, at the bottom of the page below the portion visible in Figure 16.3. This led to a page so lush with colorful photos of flowers that I could practically smell them. (See Figure 16.4.) As the words indicate, clicking any of the pictures brings up a larger and even more vivid color photo of a flower arrangement for a particular wedding. Visitors get a strong dose of Carol's style and sensibility from the 35 photos, and the only thing this page needs is a call to action. Accordingly, at the bottom of the page a new link reads, "To beautify your wedding with the living art of flowers, click here."

Figure 16.3: The revised Carol Duke Flowers page contains more than 30 changes in wording.

Figure 16.4: The top half of Carol's Wedding Flowers page illustrates the use of thumbnail photos that become larger when clicked. Its revision added a call to action at the end.

Besides the *Wedding flowers* link, Figure 16.3 also contained a *Links* link, which led to a page that seemed slapped together. (See Figure 16.5.) **Patchwork**

Farm Retreats was a dead link, and the **Daily Hampshire Gazette** and **NoHo.com** sites led an outsider to useful background and contacts in the area and therefore better fit the needs of potential bed-and-breakfast guests than of floral customers. The other two links were miscellaneous. So I removed the *Links* link from the Living Art page and added links to the **Daily Hampshire Gazette** and **NoHo.com** to the bed-and-breakfast section of Carol's site. This meant that the Links page got dropped from the site.

Figure 16.5: The contents on Carol's Links page didn't make sense for her floral business.

Attracting Stay-Over Guests

Now we turn to the bed-and-breakfast portion of Carol Duke's Web site. As noted earlier in this chapter, location represents a central factor of interest for a local business like an inn. Few people would decide where to spend weekends or holidays according to the visual appeal and verbal description of a Web site: "Honey, look at this place. It's in Akron, Ohio. Or should we go stay at the one I found the other day in Santa Fe, New Mexico?" Location thus needs to be mentioned not only in the keywords used by search engines, but also in the headline. Additionally, the location must be described using reference points that situate it clearly in the minds of people who have never been there before.

Figure 16.6 shows the top portion of the original page promoting Carol's bed-and-breakfast establishment. Someone who happened to land on this page first would not know until reading deep into the copy that Flower Hill Farm was in western Massachusetts.

The revised version includes not only the precise town and state in the headline, but also relates that town to the nearest popular destination in the second sentence. (See Figure 16.7.) For a local business seeking walk-in or drive-in traffic, a map often smoothes the way for new patrons, but since Flower Hill Farm requires reservations, guests can receive a map and directions by mail or e-mail.

The eight photos Carol selected for the Bed and Breakfast page do an excellent job of conveying both the indoor and outdoor character of the guest quarters. Below the last duo of photos, she mentions at least eight other attractions within a leisurely drive of her place. Such a catalog encourages couples or families who haven't yet decided where or how long to stay to consider Flower Hill Farm and Williamsburg worth an extended visit.

Figure 16.6: The top portion of Carol Duke's original Bed-and-Breakfast page doesn't clearly indicate her location.

Figure 16.7: The revision of the top portion of Carol's Bed-and-Breakfast page includes both town and state information.

My rationale for other revisions on this page included these points:

- The two relevant links from the Links page that was scuttled during revision—links to the local newspaper and the city site for nearby Northampton—belong on this page where Carol lists the area's tourist and cultural attractions. Those links appear on a portion of the revised page not shown here, after the recital of the area's attractions.
- Lots of words were capitalized that shouldn't have been. For instance, in "a 1790 restored Cape with attached Flower Arranging Studio and Barn," only "Cape" (short for "Cape Cod," denoting a type of house) merits capitalization in the revision. Eccentric use of capital letters undermines professionalism.
- It's best to avoid underlining for emphasis, since underlining usually marks a hyperlink on the Web. Boldface works better by itself.
- Also avoid unexplained abbreviations. Americans who travel a lot probably know that "B&B" means "Bed and Breakfast," but why exclude some travelers from overseas or Americans who don't travel much?
- Long centered lines are hard to read. The copy and photos here could have more effectively been laid out in the same staggered fashion as in Figure 16.3. Most of the centered text has been realigned on the revised page, as in Figure 16.7, but we left the offset layout for Carol's Web designer to implement.
- I matched the fonts here with the ones on the Living Art page (shown in Figure 16.3). Because the Bed and Breakfast page and the Living Art page both link from a shared home page, a shared look makes the reader feel more comfortable.
- I fixed some misleading and incomplete text about Carol's house. It's always helpful to have someone who knows your offerings well review your copy for accuracy.

Carol's recital of business terms at the bottom of the Bed and Breakfast page covers what guests need to know to book, pay for, and enjoy their stay. (See Figure 16.8.) However, the presentation was sloppy in some places and confusing in others. Problem areas that the revision corrected included these:

- Under "Cancellations" it's best to give each point a separate line. And "After that two week period" is confusing. In a list of terms like this, it's best to make each sentence independently understandable.
- What time is checkout—"After 3" or at 11? Standard punctuation helps convey the intended meaning more clearly.

- Under "Policies," a phrase like "Possible exceptions" sets the tone for customers to ask for lots of exceptions to these policies. Rephrased as "generally," the point comes across fine without inviting hassles.

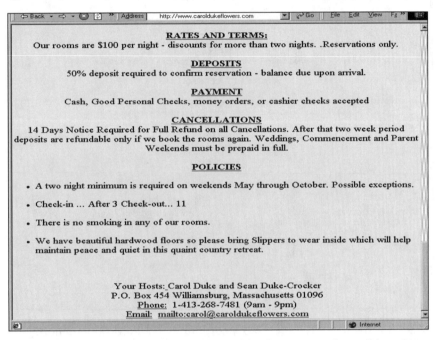

Figure 16.8: The content of the Bed and Breakfast's terms and conditions is good, but the writing was sloppy in this original version.

In addition to fixing those problems, the revision of the Bed and Breakfast's rates and terms ended with a link to Carol's Living Art page. (See Figure 16.9.) This link encourages those who happen upon this page first from a search engine or link and those who began at the home page to explore further.

A Work in Progress

A Web site is never finished. It evolves. However, it's not appropriate most of the time to bring this to the explicit attention of your site visitors. The **Flower Hill Farm** site originally included seven links at the top of the Living Art page (refer to Figure 16.2), five of which led to a more attractive-than-average under-construction page. Extra pages and new links can easily be added later, so the revision, shown in Figure 16.3, leaves out the not-yet-ready links and omits the page asking visitors to come back later. Remember, people coming to a site like this for the first time are not going to feel the absence of very optional features: "Gosh, where's the page on Carol's workshops?" "Why doesn't she include her press clips so that I can see them?"

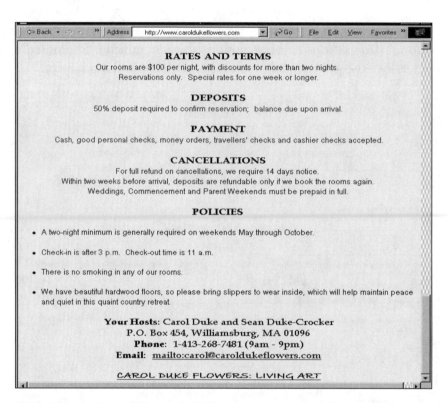

Figure 16.9: This revision of Figure 16.8 incorporates standard punctuation, a neater layout, and a link to Carol's other business.

CHAPTER SEVENTEEN

Internet Services

Web sites with services relating to people's use of the Internet tend to involve distinctive challenges. The services usually consist of something that could not have been delivered, or even described, a few years earlier. Usually too, the services are highly technological, raising the temptation to use jargon, such as search-engine optimization, uptime validation, or domain-name transfers, that are not clearly understood by the target market. As explained in Part I, *Crucial Website Elements,* people excited about their product usually overestimate the extent to which others understand their specialized language. When the intended audience consists of nonspecialists, jargon becomes even more of a critical obstacle to communication. Additionally, with Internet services, the firm is often as new as the services delivered, sharply raising the issue of trust and whether the firm really can perform as promised.

This makeover discusses:
- *Why and how you must explain a technical service to nontechnical people*
- *How to make buried pages more accessible*
- *How to organize an online portfolio*
- *What to say to avoid misunderstandings of what you do*

The "What" and "Why" of Streaming Media

WBC Imaging (http://www.wbcimaging.com/) provides affordable add-on video and audio services for Web sites. In the trade, this is called *streaming media* because, so long as the correct plug-in is installed, the audio or video plays for the viewer in a continuous stream, in contrast to other methods of delivery that require complete downloading of the audio or video file before the playing of the file. WBC has two audiences: business people who don't necessarily understand much about the Web or associated technologies, and Web designers who don't know much about audio/video technologies. This is a far cry from nerd-to-nerd selling.

We have to assume that both of these audiences care more about results—that is, getting a better response from their Web site—than about the technical means to get there. The term streaming media may not ring a lot of bells with clients. They probably think more in terms of getting audio and video features onto their site. We must also assume that potential clients will need to feel safe asking this company dumb questions, because they're buying a technical service, yet are not techies themselves.

Thus, two issues take on paramount importance on WBC's home page. (See Figure 17.1.) Most fundamentally, technically unsophisticated visitors need to understand at a glance that WBC offers on-site audio and video installation to rev up the selling power of Web sites. Once that point hits home, visitors need to understand that with WBC Imaging, adding audio or video features does not cost a fortune.

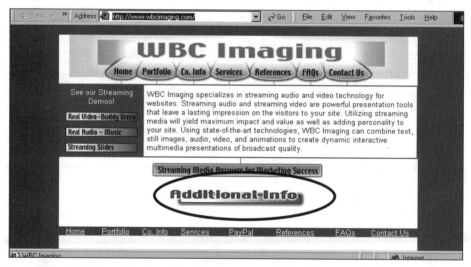

Figure 17.1: WBC Imaging's original home page (http:// www.wbcimaging.com/) needs changes to appeal to nonspecialists.

Making the first point requires delving deeply into the benefits of adding audio or video to a Web site, which include the following:

- Giving the company more personality, enabling a powerfully direct appeal to visitors
- Providing instant, on-demand access to pre-existing audio/video/ multimedia sales or training tools
- Making the company's products, services, and personnel come alive at the Web site

- Giving prospective clients the next best experience to actually being there
- Conveying a multisensory experience with emotional immediacy
- Multiplying the entertainment value of a site
- Boosting persuasiveness by showing how the product functions in real life
- Instigating an astounding 70% click-through rate and 49% buy rate for some pages with streaming media

Without appealing to such benefits, WBC can sell only to those who are already completely persuaded that they need audio/video/multimedia at their site and are merely searching for a supplier. With these benefits made clear, WBC has the opportunity to rein in visitors who are not yet convinced that audio/video/multimedia would benefit them. The site also requires clear signals right from the outset that streaming media is within clients' budgets.

In analyzing those aspects of this business that mattered most to potential customers, I came up with these ideas to highlight in the site's headline or tag line:

- Broadcast quality/"wow" value
- Audio/video
- Affordable
- Helps close the sale

The top of Figure 17.2 shows a new marketing pitch that combines these features and precedes the company name. Then the revised copy in the box makes a brief case for streaming media as a marketing tool and for WBC as the provider of choice. The new and revised copy made the original line, "Streaming Media Answers for Marketing Success" redundant, so that got cut. Besides, that element had been misleading, since it appeared to be a link but wasn't. Note, too. the friendlier tone of the revisions.

Figure 17.2: The revised version of WBC Imaging's home page contains copy that provokes excitement about the company's services.

Fixing Navigation Problems

In addition to the home page, the WBC Imaging site included, as indicated in the set of links under "WBC Imaging," a Portfolio page, a page of background on the company, a list of services, a page of client quotes (which could be better titled "Testimonials" than "References"), a Frequently Asked Questions file, and a page with contact information. In addition, the three links in the left column immediately opened demos of streaming video, audio, and slides.

In the bottom row of links, the *PayPal* link presented several problems. PayPal is a service that enables merchants without standard Visa/MasterCard accounts to take payments online. It seems peculiar for a service firm to draw attention to an alternative payment system before clients are ready to buy. In addition, this extra link appeared only on the home page. After speaking with Ronni Rhodes, co-owner of WBC Imaging, we decided that it would be best to keep the page enabling clients to pay via PayPal, but to remove the link. Clients never engaged WBC without substantive e-mail or phone contact, or both, and WBC could provide clients the exact URL for the unlinked PayPal page when they were ready to pay.

Only on my fourth or fifth visit to this site did I click the *Additional Information* link that you can see toward the bottom of Figure 17.1. Because of the unobtrusive location and vague wording, it did not attract much attention. Visitors might assume that it led to the portfolio, the FAQ, and so on. However, this link actually opened the page you see in Figure 17.3, which in turn led to ten articles, an explanation of the workings and benefits of streaming media, and three more articles by the broadcast engineer who co-owns the company. Since Ronni Rhodes said that that link wasn't clicked often, it was important to make those resources available in a different way on the revised home page. The revised page, shown in Figure 17.2, therefore includes two new links in the left-hand column: *Why Streaming Media* and *Expert Perspective*, which present more information on streaming media and all the articles. Because the two new links replaced the invitation "See Our Streaming Demos," the titles for the links to samples are now "Sample Streaming Video," "Sample Streaming Audio," and "Sample Streaming Slides."

Presenting a Portfolio

Although WBC's portfolio requires that the visitor have plug-in programs to view or listen to samples of its work instead of merely clicking and looking, it is otherwise analogous to the online portfolio found on the sites of visual artists and ad agencies, saying in effect: Here is what we've done for clients and the sort of thing we could do for you. (See Figure 17.4.)

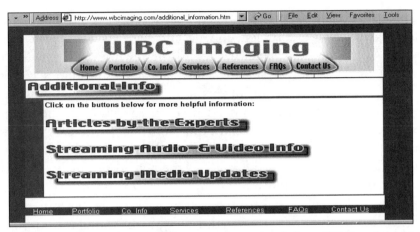

Figure 17.3: Clicking the obscure *Additional Information* link on WBC's original home page brought up this page, which in turn brought up 13 valuable articles and an explanation of the workings and benefits of streaming media.

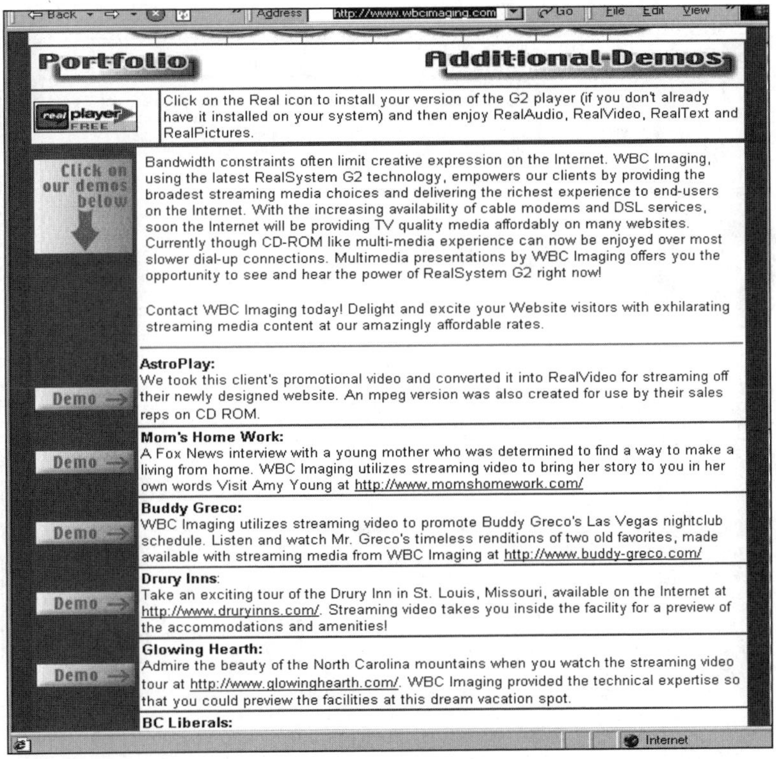

Figure 17.4: The "before" version of WBC's Portfolio page, below the site's name plate, could make it easier for readers to understand how these sample sites benefited from adding streaming media.

In this case, the introductory blurbs for each sample could do a better job of highlighting the type of problem-solving and benefits that particular project represents. Compare the original page with the rewrites in Figure 17.5, where more engaging, descriptive phrases take the place of headlines consisting of names. The overall introduction to this page was confusing and distracting, so we simplified it. Potential clients don't need an education in the prospects for greater Internet bandwidth. In addition, someone particularly interested in streaming audio shouldn't have to read all the blurbs to discover the two audio samples lurking at the end of the page, so the revised site makes it possible for someone to go directly to the audio samples from the opening paragraph. Also, the *Additional Demos* link makes more sense placed at the bottom, after readers have at least scanned the demos offered. Finally, highlighting the purpose of each sample made it clear that two of the samples had the same purpose. The revision therefore omits the redundant example.

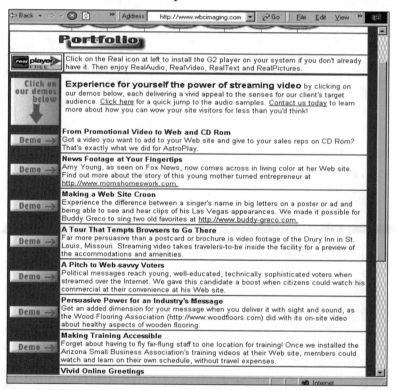

Figure 17.5: Note the new descriptive headlines for each demo in the "after" version of WBC's Portfolio page.

Marketing Copy for a Technical Service

WBC's page profiling its services (see Figure 17.6) needed a major overhaul, from its misleading headline to its missing call to action. Ronni Rhodes said that people mistakenly thought her company did Web design, and the headline on this page referring to Web design is one reason they got that impression. The opening quote is off target too, because it fails to give readers a reason why streaming media is worth adding to their Web sites.

Figure 17.6: The "before" version of WBC's Services page has a headline that misrepresents the company's true purpose.

Scanning the articles posted elsewhere at the site led to a more motivating and appropriate quote. We also refashioned the headline to hammer home the theme that on-site audio and video represented a smart investment. (See Figure 17.7.) Ronni also mentioned that it needed to be clearer at the site that WBC didn't do audio or video production, but merely worked with already created tapes or files, so the fourth paragraph now includes words to that effect.

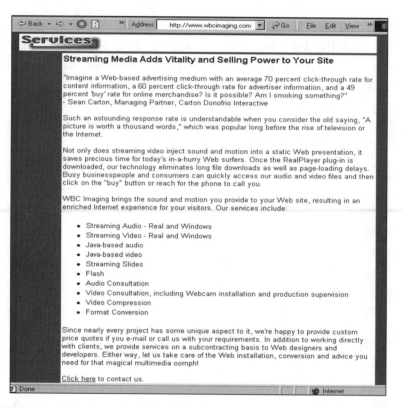

Figure 17.7: The "after" version of WBC's services page has a revamped headline, copy that stresses the tangible benefits of streaming media, and the new call to action at the end.

In the new version, the list of services is just as easy to pick out as in the old. This is important, because WBC needs to appeal not just to those who still need to be sold, but also to those trying to ascertain quickly whether this firm performs a specific service they already had in mind.

The only other significant change this Web site needed was making the previously well-hidden articles accessible from the new home page's *Expert Perspective* link, except for one article to be linked from the *Why Streaming Media* link.

GLOSSARY

above the fold—The portion of a Web page visible without scrolling vertically; the term is derived from what a passerby sees of a folded newspaper.

advertorial—Advertising copy that reads like editorial material and is laid out like an article rather than an ad.

affiliate program—A setup in which a Web site earns commissions by sending buyers to another site; the first site is an affiliate of the second site.

alt tags—Labels on Web site photos and graphics that can be read by text-only browsers and browsers for the visually impaired.

banner ad—An ad at a Web site enticing readers to click to visit another site.

benefit—In Web marketing copy, text that explains the advantages to the buyer of a specific product or service.

breadcrumbs—Words and symbols indicating categories clicked from the home page to the page currently in view; this term derives from the Hansel and Gretel fairy tale.

brochureware—A derogatory term for a Web site that simply reuses text from print brochures without modification.

browser—A program, such as Netscape or Internet Explorer, that enables you to view sites on the World Wide Web.

bullets—Points arranged in list fashion, with a symbol, such as a filled-in circle, marking each point.

call to action—In marketing copy, a sentence inviting, asking, or telling the reader to take a particular action.

chat, live—A utility enabling real-time typed exchanges, such as between a shopper and a representative of a Web site, when the shopper has a question about the site.

check boxes—Boxes that a user can check, as many as appropriate, to indicate options for an order form, registration form, or survey.

content—Articles, photos, cartoons, or other features of value to readers.

cookie—Information placed on the user's computer by a Web site to identify the user and options selected; used by many shopping carts and tracking systems.

copy—Writers' lingo for promotional text.

copyright—Legal ownership of creative work.

dial-up—A low-speed method of Internet access through telephone lines.

directory—On the Web, a service that categorizes Web offerings so that visitors can find online resources.

discussion list—A participatory mailing list, distributed by e-mail, that facilitates the exchange of ideas between like-minded individuals.

domain—The part of a Web address that follows "www." and ends in ".com," ".org," ".net," and so on, for example, "amazon.com" or "loc.gov."

download—The process of transferring files to one's own computer from the Web.

drop-down menu—Options offered through a rectangular box that turns into a list of choices when clicked; also called a pull-down menu.

e-book—Book-length material that can be read on one's computer or a special reader or printed.

e-mail newsletter—Publication sent by e-mail to subscribers on a regular schedule.

eyebrow headline—A headline above a headline in much smaller type and usually underlined.

FAQs—Frequently Asked Questions; a common format on the Web for organizing information in a question-and-answer format.

feature—In marketing copy, text that describes the objective properties of a specific product or service, such as "flexible" or "bright blue" for a pen.

firewall—A security feature that prevents unauthorized access to computers connected to the Internet.

font—A typeface, such as Times Roman or Helvetica, offering a complete set of letters and numbers in one style.

frames—Technique offering the juxtaposition of two or more partial pages from the same site on the screen at one time.

high-speed Internet access—Fast connection to the Internet via technologies such as DSL, cable modem, satellite, or ISDN.

home page—A site's main page.

HTML—HyperText Markup Language; a coding system that translates text, files, and commands into graphically interesting Web page layouts.

HTML e-mail—E-mail that resembles a full-color, graphical Web site complete with links.

hyperlink—A segment of text or a picture that takes the user to another page upon clicking it.

ISP—Internet Service Provider; a company that provides users with access to the Internet.

justified text—Text that is straight along both the right and left margins.

link—See *hyperlink*.

live chat—See *chat, live*.

listserv or listserve—See *mailing list*.

mailing list—A system for disseminating information by e-mail to many subscribers simultaneously.

media release—See *press release*.

meta tag—Information encoded into a Web page enabling it to be properly indexed by search engines.

modem—A device that connects a computer to the Internet or to other computers via telephone lines, cable, or a wireless service.

name plate—Text at the top portion of a Web page, signaling the purpose of the site and identifying who runs it.

news release—See *press release*.

opt-in—A system that sends e-mail to only those who request it.

opt-out—A system that requires users to request *not* to receive information.

plug-in—A program that a visitor needs in addition to a browser to view or experience a site or certain of its features.

portal—A site set up to function as a come-here-first location on the Web.

press release—A document that presents a newsworthy story to editors, producers, or reporters; also called media release or news release.

pull-down menu—See *drop-down menu*.

purchase order—A form from a corporation, governmental unit, or nonprofit organization, such as a school, that officially and reliably approves a specific purchase.

radio button—One of a series of circles and labels requiring the user to select one option of several.

ragged-right margins—In contrast to justified text, this style of text is uneven on the right side, although lined up evenly on the left.

registration—A process by which Web site visitors type in their contact information, choose a password, and perhaps answer some questions for access to site features.

sans serif—A font without horizontal extenders on the letters; easier to read online than a serif font.

scroll bar—A sliding device in a window that enables you to travel down a page or a frame at a Web site by clicking, or clicking and dragging.

scrolling—Going down or across a long or wide Web page.

search engine—A Web site that indexes Web content and allows visitors to search what it has indexed.

secure server—A computer host that uses encryption to safeguard its sites' data.

serif—A font with horizontal extenders on the letters; more difficult to read online than a sans serif font.

shopping cart—A Web-based system for choosing items that the user can pay for in one batch.

spam—Unsolicited bulk e-mail, despised by many Internet users; term derives from a Monty Python comedy skit.

tag line—A marketing pitch that follows a company's name at a Web site or elsewhere, such as "We never sleep, so you can" for **247sitewatch.com**.

thumbnail—A small photo that when clicked opens up a larger one.

URL—Universal Resource Locator; a complete Web address of the form *http://www.yourdomain.com/file.htm*.

usability—The extent to which visitors can actually use a site as intended.

Web form—A page with blanks requesting information that the user fills out and submits, to buy something, register, or request a call back.

Web forum—An online message board designed to facilitate user participation.

Web page—A unit of information that can be viewed on the Web without clicking any links.

Web site—A group of Web pages sharing the same general identity and usually the same domain.

white paper—Article setting forth relatively objective views and recommendations on a business or technology topic.

Makeover Checklist

Use this checklist to assess your existing site, to help plan revisions, and to check that you've done your job well when revamping a site. The answer to each question should be yes.

First Impressions

When visiting a site for the first time, Web surfers need to get their bearings quickly and decide whether the site is worth exploring. If they feel confused or something turns them off, you will have lost the benefit of that traffic forever. Check your site for the following to make sure you make the best first impression:

- Can someone get to your domain by typing either "www.yourdomain.com" or "yourdomain.com"? (If not, your Webmaster or Web-hosting company should be able to arrange this.)
- Will someone arriving at your site with no prior knowledge of your enterprise understand at a glance the purpose of the site?
- Is it immediately clear who's behind the site?
- Are the color scheme and overall look of the site consistent with your desired business image?
- Is the difference between advertising banners for third parties and your own material crystal clear?
- If someone arrives first at an inner page of your site, will they know at a glance whose site it is and what its purpose is?
- Do inner pages match each other and the home page in overall look?
- Does your site have a visual and verbal personality, so that it differs recognizably from sites of competitors?
- Have you spell-checked your text and had it proofread by someone with an excellent command of English?

- Have you considered foreign-language versions of your site to welcome international visitors? (See Figures A.1 and A.2.)

Figure A.1: The home page of the Louvre museum, in French (http://www.louvre.fr/), offers links to versions in English, Spanish, and Japanese.

Figure A.2: Clicking the Japanese-language link in Figure A.1 brings up the Louvre's home page content fully translated into that language, along with links to the other three languages.

- Are your color choices such that someone with imperfect eyesight can still read the text?
- Is the text presented in a readable font size, with columns that do not stretch the entire width of the browser?
- If you use a background other than solid white, is the text readable without strain?

- Can someone accessing your site with a 640x480 screen resolution get the gist of what you're up to at a glance?
- If you provide local services or run local events, would it be clear to a first-time visitor from some other part of the world exactly where you operate?

Functionality

You can have the richest content and sleekest look, but if the site doesn't work properly for all your visitors, those virtues don't do you much good. Use this list to ensure that your site functions at its best:

- Does the site load quickly?
- If you have lots of graphics on your home page, are they in formats that load quickly?
- Do you check your links to other sites periodically and remove or change those that don't work?
- If you offer a Flash-animated introduction, have you provided visitors not using Flash an alternate way in to your site?
- If certain features of your site require plug-in software, have you provided an overview of your site that's accessible to those without the plug-in, as well as a link for obtaining the plug-in?
- Have you made your site accessible to handicapped visitors?
- Have you included meta tags behind the scenes so that the site and important pages can be properly indexed by search engines?

How Quickly Does Your Site Load?—*Unless you have several different kinds of Internet connections at your office, you'll need more than a stopwatch to determine how quickly your site loads. Visit these sites to assess loading time and learn how to make your site quick on the draw:*

Net Mechanic, http://www.netmechanic.com/cobrands/click2commerce/load_check.htm

Virtual Stampede, http://www.virtualstampede.com/tools.htm

Web Site Garage, http://websitegarage.netscape.com/

Accessibility to the Disabled—The United States alone has 54 million people with disabilities, many of whom have the same needs and desires to surf the Web and use e-mail as able-bodied folks. Despite new technologies making it easier for people with disabilities to use computers, Web marketers unknowingly throw up obstacles that function like the stairs, low lighting, and lack of sign-language interpreters that often make things difficult for people with disabilities in the real world. The following sites explain what you can do to make your site accessible to those with visual, mobility, and other kinds of impairments, including providing text equivalents for each graphic element at a site, providing headings for frames, and ensuring that color choices communicate equally well in black and white:

Accessible Web Authoring Resources and Education Center, http://aware.hwg.org/

International Center for Disability Resources on the Internet, http://www.icdri.org/

Internet Society, http://www.isoc.org/isoc/access/

Marketing Copy

Make sure your wording speaks directly and meaningfully to your target market with benefits and details that increase your trust quotient. Good marketing copy also heads off questions, doubts, and objections. Check your site for the following to ensure that you clearly communicate your message:

- If you make promises at your site (about updating frequency, quickness of response, and so on), is each of these promises regularly fulfilled?
- Do you use the word *you* more often than *we* or *I*?
- If you know who visitors are, do you refrain from addressing them by name until they've knowingly provided you with that information?
- Is the tone of your site friendly rather than bureaucratic, cold, or negative?
- Do you remind people to bookmark your site? (See Figure A.3.)
- To increase your credibility, have you posted testimonials?
- Are descriptions of your products and services understandable to people who know much less about your industry than you do?
- Do you either avoid jargon that many in your target audience won't understand or provide explanations of insider terms?
- Have you had your marketing copy reviewed for possible legal liability issues?

Test Your You-ness—At http://www.futurenowinc.com/wewe.htm, *Future Now, a company that specializes in converting Web site visits into sales, provides a cool tool for assessing the degree to which you focus on customers rather than on yourself. You just type a URL and that site's company name; then you click a button to learn your customer-focus score. Anything above 50% shows that you're on the right track in referring more to you than to I or us.*

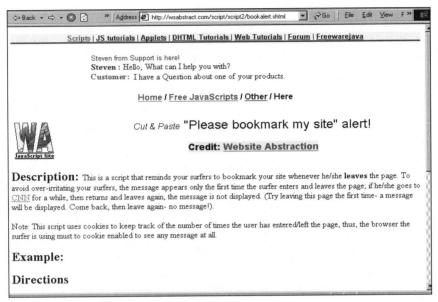

Figure A.3: Website Abstraction (http://wsabstract.com/script/script2/bookalert.shtml) offers a free "Please bookmark my site" alert that appears when someone leaves.

Some Legal Issues to Consider—*A carelessly thrown up Web site can land you in a heap of legal trouble. Among the many legal pitfalls an attorney can steer you away from are these:*

- *Trademark misuse or infringement*
- *Violation of the Children's Online Privacy Protection Act, which regulates what kinds of information sites can collect from children*
- *Misleading advertising*
- *Invalid user agreements*
- *Unexpected tax liabilities*

To find a qualified attorney, consult Lawyers.com (http://www.lawyers.com/) and select "Internet Law" as a practice area.

- If your site has more than one target audience, have you devised ways to appeal to all of them?
- Can readers figure out quickly from your site what differentiates you from your competitors?
- Have you anticipated and headed off questions or objections readers might have about your offerings?

Timeliness

As time relentlessly marches on, various elements at your site become outdated. Vigilance is necessary to maintain credibility. Use this list to ensure your Web site remains current:

- Have you updated the copyright notice for your site to the current year?
- Have you removed announcements for events that have already taken place?
- When someone points out a mistake or typo at your site, do you correct it immediately?
- When you receive other feedback on your site, do you collect it and act upon it promptly when appropriate?
- If you have timely copy or specials tied to the calendar, is it clear that you also offer products and services of year-round interest?
- If you have seasonal photos or graphics, have you updated them to match the current season? (See Figure A.4.)

Figure A.4: Snowflakes graced the Promaster home page (http://www.promaster.com/) on Memorial Day, considered by many the start of summer.

Navigation and On-Site Search

Make it easy for people to find their way around your site with intuitive and functional navigation labels. Where appropriate, provide a search utility as well. Use the following list to check the search and navigation elements on your site:

- Can someone get around your site and out of it without being constantly bombarded by pop-up screens?
- From every page of the site, can a visitor return to the home page—or visit it for the first time—with just a click?
- Can someone reach the most popular and the most urgent pages at your site in just one click from your home page?
- Have you used clear, descriptive navigation labels instead of icons or cryptic phrases?
- Do you use standard navigation labels for standard Web site elements, such as "Shopping Cart," "Press Room," "Contact Us," and "Home"?
- For each type of users in your target audience, have you thought through what they would want from your site and made it easy for them to zoom right to that?
- If your site includes many layers of content, can users find their way back to higher levels by following "breadcrumbs"? (See Figure A.5.)

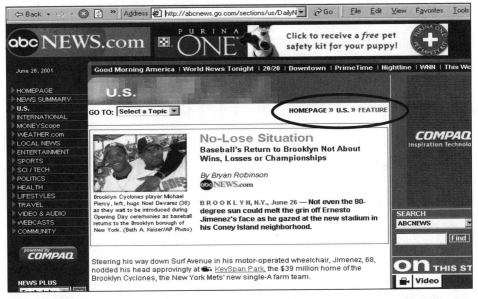

Figure A.5: On this page of ABCNews.com (http://www.abcnews.com/), the breadcrumbs can be found just above the article headline, indicating that the Back button would take the visitor back to the U.S. page, and then the home page.

- If you use pictorial navigation options, like a map, can people readily find the proper place to click?
- On different pages of your site, do you use the same words for the same links?
- Do your links change color after users have followed them?
- If your site has more than 50 pages of content, have you installed a Search box?
- If you offer a Search box, have you included easy-to-understand instructions for using it?

Your Online Catalog

You can't just say "Buy my stuff!" and expect to receive orders online. The following details have to be installed at exactly the right junctures in the shopping process:

- Are prices clearly indicated and unambiguously explained?
- Are shipping prices and return policies clearly indicated, prior to the point where shoppers are asked to enter their credit-card information?
- Do you state whether you ship internationally, and if so how and for how much?
- Have you made provisions for people who prefer to pay by check, by money order, or (for educational or governmental institutions and some corporations) by purchase order?
- Can people place an order by phone or fax as well as online?
- Do you prompt customers to inquire about special deals, such as bulk orders, overnight shipping, customization of your products, reprints of site contents, and so on?
- Do you either inform shoppers at the site which items are not in stock or immediately inform people who have ordered something for which they'll have to wait?
- Have you posted guarantees that are explicit, understandable, and reasonable?
- Do you present items in categories that allow someone with only a vague idea of what they want to find something suitable?
- When visitors place items in their shopping carts, is that immediately and unmistakably apparent to them?
- If you have more than four dozen products, do you have a search facility so that people can find the particular items they want?

Order Forms

Even off the Web, order forms are difficult to construct well. Online, you have dozens of minutiae, such as those listed here, to watch for:

- Do you provide a link to your FAQ from the order form?
- Does the secure-server icon appear on your secure-server pages?
- Do you remind shoppers to print their order form for their records?
- If the charge will show up on buyers' credit-card bills under another name than the name of your site, do you so inform them?
- Do you provide shoppers with an order number so that they'll have an easier time asking follow-up questions?
- Have you clearly and explicitly informed shoppers before they order when they can expect delivery?
- Can shoppers track their own packages, and if so, have you made it easy for them to do so?
- Have you tested the usability of your online ordering procedure by placing an order yourself?
- Have you designed your order form so that shoppers need to enter each bit of information only once?
- Do shoppers have the opportunity to review their entire order, including the final price, before submitting it?
- Can shoppers easily change quantities or delete items from their shopping cart without beginning to shop all over again?
- Do you inform buyers after they submit an order when they can expect delivery?
- Can someone whose country does not have ZIP codes, states, or ten-digit telephone numbers still place an order?
- Do your error messages, arising from an improperly filled out order form, explain clearly what the user needs to do to fix the problem?
- Have you made it clear that shoppers do not need to register as members to buy from you?
- Does the order form include enough space for people to type unusually long addresses or names?

Registration, Subscription, or Leads Forms

At many sites, the goal isn't making sales but collecting subscribers, members, or inquirers that turn into clients. How you go about getting people to respond has a huge influence on your results. Check your site for the following to increase your chances of meeting your goals:

- If you're requesting personal information, have you made clear why and what you will do with it?
- If you distribute information to an e-mail list, do you include an unsubscribe link that reliably works?
- Have you posted an easy-to-find, easy-to-understand privacy policy?
- When asking people to subscribe to something, do you tell them what they'll be receiving and how often?
- If you require free registration for access to some site features, have you emphasized that registration is free?
- If you require registration for access to some site features, have you described your registrants-only features in appetizing detail for those pondering registration?
- If you are selling ads on your site, have you provided a leads form for potential advertisers? (See Figure A.6.)

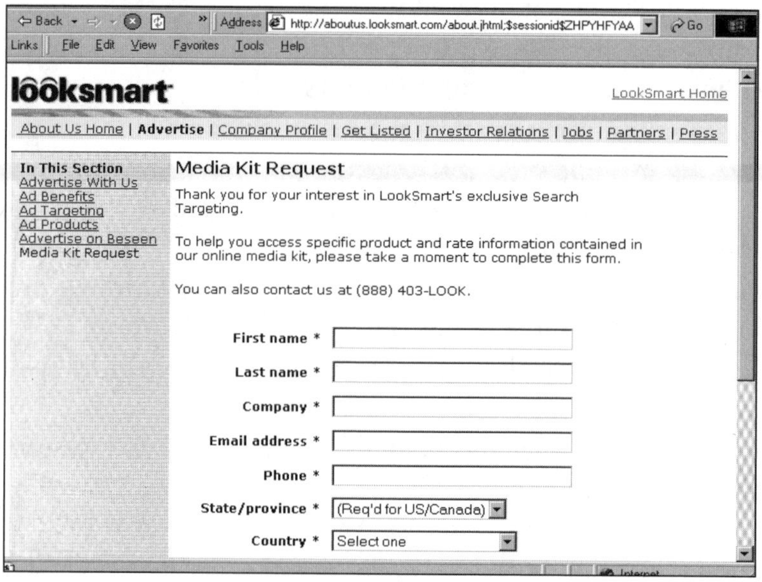

Figure A.6: LookSmart (http://www.looksmart.com/) promises potential advertisers a media kit after they fill out and submit this form.

Content

Useful content presented well makes it easier to attract visitors through media coverage, traffic from search engines, and links from other sites. Check the following content-related issues on your site:

- Have you made sure valuable content is featured prominently rather than buried deep within the site?
- For greater involvement of visitors, have you created interactive content, such as quizzes, calculators, or surveys?
- Is every bit of content at the site, including downloadable Adobe Acrobat (.pdf) files, branded with your company's identity?
- Where you use lots of photos, have you provided thumbnail shots and enabled people to see larger versions with a click?
- Where appropriate, have you enabled clients and prospects to exchange tips with one another through an online forum?
- Are photos clear, sharply focused, and useful?
- Do you regularly freshen content so that people have reason to return to your site?
- Does each major page at your site have a proper title that shows up in the visitor's browser as well as, embedded in the HTML code, keywords, and a description for the search engines?
- When your site includes a lot of content, is it clear which item is the newest?
- At a content-heavy site, have you provided easy-to-e-mail and easy-to-print versions of your articles?
- Do you offer one or more FAQ pages, either about your topic or about your products and services?

Credibility

Your Web site should include as much of the following information as possible to bolster the claim that you know what you're doing:

- Do you offer bios of leading executives of your organization as well as information about the company?
- Have you included testimonials from satisfied customers or clients?
- If you have recognized, impressive organizations among your clients, have you provided a client list at your site?

- If testimonials and a client list aren't possible because of the type of work you do, have you created problem–solution case studies?
- When you've received significant media attention, have you included links to or information about that coverage?

Accessibility Through Contact Information

Don't make the mistake of hiding behind convenient-for-you Web forms. You'll improve response rates when you provide lots of avenues, listed here, for people to reach you:

- On every page of your site, is it clear how someone could get in touch with you?
- For contact e-mail addresses, do you provide names (bruce@mnop.com) rather than functions (sales@mnop.com)?
- Do you respond to all e-mail inquiries or form submissions within 24 hours?
- If visitors have suggestions, comments, or corrections for your site, is it clear where they should submit them?
- Do you provide a telephone number and physical address to reassure visitors that your organization is reputable?
- If you have a toll-free number, do you also provide a regular phone number for use by overseas callers?

Recommended Books and Web Resources

Much as I would like to have the last word on Web sites, scads of other books and sites offer perspective, advice, tips, tools, and resources that help your so-so site become spectacular. Enjoy, and good luck!

Books

In contrast to the now-ness of the Web, books offer a more leisurely and concentrated opportunity to bone up on marketing, writing, and design perspectives. The following volumes are more likely than most to stand the test of time.

Books on Marketing Fundamentals

Caples, John, *Tested Advertising Methods,* fifth edition. Upper Saddle River, NJ, Prentice Hall, 1998. ISBN 0-130-95701-1. This book is the best ever written on the crafting of headlines. The classic advertising campaigns it portrays are as fascinating as its marketing principles.

Hodgson, Richard S., *The Greatest Direct Mail Sales Letters of All Time.* Chicago, Dartnell, 1986. ISBN 85013-155-3. These letters long predate the Internet, but they're masterpieces of wordsmithing and salesmanship worthy of study.

Levinson, Jay Conrad, *Guerrilla Marketing Excellence: The 50 Golden Rules for Small-Business Success.* New York, Houghton Mifflin, 1993. ISBN 0-395-60844-9. Whether you're a pipsqueak business or a multinational giant, this book contains marketing wisdom on figuring out how to appeal to customers, the danger of humor, the importance of tracking competitors, the power of specificity, and much more.

Reis, Al and Jack Trout, *Positioning: The Battle for Your Mind,* second edition. New York, McGraw-Hill, 2001. ISBN 0-071-37358-6. This classic work describes how to stand tall in a field of similar competitors.

Yudkin, Marcia, *Persuading on Paper: The Complete Guide to Writing Copy That Pulls in Business.* Haverford, PA, Infinity Publishing, 2001. ISBN 0-7414-0610-1. Learn more about features versus benefits, how to choose words that get your message across, and jazz up your copy creatively.

Books on e-Business

Bick, Jonathan, *101 Things You Need to Know about Internet Law.* New York, Three Rivers Press, 2000. ISBN 0-609-80633-5. Stay out of trouble and protect your intellectual property rights on the Net with these answers from an attorney to questions about Internet contracts, online privacy, domain names, digital signatures, linking, and more.

Easton, Jaclyn, *StrikingItRich.com: Profiles of 23 Incredibly Successful Websites You've Probably Never Heard Of.* New York, McGraw-Hill, 1999. ISBN 0-071-35579-0. This book contains eye-opening case histories of small- to medium-sized Web businesses in a range of industries. For a course on what works on the Web, read the profiles and then tour the sites.

Garfinkel, Simson, *Database Nation: The Death of Privacy in the 21st Century.* Sebastopol, CA, O'Reilly, 2001. ISBN 0-596-00105-3. If you're not sure whether customer privacy matters, you'll find the big picture here—and why threats to privacy are frightening to most people.

Godin, Seth, *Permission Marketing: Turning Strangers into Friends, and Friends into Customers.* New York, Simon & Schuster, 1999. ISBN 0-684-85636-0. Read persuasive arguments about why Web companies should have permission before marketing by e-mail to prospective or current customers and respect promises made to their site visitors.

Silverstein, Barry, *Business-to-Business Internet Marketing,* third edition. Gulf Breeze, FL, Maximum Press, 2000. ISBN 1-885068-50-6. Learn how to generate leads, sell online, and serve customers through a B2B Web site and e-mail.

Sterne, Jim, *World Wide Web Marketing,* third edition, New York, John Wiley & Sons, 2001. ISBN 0-471-41621-5. Light delivery, important message. Discusses personalization, customer service, usability, measurements of success, and other topics vital to getting a good return on your site investment.

Books on Site Promotion

Helmstetter, Greg, *Increasing Hits and Selling More on Your Web Site.* New York, John Wiley & Sons, 1997. ISBN 0-471-16944-7. Read these sound strategies for making your Web site a success. Learn how to submit to search engines, solicit links, buy and sell ads, use e-mail effectively for promotion, and more.

Kent, Peter and Tara Calishain, *Poor Richard's Internet Marketing and Promotions,* second edition. Lakewood, CO, Top Floor Publishing, 2000. ISBN 0-930082-00-2. This practical, comprehensive guide to promoting your site offers hundreds of low-cost strategies that get the job done.

Marckini, Fredrick, *Search Engine Positioning.* Plano, TX, Wordware, 2001. ISBN 1-556622-804-x. The hype on the cover—"Search positioning is everything!"— is a turn-off; but if you want your site to come up in search engines, this book is packed with guidance on how to do it. The book includes tips for choosing keywords, tweaking pages, and submitting to specific search engines and directories.

Yudkin, Marcia, *Internet Marketing for Less than $500/Year.* Gulf Breeze, FL, Maximum Press, 2000. ISBN 1-885068-52-2. Yes, you really can create a buzz about your online business and attract traffic to your site without spending a fortune. This book describes newsletter, schmoozing, e-mail, publicity, and Web content tactics that bring you more customers and clients from around the world.

Yudkin, Marcia, *Six Steps to Free Publicity—And Dozens of Other Ways to Win Free Media Attention for You or Your Business.* New York, Plume/Penguin, 1994. ISBN 0-452-27192-4. To get media coverage for your Web site, learn the basics of how to write and send news releases and deal effectively with reporters. Ideas on creative angles presented here will make your site or e-business sound, newsworthy, and dramatic.

Books on Usability

Dalgleish, Jodie, *Customer-Effective Websites.* Upper Saddle River, NJ, Prentice Hall, 2000. ISBN 0-13-087827-8. This book explains 17 customer imperatives, 11 best practices, procedures for site testing, and gives examples of Web sites meeting the guidelines.

Donnelly, Vanessa, *Designing Easy-to-Use Websites.* Reading, MA, Addison Wesley, 2000. ISBN 0-201-67468-8. Learn more about how to create a simple, efficient, intuitive site. This book concentrates more on methods of analysis and testing than specific real-life solutions.

Krug, Steve, *Don't Make Me Think.* Indianapolis, IN, New Riders, 2000. ISBN 0-7897-2310-7. This is a compact and well-written introduction to the concepts underlying Web usability.

Nielsen, Jakob, *Designing Web Usability.* Indianapolis, IN, New Riders Publishing, 2000. This brilliant, persuasive commentary on how Web sites go wrong and what it takes to make them work for users is indispensable for anyone involved with Web sites. At the least, you'll want to find out why a typical comment from designers who reviewed this book at Amazon.com is, "If I ever see this guy in public, I would spit in his face."

Books on Web Design

Benun, Ilise, *Self-Promotion Online: Marketing Your Creative Services Using Web Sites, E-mail, and Digital Portfolios.* Cincinnati, OH, North Light Books, 2001. ISBN 1-5810-069-x. This gorgeous book for designers tells how to create Web sites for marketing design services.

Callahan, Evan, *Troubleshooting Your Web Page.* Redmond, WA, Microsoft Press, 2001. ISBN 0-7356-1164-5. Paragraphs or bullets won't line up? Images look lousy? Forms come in blank? Identify your problem and discover the solution in this book.

Flanders, Vincent, and Michael Willis, *Web Pages that Suck: Learn Good Design by Looking at Bad Design.* Alameda, CA, Sybex, 1998. ISBN 0-7821-2187-x. If you haven't had your fill of Web site "don'ts," you'll enjoy this book, which points out site design follies with full-color examples.

Kim, Amy Jo, *Community Building on the Web.* Berkeley, CA, Peachpit Press, 2000. ISBN 0-201-87484-9. If you want your Web site to engage and involve visitors to the extent that they coalesce into a long-lived online community, use this outstanding book as your guide. The book discusses the successes and stumbles of scores of sites and dispenses wise perspective from someone who understands what makes user communities work.

Navarro, Ann, *Effective Web Design,* second edition. Alameda, CA, Sybex, 2001. ISBN 9-7821-2849-1. This book covers much more ground than most Web-design guides, including accessibility to the disabled, browser compatibility, frames, style sheets, and how to use XHTML, the successor markup language to HTML.

Parker, Roger, *Guide to Web Content and Design.* Foster City, CA, Hungry Minds, 1997. ISBN 1-558-28553-9. This book is what you get when a sure-footed design guru turns his attention to the Web. It contains a useful overview of principles of Web design for small-business owners and others, with color shots of the sites discussed.

Veen, Jeffrey, *The Art & Science of Web Design.* Indianapolis, IN, New Riders, 2001. ISBN 0-7897-2370-0. This problem-solving guide to workable Web sites focuses on how to design for speed of loading, multiple browsers, consistency, and usability.

Williams, Robin, and John Tollett, *The Non-Designer's Web Book,* second edition. Berkeley, CA, Peachpit Press, 2000. ISBN 0-201-71038-2. This fun, educational read has both technical instructions for Web design (geared to the Mac, with gestures toward PC users) and aesthetic guidelines. The engaging self-test quizzes after each chapter and charming illustrations and design lighten up the load of learning.

Books on Web Site Structure and Navigation

Andres, Clay, *Great Web Architecture.* Foster City, CA, IDG Books, 1999. ISBN 0-7645-3246-4. You'll find a wealth of examples and general principles here for structuring Web sites for distributing content, selling, or branding. The detailed analysis of sites is illuminating.

Fleming, Jennifer, *Web Navigation: Designing the User Experience.* Sebastopol, CA, O'Reilly, 1998. ISBN 1-56592-351-0. This book offers general principles, specific suggestions, and examples for sites focused on shopping, community, entertainment, company identity, learning, and content.

Morris, Mary E.S. and Randy J. Hinrichs, *Web Page Design.* Mountain View, CA, Prentice Hall, 1996. ISBN 0-132-39880-x. The strongest portion of this book concerns Web site structure, with lots of planning aids for useful navigation and content.

Reiss, Eric L., *Practical Information Architecture.* Reading, MA, Addison Wesley, 2000. ISBN 0-201-72590-8. Reiss describes useful methods and principles for deciding on the structure of a site and appropriate navigation categories with an emphasis on the processes of brainstorming, refining concepts after testing, and meeting audience needs.

Books on Web Technicalities

Kent, Peter, *Poor Richard's Web Site: Geek-Free, Commonsense Advice on Building a Low-Cost Web Site,* second edition. Lakewood, CO, Top Floor Publishing, 2000. ISBN 0-9661032-0-3. Overcome the technical challenges involved in building a Web site without spending a fortune on hired help and consultants. Lots of free programs and services listed here that do the job of commercial counterparts costing thousands of dollars.

McComb, Gordon, *Web Commerce Cookbook.* New York, John Wiley & Sons, 1998. ISBN 0-471-19663-0. Read this book for technical instruction on password protection, secure servers, forms processing with CGI, traffic log analysis, and the foiling of hackers.

Ray, Deborah S. and Eric J. Ray, *HTML 4 for Dummies: A Quick Reference,* second edition. Foster City, CA, IDG Books, 2000. ISBN 0-7645-0721-4. Keep this little comb-bound manual handy for looking up ways to tweak HTML code and decipher unfamiliar HTML tags.

Books on Web Writing and Content

Goldstein, Norm, editor, *The Associated Press Stylebook and Briefing on Media Law.* Reading, MA, Perseus Books, 2000. ISBN 0-738-20308-4. Follow the guidelines in this book to standardize your site's writing in "AP style," used by most newspapers and many magazines.

Levine, Rick, Christopher Locke, Doc Searls, and David Weinberger, *The Cluetrain Manifesto: The End of Business As Usual.* Cambridge, MA, Perseus Books, 2000. ISBN 0-738-20431-5. "Markets are conversations," runs the argument of this book. It offers an impassioned diatribe against the bureaucratic voice common at Web sites and in business writing in general.

Lewis, Herschell Gordon, *On the Art of Writing Copy: The Best of Print, Broadcast, Internet, Direct Mail,* second edition. New York, Amacom, 2000. ISBN 0-814-47031-9. This veteran copywriter understands more about the nuances of words than most writing authorities, living or dead.

Pirillo, Chris, *Poor Richard's E-mail Publishing: Creating Newsletters, Bulletins, Discussion Groups, and Other Powerful Communication Tools.* Lakewood, CO, Top Floor Publishing, 1999. ISBN 0-9661032-5-4. Pirillo has compiled surprising case studies and detailed resources for online publishing in the format of e-zines, e-mail newsletters, and discussion lists. Find out how to get and keep subscribers and stay out of technical hell.

Tomsen, Mai-lan, *Killer Content.* Reading, MA, Addison Wesley, 2000. ISBN 0-201-65786-4. This book provides a conceptual framework for building a site around content to make it usable, meeting audience needs, protecting intellectual property, and turning content into revenue.

Venolia, Jan, *Rewrite Right!,* second edition. Berkeley, CA, Ten Speed Press, 2000. ISBN 1-580-08239-4. This handy, compact manual covers the mechanics and general concepts of clear, concise writing.

Web Resources

What follows are Web sites that offer information or tools that help turn your Web site into a smoothly functioning, magnetic marketing machine.

Web Design Tutorials

ArticleCentral.com http://www.articlecentral.com/. More than 1,400 articles on Web development and design topics.

Builder.com http://www.builder.com/. How-to tips from basic to advanced topics.

Gettingstarted.net http://www.gettingstarted.net/. Basic and advanced lessons, along with interactive try-it-yourself quizzes.

HTML Goodies http://www.htmlgoodies.com/. Tutorials on creating forms, frames, images, colors, buttons, banner ads, and more.

SitePoint http://www.sitepoint.com/. Instruction on the finer points of creating Web sites.

Web Designer's Paradise http://desktoppublishing.com/webparadise.html. Advice, articles, and utilities for Web designers.

WebDeveloper.com http://www.webdeveloper.com/. Advice on using the advanced programs that get Web sites to do cool things.

Web Developer's Virtual Library http://stars.com/. Tutorials here are conveniently divided into beginner's and advanced.

Webmonkey http://www.webmonkey.com/. Tutorials accessible to nontechies on Web design and programming.

Web Page Design for Designers http://www.wpdfd.com/. Stylishly presented lessons full of pizzazz and good sense.

WebReview.com http://www.webreview.com/. Articles and columns for Web authors, designers, developers, and strategists.

Zen and the Art of Web Sites http://www.tlc-systems.com/webtips.shtml. A charming one-stop tutorial on designing your site.

Clip Art Sites

ArtToday.com http://www.arttoday.com/. Free access for 3 days to more than 1 million downloadable graphics.

ClipArtConnection.com http://www.clipartconnection.com/. Free animations and static images for your site.

CoolGraphics.com http://coolgraphics.com/. Free arrows, buttons, bullets, digits, icons, and more.

Barry's Clipart Server http://barrysclipart.com/ClipArt/. Thematic sketches, in black and white and color that you're free to use.

Free Web Site Goodies

Atomz.com http://www.atomz.com/. This free search engine for your Web site returns good matches to search terms provided by your visitors. You can set up your account so that the search engine indexes your site on a regular basis, such as weekly.

CGI For Me http://www.cgiforme.com/. Get a graphic that counts down to any date you choose, other interactive elements, free.

CGI Scripts...To Go! http://www.virtualville.com/library/scripts.html. Free bulletin boards, chat rooms, shopping carts, and so on.

Coolboard http://www.coolboard.com/index.cfm. Free, customizable message boards for your site.

Forum Company http://www.forumco.com/. Discussion boards for your site that they say can be up and running, free, in 5 minutes.

Free JavaScript Shopping Cart http://www.nopdesign.com/freecart/. You may need programming savvy to install this free shopping cart at your site.

FreeScripts.com http://www.freescripts.com/scripts/. This site's free electronic postcard script is interesting.

FusionBot http://www.fusionbot.com/. Free on-site search engine for up to 250 pages.

HumanClick http://www.humanclick.com/. Free customer-service chat utility.

Livehelper http://www.livehelper.com/. Free text chat set-up for customer service purposes.

Matt's Script Archives http://www.worldwidemart.com/scripts/. A popular source of free guestbooks, forms, visitor counters, more, to add to your site.

PicoSearch http://www.picosearch.com/. This free search engine for your site provides sophisticated options for your visitors.

Steve's Free Shopping Cart http://www.stevespages.f2s.com/. A free shopping cart to install and use at your site.

Browser and Page Check Resources

AnyBrowser http://www.anybrowser.org/campaign/. Explains why and how to make sure your site can be viewed by every browser.

Bandwidth Conservation Society http://www.infohiway.com/faster/. Tools and tips for making your pages faster loading.

Browser Photo http://www.netmechanic.com/browser-index.htm. Inexpensive product that shows how a page looks in 14 browsers or browser versions.

BrowserWatch http://www.browserwatch.internet.com/. Browser news, data, and statistics.

Dr. Html http://www.drhtml.com/. Diagnose page-loading slowdowns here.

HTML-Kit http://www.chami.com/html-kit/. Free downloadable program that checks for errors in your HTML code.

WDG HTML Validator http://www.htmlhelp.com/tools/validator/. Make sure you don't have mistakes in your page coding.

W3C HTML Validation Service http://validator.w3.org/. Find out whether your page conforms to HTML standards.

Web Site Garage http://websitegarage.netscape.com/. Free browser-compatibility, load-time, and dead-link check.

Usability Resources

Bad Human Factors Designs http://www.baddesigns.com/. Entertaining introduction to the usability perspective and one of the best content presentations on the Web.

UsableWeb http://www.usableweb.com/. Nicely categorized links to online information about usability.

Useit.com http://www.useit.com/. Six years of invaluable columns and observations from Mr. Usability, Jakob Nielsen.

User Interface Engineering http://www.uie.com/. Jared Spool's usability research firm offers some valuable free articles here.

Disability Access Resources

Accessibility http://www.htmlhelp.com/design/accessibility/. Philosophical background and practical tips for Web-site accessibility.

Bobby 3.2 http://www.cast.org/bobby/. Test whether your site works for the disabled.

Designing More Usable Web Sites http://trace.wisc.edu/world/web/. Guidelines and explanations for accessibility to the disabled.

Content Sources and Resources

AccuWeather http://www.accuweather.com/. Weather newsfeeds for U.S. regions, cities, and specialty forecasts, such as for aviation.

Become a Quiz Whiz http://www.yudkin.com/quizwhiz.htm. More than a dozen quiz types with examples and quiz-making resources.

Click for Content http://www.clickforcontent.com/. Free cartoons, jokes, horoscopes, and articles.

Content Exchange http://www.content-exchange.com/. News and articles on buying and selling content, and content-for-sale and to-buy postings.

Content Wire http://www.content-wire.com/. Worldwide content, news, and resources.

FreeSticky http://www.freesticky.com/. Free games, lottery results, stock market news, maps, and so on.

InternetContent.net http://www.internetcontent.net/. Commentary and news on the content front.

iSyndicate http://www.isyndicate.com/. Free and for-fee content from more than 1,200 well-known and little-known providers.

Moreover http://w.moreover.com/. Free newsfeeds for your site in more than 300 categories.

OnlineWeather.com http://www.onlineweather.com/about/. Weather newsfeeds for the United Kingdom and Ireland.

Zoomerang http://www.zoomerang.com/. Free customizable surveys for your site.

Writing Resources

Edit-Work.com http://www.edit-work.com/. Guidelines for creating a consistent, correct writing style on your site.

Grammar Hotline Directory http://www.tc.cc.va.us/writcent/gh/hotlinol.htm. Yes, people will answer your pesky grammar questions free. Learn where and how.

Internet FAQ Archives http://www.faqs.org/. Directory of hundreds of informational FAQs with formats you can borrow.

Resources on Copyright

Australian Copyright Council http://www.copyright.org.au/. More than 50 downloadable documents explaining Australian copyright regulations.

Canadian Copyright Information http://www.edu.gov.mb.ca/metks4/instruct/iru/pubs/web/c/. Authoritative information and links for Canadian citizens.

The Copyright Website http://www.benedict.com/. Info on copyright for visual, audio, digital artists, outlaws, and law-abiding citizens.

MIT's Copyright FAQs http://web.mit.edu/cwis/copyright/faq.html. Learn what you can and can't copyright and how, what counts as fair use, and more.

U.S. Copyright Office FAQ http://www.loc.gov/copyright/faq.html. Official guidelines from the U.S. Copyright Office.

Trust-Building Resources

BBBOnLine http://www.bbbonline.org/. Offers a Reliability Seal and Privacy Seal.

TRUSTe http://www.truste.com/. A well-received privacy seal program.

Internet Content Rating Association http://www.rsac.org/. A rating service that helps protect children on the Internet.

SafeSurf http://safesurf.com/. Self-rating system that indicates whether any site content may be unsuitable for children.

Resources on Privacy and Opt-in Issues

"Spam & Privacy Information for B2B Marketers" by MarketingSherpa.com http://b2bmarketingbiz.com/sample.cfm?contentIS=1620

"Speaking The Opt-In Language" by Kim MacPherson http://clickz.com/article/cz.970.html.

"Ten Rules for Permission-based E-mail Marketing" by MessageMedia http://www.messagemedia.com/rc/ten_guides.shtml.

"Don't Be a Sneak" by Eric Ward http://www.netb2b.com/cgi-bin/netb2b/article.pl?id=851.

Cookie Central http://www.cookiecentral.com/. News, background, FAQs, and commentaries on cookies and privacy.

Electronic Privacy Information Center http://www.epic.org/. News and resources on online privacy.

Mail Abuse Prevention System http://maps.vix.com/. Organization that sponsors the Realtime Blackhole List of domains that send spam.

Privacy Place http://www.privacyplace.com/. News, information, and commentary on privacy, online and off.

Privacy Resource Guide http://www.truste.com/bus/pub_resourceguide.html. Free Model Privacy Statement and Site Coordinator's Guide.

Internet Marketing Educational Resources

ClickZ Today http://www.clickz.com/. Awesome archives on every aspect of Internet marketing.

eMarketer http://www.emarketer.com/. Internet statistics and analysis useful for planning and marketing.

MarketingSherpa.com http://marketingsherpa.com/. Rich source of Internet marketing case studies from many industries.

WebAdvantage http://www.webadvantage.net/tip_archive.cfm. Well-categorized and well-written articles on Internet marketing.

Wilson Internet http://www.wilsonweb.com/. The largest collection of Internet marketing articles and resources online.

Internet Marketing Discussion Lists

I-Advertising http://www.internetadvertising.org/. Discussion of online advertising.

I-Content http://www.adventive.com/lists/icontent/. Discussion of creating, selling, buying, and distributing content online.

I-Design http://www.adventive.com/lists/idesign/. Discussion of Web-design problems and solutions.

I-PR http://www.adventive.com/lists/ipr/. Discussion of online and offline public relations.

I-Sales http://www.adventive.com/lists/isales/. Discussion of online sales and marketing techniques and philosophy.

Online Ads http://www.o-a.com/. Discussion of online advertising.

Online Publicity Services

eReleases http://www.ereleases.com/. Reasonably priced e-mail distribution of news releases to opt-in journalists.

Internet Media Fax http://www.imediafax.com/. Targeted distribution of media releases by fax.

InternetNewsBureau.com http://www.newsbureau.com/. Well-established press release distribution service.

Pressbox.co.uk http://www.pressbox.co.uk/. British company offering free posting of press releases, and for-fee distribution to journalists.

Press Release Network http://www.pressreleasenetwork.com/. Distribution of your release to topical or general media and Web sites.

PRWeb http://www.prweb.com/. American company offering free posting of press releases.

Search Engine Resources

FinderSeeker http://www.finderseeker.com/. Search engine for finding specialized search engines.

GoTo Suggestions http://inventory.goto.com/d/searchinventory/suggestion/. Plunk in any term and find related terms people search for, with the frequency of each.

Search Engine Colossus http://www.searchenginecolossus.com/. Master list of specialized country-specific and topic-specific search engines and directories.

SearchEngineTalk.com http://www.searchenginetalk.com/. Discussion forums on tricks and techniques for rankings in specific search engines.

SearchPower.com http://www.searchpower.com/. Directory of 16,550+ search engines.

Search Engine Watch http://www.searchenginewatch.com/. Tips, tricks, reviews, news, and opinions concerning search engines.

Internet Law Resources

BickLaw.com http://www.bicklaw.com/. Articles on legal aspects of e-business.

Ivan Hoffman, B.A., J.D. http://www.ivanhoffman.com/. More than 100 readable articles on Internet and intellectual property legal questions.

Law for Internet http://www.lawforinternet.com/. Stay out of jail free with the advice of this site.

Nolo Law for All http://www.nolopress.com/category/ilaw_home.html. FAQs on the law and domain names, Webmastering, trademarks online, privacy, and more.

Smart Fast http://www.smartfast.com/Newsletters/newsletters.htm. Jean Sifleet, J.D., CPA, offers tips on common questions of Internet entrepreneurs.

INDEX

FREE INFORMATION ABOUT SETTING UP AND PROMOTING A WEB SITE

http://www.TopFloor.com/

If you are setting up a Web site, or if you have a Web site and you want marketing and promotions advice that really works, visit http://www.TopFloor.com/.

You'll find free information of all kinds: questions to ask a hosting company, the top 10 mistakes to avoid when setting up a Web site, 8 reasons why you should create your own online community—plus links to hundreds of Web sites with services that will help you set up and promote your site, several chapters from each book in the *Poor Richard's Series*, and much more.

Also, sign up for the free e-mail newsletter, *Poor Richard's Web Site News*. With more than 60,000 subscribers in over 80 countries, this is one of the most respected newsletters on the subject.

You can read back issues and subscribe to the newsletter at http://www.PoorRichard.com/newsltr/, or to subscribe by e-mail, send an e-mail message to subpr@PoorRichard.com.

The Main Page:
http://www.TopFloor.com/

The Newsletter:
http://www.PoorRichard.com/newsltr/

E-mail Subscriptions:
send a blank e-mail message to subpr@PoorRichard.com